PROLETARIAN JOURNEY

A Da Capo Press Reprint Series

CIVIL LIBERTIES IN AMERICAN HISTORY

GENERAL EDITOR: LEONARD W. LEVY
Claremont Graduate School

PROLETARIAN JOURNEY

NEW ENGLAND

GASTONIA

MOSCOW

FRED E. BEAL

DA CAPO PRESS • NEW YORK • 1971

A Da Capo Press Reprint Edition

This Da Capo Press edition of
Proletarian Journey
is an unabridged republication of the first
edition published in New York in 1937.

Library of Congress Catalog Card Number 70-146158

SBN 306-70096-4

Copyright, 1937, by Hillman-Curl, Inc.

Published by Da Capo Press
A Division of Plenum Publishing Corporation
227 West 17th Street, New York, N.Y. 10011

All Rights Reserved

Manufactured in the United States of America

PROLETARIAN JOURNEY

Fred E. Beal on stand; Judge Barnhill presiding. Gastonia,
N. C., 1929.

PROLETARIAN JOURNEY

NEW ENGLAND

GASTONIA

MOSCOW

FRED E. BEAL

1937

HILLMAN-CURL, INC.

New York

CONTENTS

ILLUSTRATIONS

WORD FROM NOWHERE

THIS BOOK is not the tale of a fugitive from a chain gang. It is not an account of experiences at some Devil's Island. True, there is a twenty-year prison sentence hanging over me in North Carolina. But the reader will not find in these pages the familiar scenes from the life of an escaped prisoner who has known the darkness of a dungeon and the whip of a cruel taskmaster.

I am a fugitive from two worlds, the world of capitalist justice and the world of Bolshevist justice. The darkness which I have known is deeper than that of any dungeon; it is the darkness of civilization in eclipse. The cruelty which I have witnessed is more terrifying than that of any heartless keeper; it is the cruelty of putting mankind in chains.

In the hemisphere in which I was born, to the accompaniment of an industrial order propelled by greed and piloted by exploitation, I was framed by a power greater than that of the State of North Carolina. In the hemisphere to which I fled in search of the new freedom, I was crushed by a dogma more soulless than the walls of any penitentiary.

My lifetime was dedicated to the ideals of a new democracy, a new freedom, a new justice. Almost from my childhood, from the day I went to work in the mills, I was captivated by the vision of a new order of things. I joined the bands of rebels whose eyes seemed to be fixed upon a new dawn for man. I believed that our little legion would grow into an invincible army. I gave all I had to my faith. But my comrades-in-arms bartered their dreams for new idols, new in their war paint only. Nothing is left of their rebel spirit. My early vision remains with me.

The vindictive forces of capitalism would be pleased to capture me and put me behind bars. The vindictive forces of Stalinism would be glad to deliver me into the arms of their professed enemy. Indeed, they have attempted to do so. There is no refuge for me between the two worlds. There is no haven for those who suffer for true liberty.

There are fugitives from justice who can confidently expect protection beyond the pale of their persecution. The fugitive slaves from the South had the shelter of the Abolitionists in the North. The fugitives from Czarist Russia found sanctuary in Great Britain and the United States. The Communist fugitive from a capitalist country and the Fascist fugitive from certain areas can look forward to the aid of their respective dictatorships. Even the common criminal fugitive can still arouse the sympathy of some humanitarian women's clubs and ministers.

I am no such fugitive. There is no anchorage for me, except that of loneliness. And my tragedy is not that of a lone human being. For it would not be unbearable to spend twenty years in prison in the belief that outside a new world was in the making, a world without prisons. Many have done this before me. But to be buried for life amidst a deathly silence without! It is the tragedy of a lonely humanity.

All my life has been spent in the labor movement, in an effort to broaden and enrich the horizons of myself and my fellow-workers. I fought for the good of the toilers of the earth, the creators of all the fruits of civilization. I led strikes, marshaled picket lines; I organized demonstrations of protest and cheerfully shared the cells of many a prison in my battle for justice to labor.

If ever a man was prepared to believe completely in the Soviet Union, that man was I. When I went to Russia, pending the appeal of my case and that of the other Gastonia victims, it was with the feeling that twenty years in jail upon my return would be less bleak after seeing the realization of my life dream under Communism.

I did not know then that to tell the truth, even the truth about Stalin's Communism, meant ostracism by those who would build a better world. I could not know that one who had been condemned unjustly to many long years in prison by the capitalist system would be forsaken by the assumed enemies of capitalism if he returned from the Soviet Union with the truth as he saw it. I did not know that the sworn friends of liberty had two brands of truth, one for private consumption and the other for public display.

Had I known it all, I would have done exactly the same. For I take it as an axiom that humanity will advance and that American labor will know what to do for the salvation of the country only if the unadulterated truth is presented. In the world of my erstwhile dreams I found that the truth had long since been exiled. But it can still raise its voice now and then in the world which imposed upon me a twenty-year jail sentence on account of my struggle for economic justice to the producers of all our wealth.

If not for this fact—the lingering faith in my native America which I love—I could have chosen the career of a Soviet bureaucrat for the rest of my life. I could have stilled the cry within me in the fleshpots of the new exploiting class living off the Russian 'laboring masses. That road was open to me. In fact I was on it. If I turned my back upon the temptations it had to offer in exchange for the existence of a hunted fugitive, it was because I chose to remain true to myself, and true to the truth.

The Greatest Rebel of all time said: "They shall know the Truth, and the Truth shall make them free." I know of no better guidepost in this age of .institutionalized hatred and cultivated confusion for those who would seek the light of a real brotherhood of man.

FRED E. BEAL.

Nowhere,
May 1, 1937.

BOOK ONE

NEW ENGLAND

I. THE HEN-COOP

1

THE start-whistle blew. At once the room became a hive of activity with hundreds of revolving spindles sounding like the b-z-z-z-z of a million bees. I was standing in the Crescent Worsted Mill between two rows of machines waiting, with a note in my hand, for the man that did the hiring.

The spinners moved in and out between the spinning frames trying to keep up their ends. How nimble their fingers were in piecing-up, and how carelessly they threw the white and colored strands of waste from rollers to their shoulders. It was thrilling to watch the skill of these spinners. I thought it must take years to learn how to do this work.

My attention was drawn next to a twisted sort of man in black jumper and overalls at the other end of the room. He was yelling the words, "Doff! Doff!" As if this was not noise enough, he supplemented it by putting his forefinger and thumb into his mouth and letting out a penetrating whistle. This seemed to have the desired effect because four girls came running to where he was standing. Silently he pointed to an idle frame and the four girls went to work replacing full bobbins of yarn with empty ones from a wire rack above their heads.

Suddenly a voice thundered, "God damn it, get a move on there!"

The thunderer was a man past fifty, wearing a faded blue jumper and patched overalls, each patch a different shade. He was addressing those working with the twisted man.

I decided he was the boss ... the one I was to show the note to, because, I thought, no one else would dare use such language. Seeing him come my way I fidgeted with the note. With me were two other hands also seeking work. One was a girl of twenty and the other a red-headed Irish boy of my age. The girl was hired immediately and disappeared among the frames.

The boss turned his attention to the Irish boy and me.

"S'pose you two red-'eaded buzzards are lookin' for a job." He put this in the form of a statement and not a question, in the manner of a man used to hiring people. I still fidgeted with the note. The Irish boy opened up negotiations.

"Yeah, Mister Breathweight."

"Hi'm not Mister Breathweight," the boss corrected with a growl. "My name's Binns, James Binns. The 'elp 'ere calls me Jimmy."

"Yeah, me fadder says to me: 'Reddy boy, if yer goes to the Hen-coop an' lands a job, yer Pop will be in better spirits.' "

Boss Jimmy examined Red through slitted eyes.

"You're h'old man Kelly's kid, aren'tcha? ... Yes, thought so. Spends all 'is time at Gilligan's bar lookin' for spirits ... Hi'm goin' to tike you on, but don't you give that shiftless h'old man of yours a penny, see? Wait, an' I'll show you wot to do."

2

I handed the note to Binns. It was a brief but formidable introduction from the owner of the mill, and read:

Dear Binns:
See that the bearer of this note is put to work at once from the bottom up. He is fourteen years old. I have his school papers.
Sept. 12, 1910.   *John Breathweight.*

Binns held the note of introduction to the light and squinted.

"Humpf!" he grunted. "Humpf. It looks like old tightwad's writin' all right." He mumbled these words half to himself. "S'pose I got to make room for you h'even though there ain't no place."

I felt relieved. The first part of the ordeal was over. I was hired. But Binns was still talking, and pointing: "See those fourteen frames? Well,—it's one kid's job to set bobbins on all o' them, but neow Hi've got one kid more than I kneows wot to do with, Hi'm goin' to divide up the work,—see?"

He let fly a gob of tobacco juice. It splashed against the legs of the spinning frame.

"Now, you two buzzards, come along with me and I'll show you the bobbin-bin an' whereh'bouts to stick the bobbins."

My heart was pounding from fear that it would be difficult to learn how to run the complicated machinery. Some grown fellows in my neighborhood had said it took years to become a good machinist. I wondered how long it took Binns to learn the trade. He seemed so sure of himself, stopping, on the way to the bobbin-bin, to give orders to his help. His legs, shaped like barrel staves, caused Red Kelly and me to smirk at each other behind his back.

At the bobbin-bin Jimmy gave out another one of his statements of fact: "S'pose you kids kneow nothin' about the trade." He tugged his scrubby-bearded chin thoughtfully while Kelly and I gazed at the mountains of bobbins in three bins rising to the height of my shoulders.

"I kime h'all the way from H'England, left a good 'ome to show you bloody-well Yankees 'ow to run a mill ... but I'm not 'preciated round 'ere. Do your work, lads, and we'll get orn ... just 'ang your coats on a nail over there an' roll your sleeves."

Another gob of tobacco juice left his mouth. This time the bobbin-bin was on the receiving end.

Binns gave us each a leather basket, rounded to fit our bodies with strap attachments two inches in width to go over our shoulders. He instructed us to fill the bags with bobbins and come with him. I struggled with the load behind Binns. As soon as he stopped I rested it on a yarn truck.

"Eddy," he said to a fellow kneeling on the floor turning a wheel that lifted a whole side of bobbins at one time, "show these kids 'ow to set bobbins."

Eddy stood up. His pocket bulged with oily waste and wrenches of various sizes. "This is the way it's done," he said, pleasantly, taking eight bobbins in each of his large hands from my basket. "Place the bobbins, with their heads *down,* on this here bobbin rack. It's easy when you catch on."

He warned me to keep my fingers away from moving gears. "They'll bite 'em off," he chuckled. "Once a girl, right here in this room, caught her hair between two gears and oh, tst tst tst, what a mess: it just naturally pulled her hair out by the roots."

I was glad I didn't have long hair like the girls.

3

All that was required of me was to keep the bobbin racks filled on eight frames. I counted 208 bobbins to a frame. Though the job was simple, it kept me moving all the time because the frames doffed on the average of once an hour. After the doffers swapped a full bobbin for an empty one, the yarn boy took them off and I had to set the bobbins all over again.

At first I was clumsy with my basket of bobbins and broke many "ends" for the spinners to piece-up. Under the circumstances the spinners were very kind to me, helping me with the bobbin setting, but I suspect the chief reason was to get me out of their alley and save the ends. Red Kelly, who likewise had eight frames to set bobbins on, caused a commotion when he broke down a whole row of "ends" during the first hour of his career. He wanted to see what would happen to a bobbin if stuck between two moving gears. Having no particular gears in mind, he placed a thin bobbin between the two that moved the rollers and all "ends" broke at once. The spinner was on the other side of the frame, so Kelly just watched with impish delight the waste pile higher and higher on the rollers as the soft yarn worked its way down from the rovings. The result of Kelly's experiment was to send Mr. Binns on a rampage. "For tuppence I'd fire you," he shouted to Kelly, and then set to work rounding-up spinners to piece the ends.

4

The help had a special name for this little mill that was not recorded in the Textile Blue Book. They called it the Hen-coop because Patrick Shanahan, the strawberry-nosed watchman, kept his chickens in the mill yard.

I will always remember the Hen-coop as the first place in which I doubled my output without a corresponding increase of wages. This came about when I organized my bobbin setting in such a manner as to give me rest periods. The machines were fast but I was faster. And by a continued accidental bumping of my basket against "ends," thereby creating an accumulation of waste on the rollers, I received assistance from the spinners, glad to get me out of their alley. By such planning I earned a fifteen-minute respite from my labors every hour. These rest periods were sat out with Kelly, either in a dark corner behind the bobbin-bin or in the bin itself. Sometimes we rolled under an unused frame and piled boxes at the base so as not to be seen. Our motive was to keep out of Binns' sight. He had a knack of putting idle people to work.

He praised my work one day. It was my second week at the Hen-coop. "Good work, lad," he said, patting me on the shoulder. "Come out to the shed, I'll show you 'ow to pick h'out gears." The shed contained a large collection of gears; most of them scattered on the floor. Some were linked through the center on iron rods.

"When you an' Kelly get time come out here and put these gears in order," said Binns.

The number of the gear, he explained, was told by the number of its teeth. With this new knowledge in my head I went back to setting bobbins.

Before the week was over Mr. Binns was patting me on the shoulder again and again, telling me what a fine worker I was. "We are short on doffers to-day. Give them a hand, that's a good lad." The shortness on doffers continued from day to day. But I did not mind this, at the time, because I was anxious to learn how to doff.

Eddy was the fastest doffer. It was almost miraculous how he snapped the bobbin from the rack into the steel cap with the little finger of his right hand and then maneuvered it onto the spindle between the tin guards only four inches apart. The tin guards were a constant menace to his large hand but he generally came through without a scratch.

Another one of my unofficial jobs was to help old Aggie Mullan pile large spools of yarn, called rovings, on top of spinning frames. She trucked them in from the drawing room. Binns had not told me to help Aggie, but it was evident because of her advanced age and rheumatic distress that she needed help and we young people always volunteered, except when the boss was around. Not for the world would Aggie let them think she was too old for work.

Aggie had grown up in the Hen-coop. She came in with the machinery and by her constant years of toil had helped to beat a path from the sidewalk to the mill door. She, too, started at the bottom. And with the years she landed on top. She became a jackspooler. There was no higher job, for this little mill didn't go in for weaving; it sold its yarn to the big mills. With the rolling on of years, Aggie's eyesight began to fail and life began to invert itself. She went back to the drawing room, then to trucking rovings. There was one job left that didn't fit in with her early days, that of washing the oily-black slivery floor. We did our best to keep her from this reward for forty years of toil.

The last two hours of every Saturday morning were devoted to special clean-ups. The spinners cleaned fuzzy waste from their frames. Kelly and I were put to work removing, with the aid of ammonia and scraper, a week's supply of crusted tobacco juice caked around the legs of every frame. It was always pleasing to note that Binns, Eddy and Pompo respected our work to the extent of not chewing during these last two hours.

5

There was a dark corner behind the bobbin-bin in the spinning room. Strange things happened there. It appeared that the Hen-coop had quite a shocking reputation. But although tongues wagged with juicy bits of gossip, Mr. Breathweight, the strait-laced owner, did not know how promiscuously sex was intertwined with the yarn of his mill.

In one month at the Hen-coop I learned more about sex than in all the fourteen years of my life. My folks regarded the subject as vulgar and un-Christian, although they themselves were looked upon by our neighbors almost as libertines for letting my brother and me play handball on the Sabbath and read the comics in the Sunday papers.

The spinning-room artists and poets of pornography displayed their talents on the NOTICE TO EMPLOYEES signs tacked on the toilet wall. By their own statements they came there to think, but it is doubtful they thought much about rule four, prohibiting smoking, which also declared: EMPLOYEES MUST NOT READ DURING WORKING HOURS. But it was there, faded and weak in gray print. As it was more fun to break rules than live up to them, the help brought to work whatever reading matter suited their taste. For the most part it was dime novels, which passed from one hand to another until pages became worn, crumpled and finger-stained.

Then one day Binns caught Kelly reading in the shed and fired him.

"Get your h'arse up off that barrel an' get the 'ell h'out of 'ere," Binns roared.

Kelly, who had been thinking of leaving anyway, squashed a cigarette butt, and stood up: "Sure, I was goin' to jack-up anyhow."

This left Mr. Binns in a quandary. He wanted to give Kelly another chance. If he would only ask for it. But no, he was dashing off, in rather cheerful mood, for hat and coat. Binns muttered something about how he'd rather run a third-class bawdy house than a spinning room.

I was sorting gears. It so happened that I too had been doing a little reading before Binns made his appearance. To ease things up a bit, I whistled the popular tune, *Everybody's Doing It*. My back was to Binns, but I felt what was coming—more work.

"Say, lad, Hi'll arx you to double up on Kelly's frames for to-day . . . until I gets another kid." He muttered something unintelligible and went back to the spinning room.

Would I take on more work? No! In sudden rage I upset the iron rods holding the gears I had carefully sorted, and scattered them on the floor. After thus venting my feelings I sat down on the oil barrel for a little serious thinking. Should I follow Kelly's example and jack-up immediately or take on an added job?

I had never heard of a union. I had never heard of a strike. None of the hands talked of such things. Every one acted upon his own initiative.

I would ask Mr. Hoole for more wages, Mr. Hoole, the superintendent of the mill. More wages or I'd quit, I decided. With sudden emotional pride for my newly

found spirit I burst forth to slay the enemy. I found
Mr. Hoole in the drawing room, standing, with his hands
in his hip pockets. With the kind of courage that drives
men to daring deeds, I went up to him and said: "Mr.
Hoole, I want a raise."

I don't know just what I expected to hear in reply,
but an earthquake or thunderbolt would have astonished
me less than the calm way Mr. Hoole met my ultimatum.
He didn't seem at all surprised. He rocked back and
forth on his feet and moved his mouth much the same as
a cow chewing her cud.

"How much do you get now?"

"Four dollars forty-eight!"

"Hm, well next week I'll see that you get five-ten."

"Thanks, Mr. Hoole."

That was all. I walked away with a feeling that I had
been cheated. He hadn't given me a chance to unburden
myself about the many jobs that I was doing. I thought
he didn't know, but he must have known all the time,
else he would not have granted the increase without an
argument. Pompo had asked him for a raise and the
answer was, "I'll give you a raise on the toe of my
boot."

I was walking, not back to the spinning room, but
away from it, through the drawing room. I suddenly
realized how I hated that spinning room with the
grouchy work-driving Binns. And Kelly, who understood everything, was gone.

I spent over half an hour walking from room to room,
always sidetracking the spinning room. Finally I wound
up in the twisting room. I knew that Binns would be
raving because the frames were not set. There was nothing else to do but go downstairs and face the music.
Binns met me at the bottom of the stairs, livid with rage.

Spinning room workers of the Crescent Worsted Co. (Hen-Coop), Lawrence, Mass., 1910. Front row, left to right, Pompo and Beal; Eddy on extreme right. Jimmy is elderly man on right, standing.

Private Fred E. Beal, (left), 5th Co., 2nd Bat. Camp Devens, March 24, 1919.

Fred E. Beal, just after spending "time" in the New Bedford jail, 1928.

"Cristalmighty, where the 'ell 'ave yer been? The goddam frames are all stopped!"

I made no reply. This angered Binns who was within arm's reach of me. He grabbed my hair.

"Won't h'answer, eh? Well, Hi'll show *you* ... Hi'll pull your blasted red hair h'out by the roots!"

He seemed to be carrying out his threat. I kicked and squirmed but he held me at arm's length and my efforts were mostly wasted. The great moment came when I landed a forceful kick just below his knee-cap. He released his hold on my hair and took hold of his knee; it must have been quite a blow, because he danced around on one leg, groaning.

Yet when the pain subsided, instead of firing me with a final outburst of profanity, he said mildly: "Go back to work, lad."

But I was too outraged,—too full of turmoil to listen to reason. I quit.

II. BACKGROUND OF A RADICAL

1

I AM a Yankee. I do not say this with any jingoistic pride in my accident of birth. I state it merely as a fact which explains the thing I am and the things I have done. A Yankee is a distinct type of human being and I am that type, as my parents were before me and theirs before them. My father never had a radical thought in his head, yet he took it for granted in a simple way, which the foreign revolutionary can never understand, that he had a perfect right to criticize the politics of his neighbors and the policies of local officials and national governments. In the same way, though he himself held no strong religious or social convictions, he felt that if you sincerely believed in anything, you were morally bound to preach the word to the people.

Historians call this the Puritan tradition. I think that this mixture of zealot and independent, which makes up the Yankee, is something deeper than a tradition. It is born in the blood and bred in the bone. Certainly I found it in myself long before I ever heard or read of the Puritan tradition. The little schooling I had in my childhood did not include such big words. But the essence of these words was there in my home and family.

Later in life I noticed that this spirit formed a point of difference between myself and others. This was no less true among the Irish, Italian and French-Canadian mill-workers of my native city than in Gastonia and other mill-towns of the South; no less in radical circles

of New York than in Soviet Russia. I have labored and
"struck" side by side with workers of many nations;
with them I shared jails as well as ideals. In the intimacy
of such relationships men reveal to each other both their
individual personality and their racial character. The
French-Canadians are born slaves, like the Slavs. They
have no initiative, no public spirit. The Irish, too, are a
docile race until they are aroused. Then they become
fighting mad for a brief spell and are capable of any
extreme. But they are quickly disheartened and disor-
ganized so that it is impossible to depend on them for
any length of time. The Italians are more dependable as
a group although as individuals they are very impulsive.
I think they can be more easily influenced by oratory
than any other people I have known, with the Americans
south of the Mason-Dixon line running them a close
second. The Southerners will follow a good speaker
whether he be a labor leader or a revivalist or a lyncher.
They seem to have many prejudices but no convictions
of their own and will accept, for a short while, the
opinions of any one who talks convincingly. Nearest to
the Yankee in temperament and character are the Jews,
though they are aggressive rather than independent and
fanatic where the New Englander is only zealous.

2

Like all Yankees, my relatives claim that our family
is descended from "pure" Mayflower stock. I have
always believed this to be the boast of people who have
very little else to be proud of. Considering how widely
that stock has spread in New England, I don't see how
any Yankee could very well escape the Mayflower
strain. But I have my doubt as to its "purity." In our

family, I know, it has been adulterated at least twice by
"foreigners." For my father's grandfather, Thomas
Beal, came to Massachusetts in the early years of the
Nineteenth Century and settled on a farm near Dedham where he added some fresh English blood to the
native mixture. And my mother was a Hale of New
Hampshire. The Hales, like the Beals, had one "foreigner" in the family. She was an Indian and was probably considered a great mismarriage at the time. Now
they are as proud of their Indian blood as of their Mayflower descent and of the fact that Hannibal Hamlin,
Lincoln's first Vice-President, was one of the "tribe,"
as they like to call the family. They specially cherish
those members of the tribe who are born with the
straight black hair and high cheek-bones of the Red
Man. I have the cheek-bones but am disappointingly
tow-headed.

Both the Beals and the Hales, though the latter were
better off, had been dirt farmers for generations. They
did not know poverty in its ugliest aspects, yet they
knew nothing of comfort, either. They had plenty to
eat but little beyond the simplest wants and no hope of
improving their lot. It was this that drove my grandfather to the city; or, as he said, it was my grandmother's social aspirations. The truth, I think, was that
they heard the call of industrialism and responded. The
same call was to bring millions of European peasants to
our shores and thousands of Southern mountain folk to
the mill-villages. The Yankee farmer, being closest, was
the first to hear this modern Lorelei and the first of her
victims.

The story of our family was in its main features just
like the saga of all the other failures. The farm sold for
a pittance; the heavily-mortgaged cottage in the sub-

urbs of Lawrence; the fifteen years of struggle to retain it on the inadequate wages of a railway clerk and to sustain a growing family of six children; and the final surrender which moved us from the fields and river to the "dumps" of the city. Our Yankee relatives always referred to this neighborhood near the railroad as "the patch of the dirty Irish." It was a district of ugly, crowded tenements with nasty words written in chalk on the clapboards and flies swarming around babies dressed only in smelly diapers. Though we lived there for many years, we never thought of it as "home."

3

I was eleven years old when my mother died. It was some months later, after watching a Democratic torchlight parade, that father and I stood on the Falls Bridge which spans the Merrimac River uniting North and South Lawrence and looked at the many textile mills that flanked the river banks, their hundreds of bright-lit windows reflected in the dark water. The hum of the spinning machines could be heard above the roar of the river as it spilled over the dam to turn the mill wheels. Inside men and women bustled about like so many ants busy at their mysterious tasks. I thought it would be fascinating to be one of them, working late into the night, earning money that was so scarce and so much needed.

"I hope you will never have to slave in one of those mills," Father remarked, as if in answer to my thoughts. "Keep on with your schooling as long as possible. Try to learn something that will save you from the life of a mill-hand."

But when I reached the working age of fourteen

years, there was really no choice between Father's wishes and the family's needs. The latter were far more insistent. To tell the truth, I did not care much for school and I could not bear the feeling that my father and two older brothers were supporting me when I was perfectly able to work. After a few futile weeks of trying to get a job more to my father's liking, I was on my way to the Hen-coop. It wasn't many more weeks before I was on my way out.

4

There were seventeen major mills in Lawrence. Within six months I had passed through four of them, working in the spinning room either as a doffer or at setting bobbins. On the day I quit the Hen-coop I found another job at the Ayer Mill. I didn't like the boss there, and quit again in a month. Mill jobs were plentiful; besides, it was considered the smart thing to travel from one mill to another, and brag about it.

I soon found myself in the Wood Mill, the largest worsted plant in the world. It was a mammoth building, only five years old. Among its modern devices were wide moving stairs to carry the workers to their respective rooms. When I described them to Grandma Beal, she remarked fussily: " 'Twon't be long before they'll have horse an' buggy take 'em to work." And these moving stairs were the cause of my getting walking papers from that mill. We kids thought it fun to race down the stairs when they were moving up. It *was* fun. But the watchman who caught me by the nape of my neck and seat of my pants did not think so. Four others were fired with me.

In December, 1911, I was working at the Pacific

Worsted Mill as boss-doffer. I had charge of six doffers on a section and was getting one dollar a week more in wages. The spinning room was so large it had to be divided into ten sections, with as many bosses or section-hands. I boss-doffed on section four with "Slim Jim the Burglar" for my section-hand boss. He wasn't really a burglar; he had acquired this name because he was the spitting image of Victor Potel, the movie comedian who played in the one-reel masterpiece of the same name at the Pastime Theater. We had a nickname for every one we worked with. Two of my six doffers, "Gyp the Blood" and "Lefty Louie," were named after well-known underworld characters who had spent a little time at the Concord Reformatory. "Queenie" was a fat, pimply-faced, French-Canadian girl who liked to bounce bobbins on our heads. "Tony the Wop" was a late arrival from Italy. He was only sixteen years old but he learned English fast from Gyp and Lefty. There were two others, two little girls, who could hardly reach the bobbin rack when they doffed. In fact, one of them had to stand upon a box when she doffed. She was "Little Eva," after the child heroine of *Uncle Tom's Cabin*. Little Eva and the other little girl, also a French-Canadian, were below the legal age of fourteen for working. They hid whenever "Limpy" Fallsby, woman State inspector, passed by.

I was called "Lobster;" Red Lobster at first, because of a very reddish complexion, then just plain "Lobster." I earned this name, so I was told, by being an easy-going slob. Some doffer would stay too long in the toilet or visit a friend in another part of the room. It was my job to find him or do the work. It was easier to do the work. Tattling to the boss was frowned upon by the bunch, and the boss frowned upon me when the doffers were not on the job. Our section-hand had several higher bosses, Mr. Tobin, the second hand, and Overseer Paddy Parker. Paddy was a patriarchal old man with a snow-white Vandyke. His stiff-jointed son was agent of the mill. Both knew my father. For this reason they expected more from me in the way of advancement and, as a beginner, Paddy wanted me to work in his office. It is not clear to me now why I refused; perhaps I liked the close association with the Italians that the job of doffing gave me.

Most of the spinners were Italians. From the beginning I loved the Italians, or "dagos" and "wops" as we called them. They were so warm-hearted, good-natured and excitable. After my Yankee childhood, their strange language fascinated me. Tony told me about Italy and the reason for coming to America and to Lawrence. It was on account of a poster, he said, depicting a worker, with a bag of gold in his hand, leaving the mill for a bank across the street. There were words on the poster that promised good wages and reduced fare, and it was signed by the American Woolen Company. Friends of his had left for America months before and they wrote in jest of finding gold in the streets, and Tony believed every word of it. With such an incentive, he won over his parents' consent to the trip. He was disappointed, not in America but in the broken promises. He wasn't getting the wages he dreamed of, and he hadn't found a single piece of gold in the streets.

III. STRIKE

1

I SUDDENLY discovered that I did not want to be a textile worker. I was fifteen. I went to a lecture given by Mr. Bowker, a local man, who had traveled around the world and got paid for telling people about it. I then attended many of his lectures and had visions of myself in his place. Yes, I would grow up to be a lecturer. Mill work was dreary. I would become a globe-trotter, and come back home with colored slides to prove to my friends, some of whom had journeyed as far as New York, that I chummed with the Terrible Turk and ventured into darkest Africa. I would astound my pals by all kinds of gadgets. I would press one and, after a clicking sound, a new slide would make its appearance. Let them wonder how I could ever travel so far without getting lost. I awoke from my dreams when Mr. Bowker finished one of his lectures. How did a man who had traveled around the world really look? I was curious and edged my way close to the lecturer. Indeed, he seemed different from those who stayed in Lawrence. I was sure that some day I would be a lecturer.

My father took me to see Teddy Roosevelt when he stopped in Lawrence to speak from a train platform. It was during the 1912 campaign when Teddy founded and led the Bull Moose movement. My father was all for Teddy. He would show the money-bags where to get off. "Yeah, if Teddy were President, he would give the common people a square deal!" The Old Man raged against

Wall Street and the trusts, and worshiped Teddy. After seeing Father's hero, I was surer than ever that I wanted to be a lecturer. Roosevelt had the same air about him as Mr. Bowker. Both had seen the world, and made people take notice of them.

Then one day, at noon-time, another kind of lecturer addressed the crowd in front of our mill gate. He was not dressed as well as Mr. Bowker and did not use such good language but what he said was just as interesting. This strange lecturer urged us to organize into a union, to join the Industrial Workers of the World, and to demand from the bosses more wages and shorter hours. He declared with emphasis that we, the textile workers, were *wage slaves* and that all the mill owners were slave drivers, as bad and as brutal as Simon Legree of *Uncle Tom's Cabin.*

This was news to me. I had always thought that only colored people could be slaves and that they had been freed long ago by us Yankees who fought in the Civil War. Yet there was something convincing about his talk although I could not quite understand just who were the bosses who, according to the speaker, were enjoying the Florida sunshine while we slaved in the mills for their profit. All the subordinate bosses I had ever known were working in the mill, like "Slim Jim the Burglar" and Paddy Parker.

The Irish workers did not like the speaker; the Italians did. The Irish cupped their hands to their mouths, made strange noises every time the Italians applauded, and yelled: "Ef ye don't loike this countr-r-ry, go back where ye coime fr-r-rom!"

The speaker ignored these remarks and continued: "The working class and the employing class have nothing in common. Between these two classes a struggle must go on until the workers of the world organize as a class, take possession of the earth and the machinery of production, and abolish the wage system."

Then, rudely, as if by prearrangement, the ten-minutes-to-one bells, high up in the mill's belfry, began tolling their dismal warning to us workers that it was time for us to get back to work. *"The slave bells are calling!"* yelled the I.W.W. speaker. "The master wants you back at the bench and machine. Go, slaves! But remember, these very bells will some day toll the death-knell of the slave-drivers!"

The bells tolled on defiantly.

2

That afternoon, during the rest period, we doffers talked about the I.W.W. speaker and the union he was organizing. We had good reason to talk. Things were about to happen. The State Legislature had just passed a law reducing the hours of labor from 56 to 54 per week, and there was rumor that our pay would be reduced accordingly. Our next pay day was Friday, January 12th, and the grown-up workers were talking about going on strike if wages were cut. We young people thought it would be fun to strike and made plans to go skating and sleigh-riding—all but Little Eva. She and her mother were the breadwinners of the family. Her father had lost an arm at Pingree's Box Shop two weeks after they came from Canada. They sorely needed Little Eva's weekly wage of five dollars and four cents.

Old man Dwyer, the empty rovings collector, had worked in the Pacific Mills over thirty years. There was a strike in the Pacific Mills in 1882, said Dwyer, against a wage reduction. He took part in that and lost.

"Thems that runs things gets the best of us every time," he shook his head dejectedly. "Let well enough alone." He was against going on strike. "Tain't right to be loafin'," he would say. "These Dagos, who come to this country and takes the vittels right out of our mouths by workin' for nothin' only wants more money to send home to Italy."

While the discussion was on, two Italian spinners came to me with a long white paper. They wanted me to be among the first to sign a petition against the threatened wage cut because, they said, I was American. The idea was to present Paddy Parker with a long list of those opposed to any reduction. I read the words at the top of the paper:

THE FOLLOWING PEOPLE WORKING IN THE SPINNING ROOM WILL GO ON STRIKE FRIDAY, JANUARY 12TH, IF WAGES ARE CUT—

Queenie read it over my shoulder. "Don't sign it, Lobster," she cautioned. "These Wops'll get you in trouble. You'll be put on the blacklist if you sign that paper!"

But I signed it. So did "Gyp" and "Lefty Louie."

And January 12th was only two days away.

3

On this Friday morning the atmosphere at the mill was tense with suppressed excitement. We were not sure that the company would cut our wages. We would know when the paymaster came around at eleven o'clock. The shop was full of rumors. One of these was that the big Wood Mill of eight thousand workers had already gone on strike. This almost started an immediate walk-out in our spinning room. Dwyer had it on "good authority" that we would get an increase if we stayed at work. Queenie said the priest told her not to strike.

"You goddam French-Canucks will go out if we do," snapped Gyp, "even if we have to pull you out by the tongue." Gyp was afraid his plans for skating might fall amiss.

Paddy Parker, petition in hand, called me to one side. "Young man," he said blandly, "I see your name heads this list. Did you put it there?"

"Yes, I did, because I don't think we should get a wage cut."

"You shouldn't have your name with these foreigners."

"I work with them, don't I?"

"Yes, but you want to get a better position soon, don't you? Stand by the company. I'll cross off your name."

"I'm going on strike if the others do," I said firmly.

"All right, young man, if you do, you will *never get work again in the Pacific Mills,* and I will see to it that you are blacklisted at other mills, and every other name on this list."

The threat of not being able to get work again in any of the mills made me feel miserable. Where else could I get a job? All of Lawrence to me was mills, mills, mills. And I was too young to become a lecturer. Perhaps the best thing would be to leave Lawrence and go West, to be a cowboy like those in the movies. For the first time in my life I felt fear tugging at my heart. Hadn't I promised to help out the family? And now, if I went out on strike, I would never get another job in the mills of Lawrence and perhaps Paddy Parker could stop me from getting a job anywhere. I had to make a decision in thirty minutes before the paymaster came around.

It was my habit, in a crisis, to ask God the way out—God and Jesus Christ, because I took my Sunday-school teachings seriously. I always talked with God in private. There was no thought of irreverence in me when, sitting upon the toilet seat, I asked God about going out on strike. There just wasn't any other private place.

There was a sharp whistle. It was the call that said: "Come and get your pay!"

Just like any other Friday, the paymaster, with the usual armed guard, wheeled a truck containing hundreds of pay envelopes to the head of a long line of anxiously waiting people. There was much chattering in different languages, and much gesticulation. I stood with Gyp halfway along the line. When the great moment came, the first ones nervously opened their envelopes and found that the company had deducted two hours' pay. They looked silly, embarrassed and uncertain what to do. Milling around, they waited for some one to start something. They didn't have long to wait, for one lively young Italian had his mind thoroughly made up and swung into action without even looking into his pay envelope.

"Strike! Strike!" he yelled. To lend strength to his words, he threw his hands in the air like a cheer-leader.

"Strike! Strike! Strike!"

He yelled these words as he ran, past our line, then down the room between spinning frames. The shop was alive with cries of "Strike" after the paymaster left. A few French-Canadian spinners went back to work. A tall Syrian worker pulled a switch and the powerful speed belts that gave life to the bobbins slackened to a stop.

There were cries: "All Out!"

And then hell broke loose in the spinning room. The

silent, mute frames became an object of intense hatred, something against which to vent our stored-up feelings. Gears were smashed and belts cut. The Italians had long sharp knives and with one zip the belts dangled helplessly on the pulleys. "Lefty Louie" and I went from frame to frame, breaking "ends," while Tony smashed windows. Queenie barricaded herself behind trucks and let loose a barrage of bobbins on "Gyp" who seemed determined to get hold of her tongue. It was a madhouse, a thrilling one, nevertheless.

More cries: "Strike! All Out! Strike!"

Old man Dwyer hugged his truck of rovings and Paddy Parker was at the door when we stampeded for the street. How ineffectual he looked, standing there with the petition. It was 11:45. The company wanted to keep us in until twelve, when the bells in the belfry would again ring out the noon hour, so the gates were closed. Three workers grabbed the watchman and forced him to open up. We wanted to get out before the bells rang, and we did.

We piled out onto Canal Street, singing and shouting.

It was snowing.

4

The next day I went skating with a few other strikers of my own age. We looked upon the strike as a vacation; it would be over and won in a week, especially since all the mills in the city, with a force of twenty-seven thousand workers, were on strike together. I was wondering how Paddy Parker and other mill bosses could remember to blacklist me out of twenty-seven thousand. And the more I wondered and thought about it, the less I worried. Besides, there were mills at Lowell, twenty miles from Lawrence. They couldn't keep me out everywhere. But a week went by and the strike wasn't over. I read in the newspapers that the strike was being led by a bunch of foreign anarchists and "I Won't Works" who were against God and the Government. They named the leaders: Joseph Ettor, Arturo Giovannitti, Carlo Tresca, and, as the worst of the lot, Bill Haywood, who was expected any moment to cause further trouble.

A burning desire overtook me to see these people who were against God and the Government. The strikers I had known were as much for God as I. So for the first time since the strike began I went to the mill gate. Here I found thousands of strikers massed together booing and yelling at people going to work. Yes, there were hundreds of people going to work—a complete surprise to me. I thought every one was on strike. Every time a group of these people crossed the canal bridge in front of the mill gate a roar went up from the strikers: "Scab! Scab!"

An Italian spinner recognized me. "You scab, too?" he asked.

I was near the gate. Perhaps he thought I was going in, too. "Me no work. Me stay out with you," I replied in my best pidgin English.

"Your people, shame! They work; they scab on us peoples. What's the matter, Irishee afraid of police?"

While we were talking, police were swinging their clubs on the heads and shoulders of the strikers. One policeman, on horseback, nearly drove me into the canal. They were trying to break up the mass into small groups. A man carrying an American flag called us to follow him towards Union Street. I marched with the mass, sore because that policeman tried to run me into the canal. We were marching east. Union Street crosses Canal, running north and south. On Union Street we joined with another great mass just arrived from the Wood Mill. The crowds were so large that the police practically gave up hope of dispersing them.

There was much singing and laughter. The demonstration was taking on a festive air. Then something awful happened.

A policeman fired a shot and a woman fell dead. I wasn't near the scene, but the news spread rapidly over the mass: "A woman shot ... murdered ... by a policeman ... He fired from the mill. ... Anna LoPezza shot ... Anna LoPezza murdered!"

Only my mother's death seemed to me a greater tragedy in my life than the killing of this unknown Italian woman. Some of my Sunday-school friends laughed at me because I was so sad over the death of Anna LoPezza. "She's only a Dago," said one. "She probably shot at the cop first," said another. She was a Catholic, but Father O'Reilly stood at the cemetery gate and refused to let her be buried in that Holy Place.

All these things did not jibe with my religious training and thinking. What would Christ say about this? What would He do? It was clear to me that Christ would not be on the side of the policeman who shot Anna LoPezza. He would not curse Anna LoPezza for being a Dago. This put me in the mood of taking sides. Policemen, priests, my own minister, and the newspapers, were on the side of the devil. The only ones fighting for right were the strikers; and since the strikers were mostly foreign-born, I had to mix with them to the exclusion of my Yankee and Irish friends. Besides, most of the Irish scabbed. The most shameful scabbing was done by the French-Canadians. They scabbed on principle and thoroughly enjoyed it. It was the Italians, Poles, Syrians and Franco-Belgians that kept the strike alive.

One day, after the militia was called, thousands of us strikers marched to Union Street again. In the front ranks a girl carried a large American flag. When we arrived at the junction of Canal and Union Streets, we were met by a formidable line of militia boys, with rifles and attached bayonets. They would not let us proceed.

An officer on horseback gave orders: "Port Arms! Disperse the crowd!"

Whereupon the militia, boys between the ages seventeen to twenty, guns leveled waist-high, moved toward the crowd. Their bayonets glistened in the sunlight. On and on they moved. The strikers in front could not move because of the pressing of the crowd behind them. It looked as if the murder of Anna LoPezza would be multiplied many times. And then the girl with the American flag stepped forward. With a quick motion she wrapped the Stars and Stripes around her body and defied the militia to make a hole in Old Glory.

The officer on horseback permitted us to proceed and there was no further trouble.

IV. TWO AMERICAN TITANS

1

On the battlefield of Lawrence two American titans came to grips, proletarians both. One was the son of Portuguese immigrants; the other the son of Salt Lake city miners. The child of the Portuguese workers became a mill-hand at the age of eleven; the miner's son went to work in the mines at the age of nine. The half century of their active careers spanned the era of the industrial revolution in America. Both were already legendary figures at the threshold of my own labor career, at the outbreak of the class war in Lawrence.

The orphaned Portuguese boy, William M. Wood, became the textile king of America. The Utah miner's son, Big Bill Haywood, became the leader of the most revolutionary American labor army. Both lived to see their dreams frustrated. Even in their deaths, they carried out the peculiar American symbolism of their lives. The great captain of the textile industry committed suicide at the pinnacle of his power, crushed by the emptiness of his achievements. The great leader of the I.W.W., who had forfeited his bail to escape capitalist prison in America, died a crushed and embittered man in the land of his refuge, Soviet Russia.

2

Big Bill Haywood, "the trouble maker," was coming to take charge of the strike. So the Lawrence newspapers announced. Ettor and Giovannitti, the former leaders, had been arrested as "accessories before the act" in the case of the murder of a girl picket, Anna LoPezza, in spite of the fact that they had not been at the scene of the shooting. There were others, like Carlo Tresca and Elizabeth Gurley Flynn, who rushed to Lawrence to aid the strikers. But the bosses and the newspapers were afraid most of Big Bill. He was coming to fight for the people . . . for me. Fifteen thousand of us strikers met him at the station. When he stepped off the Boston train, he was cheered and almost carried down Essex Street to the Lawrence Common where he spoke to us from the Common's bandstand.

Haywood was not an ordinary man either in stature or speech. This giant from the West, blind in one eye, had come "to meet the textile workers of the East" in a manner which portended fierce combat. With a voice loud and deep as a foghorn he opened his speech by addressing us all: "Fellow workers." I am sure most of his audience did not understand English, but they understood Big Bill. They sensed the essence of his words and applauded spontaneously when he emphasized some particular point with his large fists.

Once he looked benevolently down at us youngsters, in short pants, who had worked our way to the front of the crowd around the bandstand, and roared: "These kids should be in school instead of slaving in the mill!"

This was the only thing that Bill said that I wholeheartedly disagreed with. This was the attitude of the grown-ups. They seemed to think kids were in the way and that a strike was something for the grown-ups to settle. But I preferred the mill to school, and I was glad to be a striker.

Bill made it clear in thunderous tones that every

worker and striker should join the Industrial Workers of the World because only through organization and solidarity could we win our strike and future strikes.

It is twenty-five years since I heard his voice booming across the Lawrence Common but I recall almost every word and gesture of that speech. Particularly I remember one statement that thrilled and frightened me at that time: "Only by One Big Union of the working class and by mass action can we hope for the final victory of those who work and produce over those who exploit and sweat us for their profits. The road for us to travel is through industrial unions, not through the American Federation of Labor craft unions nor through the Republican, Democratic and Socialist Party method of voting for 'good men' who will sell us out later. I would *smash the ballot box with an ax!*"

I hadn't realized there was so much misery in America until Haywood explained it to us. New York had thousands of sweatshops where old women and nine-year-old children slaved twelve and more hours a day for a pittance. . . . In Pennsylvania miners were entombed underground twelve hours a day at starvation wages. . . . The South lynched its negroes. . . . I.W.W.'s were being tortured in Western prisons for demanding bed linen and liceless bunks in lumber camps. . . . Even work conditions in the Lawrence mills were worse than I thought. He produced pay-envelopes—I don't know where or how he got them but there were several dozen—to prove how low were the wages in our mills. How could mothers and fathers raise a family on five or seven dollars a week? And on top of this a wage cut!

My wage had been $6.16 for fifty-six hours of work. With the wage cut I stood to lose twenty-two cents, enough to buy two ice-cream sodas, a pound of candy,

a ticket to a ball game on Saturday afternoon at River-
side Park, or the price of two movies and a newspaper.
I had thought of the wage cut in these terms because I
knew it would have to come out of my spending money.
Five dollars had to go to the upkeep of the family. But
now I realized with dismay that to most of the strikers
the cut meant the loss of far more important things, of
bread and meat, of shoes and clothing and coal for the
stove. The strike took on a new meaning for me from
that moment.

Bill's voice boomed to a close with the slogan: *"All
for One and One for All!"*

The crowd went wild. He won our hearts with his
understanding of our problems. I had never heard any
one speak with such force and sincerity and with such
meaningful words. He was my hero, my God. His speech
was translated into Italian, Polish and French by other
speakers. When this was over, he came down from the
bandstand.

We kids stood looking at him in wonderment. I
touched his coat and he beamed down upon me. My hat
was off, and he said, ruffling my hair with his big hand:
"Hello, tow-head. Put your hat on, you'll catch cold."

That was all he said to me. The crowd swallowed him
up. I felt important and grinned at the other kids and
they grinned at me.

"Great guy!" I exclaimed.

They agreed.

3

There was dynamite in the Lawrence strike, but it
exploded in the wrong hands. It was the dynamite era
in the labor struggles in this country, the era of frame-

ups, of private sleuths hired to plant explosives among strike leaders. Even at this early date California had become quite expert at this practice. But New England was just learning the delicate profession and Lawrence proved an inept pupil.

One morning the arrest of three strikers was sensationally announced. The charge was that they had been discovered in possession of dynamite. The workers knew that the three men were victims of a plant. But the hue and cry raised by the officials, the press, the mill owners and the priests portended no good. And then an untutored police detective made an even more sensational discovery. The dynamite sticks were wrapped in the pages of *The Undertakers' Journal.* There was an address-label on that worthy periodical. The label carried the name and address of John J. Breen, a prominent Lawrence undertaker. This clew led the investigators right along the dynamite trail to its source, which was not the headquarters of the strikers but the very throne of the mill owners.

For Breen was promptly arrested and just as promptly lost his nerve and confessed everything. He informed the police that his instructions to plant the dynamite at the door of the accused strike leaders had come directly from William M. Wood, head of the textile trust which was determined to break this strike at all costs in order to intimidate the mill-workers throughout New England. Breen also implicated in the conspiracy Wood's close friend and builder of the great Wood Mill, the contractor E. W. Pitman. Pushed hard during the course of the preliminary investigation, Pitman committed suicide to avoid testifying against his patron and friend. This saved Wood, who was acquitted of criminal charges after a lengthy and sensational trial.

Breen, of course, was found guilty and sentenced to pay a fine of five hundred dollars which did not come out of his own pocket.

4

Billy Wood was a name to conjure with in Lawrence in the days of my childhood. At the turn of the century he had become the dominant leader of the country's textile industry as President of the American Woolen Company, a huge combine of more than sixty mills. His own plant, the largest in the world, with its moving stairs and other modern devices, overshadowed the textile center just as he dominated the rest of the mill owners. And to the mill-hands he was the symbol of all the powerful moneybags who, as Big Bill Haywood had said, were driving the American workers into slavery.

Yet Billy Wood was of true proletarian origin, much more so than I. This terror of the Lawrence strike who answered to the name of William Madison Wood was the son of a Portuguese sea cook called Jacinto. His mother had been a scrub-woman in New Bedford. Left an orphan at the age of eleven, he went to work in the mills. But he did not remain a mill-hand long. An intense and brilliant student, he learned accountancy, obtained a banking job, and rose rapidly in his new profession. He climaxed this by marrying the daughter of Frederick Ayer, one of Boston's patrician mill owners, and soon was at the top of the industry where he had started at the very bottom.

Throughout his life Billy Wood remained unostentatious in his habits, working long hours, seven days a week, at the same old desk in a very plain office. And he retained a very genuine feeling for the welfare of the

working people. In fact, he was the first great paternal-
ist of the new industrial system in America. Long before
it became the vogue among capitalists, he set up a model
housing enterprise, known as the Shawsheen Village
project. His summer camp for the undernourished children of the mill workers and his special dairy farm to
supply milk for his employees established his reputation
as a great humanitarian in his relations with labor.

"In the new social and industrial order on which we
have entered, there is no room for the selfish employer or
for the selfish worker," is the way in which Wood stated
his social philosophy. "It is my firm conviction that there
is no essential antagonism between capital and labor.
Differences of opinion may arise, but these can be ad-
justed if both parties are pervaded with a spirit of good-
will and justice."

But the applause which greeted these words throughout the land had barely died down when their sincerity
was tested by the Lawrence strike. The nation soon
stood aghast at the reign of terror let loose by the same
Billy Wood. Clubbing and jailing of strikers became
an hourly occurrence in the streets of Lawrence. Following the murder of Anna LoPezza, another striker,
John Remi, fell as the result of a bayonet thrust. A
bloody whirlwind of violence swept through the city and
Wood announced that this would be repeated until the
strike was broken. The wave of sympathy for the strikers
which swept the nation at the news of this bloodshed
was swelled by resentment against this statement. Offers
of all kinds of help and thousands of dollars for relief
of the hungry strikers poured into Lawrence from all
over the country.

One of the proposals, which came simultaneously from
several eastern cities, appealed especially to the strike

leaders because it furnished a spectacular solution to their most difficult problem. For at this time the desertions from the ranks of the strikers were due almost entirely to only one reason—starving children. The cry of hungry children for bread had driven back to the mills many workers who were in full sympathy with the strike and quite as determined as the rest of us to stick it out to the bitter end. While they were willing to suffer themselves, these men and women returned to work simply because they could no longer bear to see the suffering of their children. As the days went by and their small savings melted away, more and more parents were forced to scab and this threatened the success of the strike.

Now came the offer to adopt temporarily the starving children of the strikers. It was quickly accepted and the workers of Philadelphia arranged to take the first batch of fifty youngsters.

It was a cold morning on Saturday, February 24th, when the strikers brought their children to the Lawrence Station. Some of the tots were so small that the mothers held them in their arms. All were pale and haggard and wrapped in rags. It was both a sorrowful and a joyful occasion. Even the parents who cried at parting with their children felt that it was a step toward victory. And the crowd of several thousand workers who had come to see them off cheered the kids like heroes.

About a hundred policemen, armed with long nightsticks, mingled in our crowd. At first we thought nothing of it, though our past experiences with the forces of law and order ought to have made us wary. But as train time approached the police began to draw closer to the group of women and children. Suddenly there were cries that the militia was coming. And immediately afterward two companies were seen marching with fixed bayonets along Essex Street toward the railroad station. At the same time a file of patrol wagons drew up to the curb alongside the station.

These things created a great sense of tension in the crowd, yet still no one anticipated what was about to happen. We felt that since we were breaking no law, the cops and militia had no excuse for taking any action against us. Then some one blew a whistle and we saw the reason for the military force. The police surrounded the departing children and the militia forced the crowd back at the points of their bayonets. Then the kids were herded toward the patrol wagons, the littlest ones snatched out of their mothers' arms. They were packed in while the mothers, now fighting against the separation, were dragged screaming off to other "paddy" wagons. An ugly murmur rose from the crowd at this act of brutality. We looked in vain for rocks or bricks or any kind of weapons with which to attack the loaded rifles and glistening bayonets of the militia. Sensing the anger of the crowd, the officers ordered their men to advance and break it up. Thrusting their bayonets at the unarmed people, the soldiers dispersed the crowd.

Meanwhile the women had been driven off to the various police stations and the children taken to the poor-farm. In this the police were carrying out the orders of the mill owners. The latter realized that the arrival of the starving children in other communities would be a deciding factor in the struggle. They knew that the sympathy thus aroused would bring sufficient funds into the strikers' treasury to continue the strike longer than they could afford to carry on. So they took this means to crush a serious threat to their cause. But they had not reckoned on the American reaction to such an act of terrorism. It served the strikers' cause far more than the children could possibly have done. It brought about a Senatorial investigation after Senator Miles Poindexter, who had secretly visited Lawrence, declared: "It is like a chapter in the story of Russia's treatment of the Jews. I never expected to see such things in the U.S.A." And Victor Berger, Socialist member of Congress, denounced the action on the floor of the House: "I want to call attention to one of the most outrageous invasions of constitutional rights that has ever occurred in this country. I refer to the brutal manhandling and clubbing of women and children in Lawrence, Massachusetts, by the official and unofficial agents of the Wool Trust where the wage earners of the worsted mills are striking against extremely low wages and inhuman conditions."

The great strike became a national scandal. The then powerful Socialist Party, under Eugene Debs, pitched in and helped the I.W.W. though the two organizations were enemies. And the ranks of the workers, comprising twenty-eight nationalities, grew stronger and more solid as the strike progressed. Added funds enabled us to feed the children at home and reduced the number of scabs to a minimum. Finally, after sixty-three days, the strike ended with a notable victory for labor.

The Industrial Workers of the World emerged from the battle with an organization numbering thousands of members in Lawrence alone. I was one of them. Vaguely I understood the I.W.W. principles of the class struggle and of direct action but chiefly all that mattered to me at that time was that I had enrolled as a member in Big Bill Haywood's union. He, rather than Billy Wood, was my ideal of success.

5

The strike was a personal tragedy to the paternalistic
Billy Wood. It shattered his poise forever. The Lawrence defeat was the beginning of a series of events
which ended in the self-destruction of the woolen magnate. Wood could not again restore the paternalistic system that was so dear to him. He tried to endear himself
to the workers, but his failure was pitiful. He attacked
the profiteering merchants in Lawrence for charging
high prices to mill employees and built a company store
to sell goods at cost. On that occasion he held a big lawn
party at his Andover estate to which he invited the
workers. A half-holiday on full pay was declared that
afternoon in his mills. The Lawrence papers paid great
tribute to the benefactor who was to be received enthusiastically by his men upon his arrival in Lawrence.
Crowds of workers lined the streets when Wood came to
town. He drove through it, standing in his car, doffing
his hat and smiling, but his was a sad smile. There was
some handclapping, but there were also hoots and jeers.
Only a few hundred attended his lawn party—for the
free ice cream cones and cake.

Wood continued his welfare activities. He organized
a club in his mills, and placed a former socialist, Ignatius
McNulty, at its head. The club was to interest men in
sports, women in sewing, and to teach English to foreigners. But it failed. The radical leaders simply described it as a snare for the workers. Yet I have no
doubt that Billy Wood was really anxious to find a common bond with his men. But he was a victim of a system
stronger than himself, a system which barred common
language between the exploiter and the exploited. In
1922 Billy Wood's favorite son, who was active in social

welfare among the mill-hands, was killed in an automobile accident. There were rumors long before that the iron fist displayed by Wood in the Lawrence strike had been the cause of domestic trouble.

The finale came on February 2, 1926. The lonely old man, in spite of the $150,000,000 colossus he had welded, furnished the world the leading sensation of the day when he committed suicide at Daytona Beach, Florida. He had ordered his chauffeur to turn his car into an isolated road, and announced that he wished to take a walk by himself. Within a few seconds came the report of a pistol shot. Death was instantaneous. Thus ended the tragedy of a worker who rose to great heights but who could not rise high enough.

There were comrades of mine in the radical movement who said, at the time of Wood's suicide, that it served him right, that all of the mill owners and bosses ought to meet a like fate. Were not strikers shot to death in Lawrence and was not Billy Wood indirectly responsible for the murders? I agreed, but somehow I did not feel that way about Billy Wood's suicide. I knew all the grief he had caused, but when I grew up I also knew that Wood himself had been driven by the monster which he had helped rear. I could feel no bitterness towards the Portuguese proletarian who had become the textile king of America.

6

Two years later Big Bill Haywood died in Soviet Russia. An intimate comrade of his, a veteran of the I.W.W., told me of his tragic end. It was in the Foreign Workers' Club in Moscow that this man, whom I shall call Dan because that isn't his name, began to talk with warmth of his hero. And as I listened to the old "wobbly," I could not help drawing a parallel between the biography of this great labor leader and my own fate. I say this in all modesty for, however much we differ in achievement, the course of my life has been strikingly similar to Haywood's.

Although of colonial stock, William Dudley Haywood was born in 1869 into the most exploited class of workers in the world, the miners. His father, a native of Ohio, was working at that time near Salt Lake City and until the age of nine, when he himself entered the mines, Bill was brought up in Utah. A lad of great size and strength, he became a full-fledged miner at fifteen; at that time he had already suffered the loss of an eye from one of the many accidents of his dangerous occupation. In 1886, reading about the Haymarket riots in Chicago, he became interested in labor and for the next ten years, as he toiled in the mines and fields of the Northwest, he preached the doctrine of organization to his fellow workers. In the closing years of the Nineteenth Century he became dominant in the leadership of the Western Federation of Miners through his aggressive policy and through his advocacy of industrial unionism, the advantages of which to the workers are only now coming to be widely recognized and understood. But Big Bill became a national figure in 1901 when the Telluride strike opened a five years' industrial war in Colorado, five years marked by the most savage violence and the most flagrant abuse of the workers' Constitutional rights known in American history.

It was during this struggle that Haywood was "framed" for the murder of Frank R. Sennenberg, former Governor of Idaho, on the perjured testimony of Harry Orchard, a member of the Western Federation of Miners. Charles H. Moyer and George A. Pettibone, other officers of the Federation, were also implicated. All three were arrested in Denver and shipped across the state line without trial or extradition hearings. This act aroused the country and a national movement was soon under way to prevent Big Bill and his comrades from being railroaded to death. While in the Idaho penitentiary, Haywood was named the Socialist Party candidate for Governor of Colorado and polled about twenty thousand votes—fifteen thousand more than any Socialist nominee had ever received in that state. On July 28, 1907, Big Bill was acquitted after a sensational trial. But ten years later he was not so fortunate. In September, 1917, Big Bill was arrested for sedition because he opposed American participation in the World War. At the end of a trial that lasted four months he was sentenced to twenty years in prison and a fine of ten thousand dollars. Unlike Debs who shamed the country by serving his sentence, Haywood fled the country while he was out on bail and in 1921 arrived in Russia where he was received as a hero.

Dan told me these facts as he recalled the highlights of Big Bill's career—his glorious fight for the miners, his organization of the I.W.W., his emergence as a leader of the Socialist Party which later repudiated him because he advocated violence and direct action when he found that the reform of capitalism through political action was impossible. "Compared with Bill, to-day's revolutionary leaders are a bunch of weak sissies," growled Dan as he dropped his Communist mask for the while. "Safe behind their office desks, they plan the struggle of labor against the ballots and bullets of capitalism. They never face the cops' clubs nor the guns of the militia; they never run the danger of a frame-up

that will put them behind bars for life, like Mooney and
Billings, or burn them in the electric chair, like Sacco
and Vanzetti. Big Bill, on the other hand, never told
the workers to do something that he wouldn't do himself.
He led them to the post of danger; he didn't order them
to go there. But he made his great blunder when he
joined the Communist Party, just before he skipped
from the States," concluded Dan. "It was on the Party's
advice that he deserted the labor movement in America
and he never forgave himself nor the Communists for
this act."

"*Deserted* the labor movement?" I interrupted.
"What do you mean 'deserted'?"

"Those are Bill Haywood's own words to me. He felt,
since there were dozens of other boys in prison taking
the rap for opposing the war, that his place was with
them. So did the boys and the I.W.W., and they
told him so. But this wasn't the worst of things. Bill
wanted to go right on fighting for the workers,—for the
Russian workers,—in Russia. This led to many difficulties with the Russian Communist Party—that is, his
kind of fighting was not compatible with Soviet
methods—and they threatened to send him to Siberia!
And finally they convinced him to take a manager's job
at a southern coal mine. But the working conditions and
life of the Soviet coal miners was so terrible that Bill
returned to Moscow a sick man, disillusioned and heart-
broken. Before he died, he wrote a book in which he
told of his experiences in America and Russia. When
the book came out, the section on Russia was missing.
There was a notice that Bill died before it was finished.
But this wasn't the truth. What Bill wrote about conditions in Russia the Communists thought expedient to
suppress."

"But he was buried at the Kremlin Wall," I reminded Dan. "Surely the Communists must have thought that he deserved this high honor."

"Politics," he retorted. "The Communists hated his guts. But after all, they knew he was popular in America with the radicals. They know how to make grand political gestures . . . when the occasion is a funeral."

V. FROM WAR TO CLASS WAR

1

I WAS twenty when America entered the World War. In the months before that event, when the Allied propagandists were working up sentiment in the United States favorable to their cause, we used to talk about it at the mill and at the union headquarters. None of the boys I knew had any wish to travel three thousand miles to kill Germans with whom we had no quarrel. We all put our trust in President Wilson when he ran for re-election on the slogan of keeping us out of the slaughter in Europe. And yet a month after the inauguration we were in it.

Overnight, almost, a strange power cast its spell over the land. Uncle Sam pointed at us from every billboard with the call, "I want you!" And the men who had held the same opinion as I began to respond. They quoted the phrases of the "minute men"; they repeated stories of German atrocities, of how the Huns had been cutting off women's breasts and the arms of little children. They joined the army and the navy. Was it to make the world safe for democracy that these boys enlisted? Or did some strange virus of adventure in their blood cause them to exchange the drab overalls of the mills for the uniforms of soldiers? The girls liked the uniforms.

But I did not want to go to war. I had no desire to kill Germans even if they were guilty of all these atrocities. I read of conscientious objectors being sent to prison and wondered whether I would ever have the courage to become one. Meanwhile I heard boys like myself, who did not volunteer, denounced as slackers. I preferred being a slacker to being a killer. The newspapers carried headlines: DEBS GUILTY OF DISLOYAL ACTS. But I found Debs loyal to the best interests of the workers and he, rather than Pershing or Teddy Roosevelt, became my war hero. But I found myself lacking the courage of my hero. When in September, 1918, I was notified to appear before the local draft board, I went meekly enough. And soon I was marching up Essex Street to the North Station with thirty or forty other draftees. Bystanders applauded us *en route.* But what sticks in my mind is the face of a tall, elderly man, standing in front of the Waldorf Restaurant and picking his teeth with a toothpick. "Cannon fodder," he said to us as we marched past.

An old lady approached me at the station: "You look so young. Do you want to go to war?"

"Oh, sure," I stammered, not knowing whether to please the old lady with yes or no.

My family was there to see me off. Many people, including the draftees, were crying. The train moved on to Boston, thence to Camp Devens in the village of Ayer, Massachusetts. There was much drinking and singing on the way. *I Didn't Raise My Boy to Be a Soldier* and *Oh Say! Can You See Any Bedbugs on Me?* were the most popular songs. When we entered the town of Ayer, a hard-boiled sergeant jumped aboard and burst through our car door: "Shut up, youse guys! You're in the army now!"

And so we were.

2

The camp was crowded. I was placed in a tent with seven others. The legs of my army cot stood in pools of water. A young fellow lay plumb on his back beside me muttering incoherently, perhaps feigning he was a "nut." Other fellows said he wanted to escape going to France by being sent to the "dizzy" battalion (a place, I found out later, where the mentally sluggish or worse were sent). We played pranks on him—placed two burning candles at his head and a supposed lily on his chest, to make him look like a corpse. Whether through our assistance or not, he was sent to the "dizzy" battalion in a week.

With daybreak came reveille. The top sergeant bellowed through the barracks and out the door: "Rise and shine!" We rose but failed to shine in the bleary eyes of the sergeant whose name was Bill Grimes, a huge man with a scar on his cheek. Wiser ones said that Grimes came from the regular army, and that he had been too dumb to be made a lieutenant. I imagined he got his scar fighting in Mexico. We rookies lined up in front of the top sergeant. We still had on our civilian clothes—damp and wrinkled. Peter George, a Greek cook from Somerville, Mass., was at my right. He wore a crushed straw hat and a stiff starched collar. At my left stood, straight as a poker, Hugh Tupper, destined to be my buddy during my stay at the camp. Tupper hailed from the historic city of Lexington. He was a country mail carrier. Howard Begg, another one of my future buddies, was in the line in front. Begg, sophisticated and cynical, came from Watertown, Mass. His father was a manufacturer.

Lieutenant Peabody made his appearance, like a

prima donna, on the barracks steps, to take over the new recruits from Sergeant Grimes who had a paper in his hands with a list of names. He called them off: Adams, Ashley, Baxter, Beal, Begg, Clegg . . . And then, turning about-face to the lieutenant, "All present or accounted for."

Came the great moment. Every one was silent, while Lieutenant Peabody walked back and forth in front of us with a smirk on his lips. He was very superior, looking down upon us as if we were rugs for him to wipe his feet on. His lithe and well-proportioned body was marred by a mean-looking pug-nosed face. He started by telling us we were the worst looking lily-white rookies he had ever seen. But he had hopes: "Two weeks of dragging that ass around the field should help. I'll either make he-men out of you or you'll go home in a wooden kimono."—Afterwards Tupper named him "The Beast of Berlin," our favorite nickname for Kaiser Wilhelm.

Another lieutenant by the name of Collins was well liked, possibly for the manly jokes he often told. Collins was a wiry man, nervous, and always on the move. He had odd names for those of us who occasionally failed to understand the drill orders. We had a "moon-face," a "cheese-head," and a "bean-face." He called me "furniture-face" once when I was looking the other way during calisthenics.

One of the lieutenants lectured for an hour to us against slackers and conscientious objectors. He used every swear-word and curse in describing these people and when he ran out of insults, he barked: "Is there a conscientious objector in this crowd? If so, let him speak up or raise his hand." All were silent, while the lieutenant stood in front of us with fists doubled and posing like a prizefighter.

Then one lone lanky Maine fellow raised his hand. We all looked at him in amazement.

"You gawking idiot," shouted the lieutenant. "Are you one of those bastards?" He walked towards the Maine fellow as if to strike him.

Lieutenant Collins stopped him. "Perhaps the man didn't understand," he said.

"I think he does. Say, you . . . do you believe in fighting for Uncle Sam or not?"

"I don't believe in killing any one," spoke up the Maine fellow. He hung his head and looked at the ground as if he was ashamed to admit such a terrible thing.

"Why, you yellow bastard! We ought to hang you by the balls. You're a coward! You're yellow; that's what you are. Come out here and fight like a man!"

Collins intervened again and we marched off to the barracks.

"What a brave fellow to admit publicly his feelings against killing any one," I thought. "Why didn't I come out and say the same thing?" I could see that it took more courage to do this than to go to France and shoot Germans.

In the mess hall a few fellows clustered around the piano. Somebody began to play and sing *Home Sweet Home*. Others joined. One of the soldiers, sitting at a table and writing, yelled out: "Pipe down, you eggs, you want us all to go home?" Somehow the idea struck me that here was a way to end the war. Suppose all the soldiers in all the armies on all the fronts began to sing in their different languages the same song, *Home Sweet Home,* to the same tune. But I kept the thought to myself.

3

Influenza struck the camp a terrible blow. The dread epidemic came suddenly. The camp doctors said German agents were spreading "flu" germs in all the American camps. Our 5th company, 151st Depot Brigade, had only a dozen soldiers left for training in the field. All the others were in the hospital. I happened to be one of the dozen. Each day our group had grown smaller and smaller until, finally, all that remained were ordered to hospital work. With six others I was detailed to work with one of the undertakers. Men were dying at the rate of eighty to one hundred a day. What ghastly sights we saw. Our job was to slop dead men's intestines into a pail after the undertakers did their work. Insides were removed only from the dead who had to travel long distances—in their coffins, of course. How calm and indifferent were the undertakers, smoking and telling jokes. One of our group fainted when he had to dump the insides of a huge colored fellow into a pail.

One day I was detailed to carry the dead from the undertakers to tents or to the library which had been requisitioned for that purpose. We laid the dead on the floor and tied tags, with names and addresses, on their toes, for identification. There was a strong wind and drizzly rain and each time we passed the tents, carrying new dead, the flaps would blow up exposing the tagged toes. I was unnerved. It seemed indecent. And there was "Fat" lying on the floor of the library, dead like all the rest. "Fat" was a jolly, good-natured locomotive engineer from Maine, named McDonald. He was so stout the army could not find a ready-made suit for him. He felt embarrassed drilling in the field in civvies. One day he was taken with a pain in his side. His superiors made him drill just the same. That night he was taken to the hospital to be operated on for appendicitis, but he died a few days later from the "flu." I saw him laid out on the library floor with a tag tied to his big toe and in a uniform that at last fitted him.

Newsboys suddenly made their appearance in the camp selling papers carrying the headlines: GERMANY SURRENDERS! PEACE DECLARED! There was a scramble for the papers and some of the soldiers began to celebrate. It proved a false report. But a few days later the Armistice was signed, and the war was over. I remained in the camp for six months, however. Several hundred of us were kept as "Permanent Personnel" to help demobilize returning soldiers from France.

4

That winter another textile strike broke out in Lawrence. It was under the auspices of the Amalgamated Textile Workers' Union. Three Protestant ministers, Muste, Long, and Rotzell, were the leaders. Now and then I got leave of absence from camp to do picket duty in front of the mill gates. For these reasons I was nicknamed by the company, "Bolshevik," and by my buddies, "Dizzy." They couldn't understand why I took sides with "wops" and "hunkies."

The Y.M.C.A. secretary at Current Events, held each evening at one of the huts, always referred to the Lawrence strikers as "Bolsheviks," the word Bolshevik having become synonymous with murderer. One night he said: "The strikers in Lawrence are being led by Bolshevik murderers. It is not more wages they are fighting for but for a revolution like that going on now in Russia. Lawrence has always been known to harbor criminal leaders before . . ."

"You're a liar!" I suddenly yelled out, perhaps thinking of Big Bill Haywood. "The Lawrence workers are on strike for shorter hours and more wages, and they are not Bolsheviks, either."

The "Y" secretary was taken by surprise. And those from my company in the audience shouted: "'Attaboy, Red. That's the stuff, Bolshevik, give 'em hell."

The "Y" secretary thereafter was more careful in his description of the Lawrence workers. But his words set me to thinking and reading about the Bolsheviks in Russia. The newspapers were full of stories about the Revolution, about Lenin, about Trotsky leading armies against the Tsarist generals. In camp, too, there were lectures about Bolshevism. "Whenever you see an agitator speaking on a street corner against America pull him down, beat him up, show him that returning soldiers will not stand for Bolshevism in this country," cried one of the speakers at the Y.M.C.A. Auditorium. "The foreign Bolsheviks are on every street corner and hall in this country trying to tear down our institutions!" cried another. Most of the soldiers did not know what the speakers were talking about. Was some great foreign army about to invade America? Who these Bolsheviks were or what they looked like was a puzzle to them. I figured it out that they meant Socialists and other radicals who went on strike.

5

I kept right on helping to demobilize the incoming soldiers from France. Often in the middle of the night some of us had to get up and prepare chow for them before they got to the delousing plant. And almost any night I could hear the tramp, tramp of feet, first in the distance, then marching by our barracks. And a sorrowful lot of soldiers they were! All the adventure and poster glamour of enlistment days had gone out of them. They marched with rhythmical army cadence and discipline, but one look at them told the story. They were gloomy, tired and disillusioned. The French girls were not so free and beautiful as they had dreamed. They didn't hang the Kaiser to the sour apple tree, as they expected. And then there were rumors that the stay-at-homes had taken over their jobs.

All that the boys brought back with them were lice, obscene pictures, and venereal diseases. The lice were quickly eliminated at the delousing plant where the soldiers stripped, shaved all their hair and received a kerosene bath with a whitewash brush handled by a big negro. And the clothes received a steam bath. Then every soldier had to pass short and long arm inspection. Some were segregated to the venereal disease barracks, and others sent to barracks to wait for discharge.

When Tupper and I passed the venereal disease barracks, he said: "Jecus-cats, Dizzy, aren't you glad we didn't go to Paris now." Tupper, a devout Catholic, never used the Lord's name in vain. He always said "Jecus-cats" in place of Jesus Christ.

Where were the garlands of victory to be spread at the feet of the victorious army? Perhaps they were showered upon the boys on Fifth Avenue and Beacon Street. At Camp Devens, the victorious army only wanted to go home and go to work and get back wages in amounts equal to those of the stay-at-homes.

"All I want," said Private O'Brian, "is to get out of this man's army and go home."

"And get a job," said Private Kowalski.

"Me, too," said Knutson.

"And what about back wages?" interrupted Turovich. "They gave me a choice of Work or Fight. I chose to fight. Now I want to get paid for it."

"Me, too," said the Swede.

"Right," said Private Levy, "they're getting away with moider."

Between looking at smutty pictures and lectures against Bolshevism, war was planned on the stay-at-homes for jobs and on the government for back wages. But the privates who had been buddies for months were scattered after being discharged around the country. Their plans brought meager results. The State of Massachusetts passed a bonus bill providing one hundred dollars for every soldier. Upon my discharge from the army, May 18, 1919, I was given fifty dollars, plus railroad fare back to Lawrence. This was enough for my immediate needs.

That summer I read in the Socialist paper, The New York *Call,* about Tom Mooney who had been framed in California on the charge of planting a bomb in a Preparedness Parade. The Socialists were advocating a strike to free him ... Suffragists were fighting for the right to vote ... The Irish went wild over De Valera, the Sinn Feiner, when he came to Boston to speak ... The steel strike was on. William Z. Foster, just fresh from waging the War as a salesman of Liberty Bonds, was the leader ... American soldiers returning from the bleak Archangel front in Russia wanted to know what they were fighting for over there ... Trotsky was victoriously leading the Red Army against Kolchak ... Theodore Dreiser wrote a story called "Toilers of the Tenements."

6

I was still interested in finding out the meaning of Bolshevism, but I had a hard job of it, as I couldn't find any local Americans who claimed to be Bolsheviks. At last I came across some local radicals, holding forth on the streets of Lawrence. The first one I heard was Thomas Nicholson. He spoke on the corner of Essex and Franklin Streets every Tuesday and Saturday night between eight and ten, in competition with the Salvation Army beating the drum across the way. Nicholson was a tall, very thin man, with a face long and narrow. He wore glasses and looked something like Woodrow Wilson.

He was an Englishman by birth and an optician and clock repairer by trade. Later, when we became Comrades, I found him to be a very likeable person, always constipated, and believing that he hadn't long to live. He insisted he had a duty to perform before dying—to put his message across.

He carried his own platform in the form of a folding chair. At just the right time he'd unfold his chair in the gutter and let down a rolled sign: THE SOCIALIST PARTY, LAWRENCE LOCAL, painted in red. Then he would mount his platform and wait, looking over his slowly gathering audience, which somehow seemed to come from thin air. Some, like myself, had been leaning against a post nearby, or holding up one of the buildings, waiting for the orator to begin. I felt he was doing us workers a favor by giving us the benefit of his wisdom. He felt it, too. Before beginning he smiled down upon us benignly, as if to say: Well, I'm here again to show you how mankind can be saved. Then, with sudden speed, Nicholson would shoot out that long arm of his and yell: "I'm a rrrrevolutionist!" rolling the "r" several times over the tongue in a sort of oratorical ecstasy. When the audience recovered, he went on more mildly. He would quote Shakespeare, the Bible, Lincoln, Jefferson, and multitudes of other authorities, not forgetting Marx, of course, to prove that Socialism would be the savior of mankind. The streets were crowded, for on Tuesdays and Saturdays the business men kept their stores open late. Often passers-by gave Tom the "razz," but he was too dignified to get rattled.

Sometimes Nicholson would bring along a more prominent speaker from Boston or New York. That's how I came to hear Mrs. Elizabeth Glendower Evans of Boston and that's how I first came to know about Sacco and Vanzetti, then in prison charged with murder and waiting for the electric chair. Mrs. Evans was a picturesque old lady who kept up a constant fight to free Sacco and Vanzetti.

But by far the best and most interesting radical speaker, to me, was Samuel Bramhall, also of Lawrence and also from England. He had lived in America some forty years. Bramhall, with his great sincerity, courage, and fund of knowledge, influenced me more than any one else. He was a pest to the Lawrence politicians, as he liked to snoop around the city hall chambers and council meetings where the City Fathers were wont to plot ways and means of adding to their income. His appearances would cause a near-panic among the grafters. I heard and then met Sam during the Lawrence textile strike in 1922. I was on the picket line in front of the Pacific Print Works where I had been working before the strike when he walked up to me and asked if I would lead the line. Lead it! Of course, I would lead it.

I needed little urging from him to join the One Big

Union under whose auspices the strike was being fought. And under his guidance I began to take an active part in union affairs. In October of that year I joined the Socialist Party. Again I was committed to the theory of a class war, but this time I knew what it meant.

VI. RED HORIZONS

1

I WENT back to work at the Pacific Print Works. This
was my second time there. Moses, the boss, rehired me
because I had been in the army. I worked again as a
shearer. The job was simple. I took a fresh load of
starched cloth and ran it through the shear. When a
roll was made of it, I tied it up. It was then taken to the
print room. The cloth passed over sharp knives and
brushes which cut and brushed off the loose ends. The
machine automatically counted the number of yards.
There were seven shearers and about thirty winders in
the room. The winding machines just wound the cloth
on a roll without its passing over knives or brushes.
They went faster and for this reason the workers on
these machines received more wages. Most of them were
on piece-work.

We shearers thought we should get equal pay with the
winders because our work was harder. Even before I was
drafted into the army I had my first experience as a
strike leader as a result of that feeling. It was in the
same plant. The strike had started very simply. I had
brought the shearers together in a huddle. We asked
the winders to go on a sympathetic strike with us. They
agreed. At a certain hour one of the shearers gave a
loud whistle and we quit work. The shearing machines
stopped, and then the winders, and then the dryers,
whom we had not asked. The whole room was stopped.
I was surprised and a little scared because all eyes were

upon me. They wanted me to do the talking. Nearly all the workers got their hats and coats and gathered around the time clock. Boss Moses came along and demanded to know what was the matter. I told him that the shearers wanted wages equal to those of the winders. Then one of the winders spoke up and said they wanted more wages.

"Punch the clock *out* or go back to work," said Moses.

We punched the clock *out*. A sudden idea came to me that we should march through the print room on the way out. We did. And the men there joined us, too. Inside of a week most of the plant was out, and I didn't know what to do with the strikers. Police were at the gates every morning, but everything was peaceful. In one week the strike was won; we all received a slight increase in wages.

So here I was back again at the same machine, with a new cause to fight for—the "emancipation" of the working class. Now that I had become "class-conscious," I began organizing the "unconscious" into the One Big Union and the Socialist Party. I set about their conversion like an ancient Puritan. The same Puritanism had found expression in me before as an ardent churchman and prohibitionist, believing that booze and sin were the causes of all poverty and misery. But the Eighteenth Amendment came along and I discovered that liquor was not the cause of all evil. And during the war I had been disillusioned by the church and organized religion. They had supported the murderous conflict and it seemed to me they ought to have followed Christ's teaching and the commandment of "Thou Shalt Not Kill!" My new associates—the radicals—were against war. I read every piece of radical writings I could get hold of: Bellamy,

Upton Sinclair, Jack London and other authors. I could not understand Karl Marx.

My pre-war experience of "organizing" a strike in the "white room," gave me confidence in my ability to win people to my view. It surprised me, too, how easily I could talk people into joining the Union. I believed everything I said. My heart was in the work. I had little trouble in organizing my section. Then I started on the "dye room" below. I met with success here, too, but only among some of the foreign workers. The Irish and the Americans were too much interested in baseball and prizefights. Some of the Irish were antagonistic and called me names, such as "King of the Dagos."

2

The One Big Union and the Socialist Party were miles apart from each other in theory. The former, in theory and practice, was much like the I.W.W. The Socialist Party had a program of radical parliamentarianism only—a program of fighting for socialism through the ballot box. The One Big Union paid very little attention to parliamentary ways, but organized *all* workers under a common card. It differed from the American Federation of Labor unions both in its end and the means to this end. Its objective was a society consisting of workers and producers only and omitting the owning class. Its means were industrial unions whereas the A. F. of L. adhered to craft unions.

But there was also a fight going on within the One Big Union. On one side was the Workers' Party, a Communist organization, and on the other was a group led by Ben Legere which had no political connections, each individual being free to belong to any party he liked.

The Workers' Party crowd controlled the executive board but Ben Legere had the rank and file of the membership behind him, especially the Franco-Belgians and the Italians who were mainly syndicalists. It was literally a life-and-death struggle for the One Big Union because the Communists, under instruction from their national headquarters in New York, were intent on smashing the Union and putting its members into the American Federation of Labor. The purpose was to get as many people as possible into that organization and then "to bore from within" for control. Legere was opposed to this policy, holding that the Communists bored so hard that they worked their way right out the other side, thus destroying the Union without gaining the Federation.

What complicated matters for the Communists is that they had to play fast and loose at the same time. They were constantly telling the people that the A. F. of L. was rotten to the core and that its leaders always sold out the workers to the bosses and yet their entire strategy was to get these same workers into the A. F. of L. membership. They hoped to turn this trick by educating the masses to follow blindly behind Communist leadership and to ask no questions. Unfortunately for them their method of education consisted of distributing Marxist literature. When we got their pamphlets and papers, full of such words as proletariat, ideological, aggrandizement, manifestations, capitulate, and orientate, we pretended to understand what it all meant and let it go at that. As a matter of fact, that jargon simply made our heads twirl and we did not have the slightest idea of what it was all about.

In my opinion Ben Legere was right and I supported him. He seemed to me to be on the side of common sense and the best interests of the workers. Besides, I was a Socialist, not a Communist. I had been elected secretary of the Socialist Party local in Lawrence. This was nothing to boast about. The membership consisted of only ten persons. I was the youngest member and the only worker—all the rest were poor business men and one lawyer. They were a very passive lot, fearing to tread on the toes of the conservatives lest their business be hurt. But there was nothing timid about Legere. He was willing to fight both the Communists and the mill owners at the same time. He had a nickname for all those who were against him or his leadership in the Union. "Sto-o-ol-pigeons," he would yell at the top of his voice, "stool-pigeons." In his way of thinking there was no lower type of animal than the stool-pigeon who betrayed the plans and activities of the workers to the bosses. The Workers' Party men countered by calling those who opposed them "counter-revolutionists." They represented Soviet Russia. That was their great playing card. To be against them was to be against Soviet Russia, the Workers' Fatherland.

The result of this internal struggle was almost a standstill of activity by the One Big Union in Lawrence but our reputation was still good outside. Thus it was that when the Dover, New Hampshire, textile strike broke out in 1924, a delegation of the strikers came to us and pleaded for aggressive leadership because the United Textile Workers' Union, which was affiliated with the A. F. of L., was not conducting the strike so as to insure victory. They did not have to plead long.

3

Bert Emsley, then secretary of the One Big Union, urged me to go with him to Dover and take over the strike. I did.

Emsley was an idealist. His parents were wealthy. He had been a teacher and served in that capacity at Camp Devens during the war. He was assigned to the dizzy battalion and found that many of the supposedly feeble-minded were merely illiterate and completely ignorant men. He was terribly upset by this situation and decided to devote himself to the task of improving these conditions. After leaving the army, he found his way into the radical movement via the One Big Union. At first he was hired to teach the foreigners English, but becoming "class-conscious," he took on the job of secretary of the organization.

Bert was a short, stocky fellow who had a way with him and commanded respect. Bald on the first half of his head, he made up for it by letting his hair grow long and hang over his ears. He had done almost no speaking in public before going to Dover. I had done less. But Bert went at it like a veteran and gradually I learned to take charge of the strike committee when he was away. The strikers were Greek, Irish and French-Canadian. The young people were good fighters. They welcomed the strike. But there was very little discipline. And when I was alone I had difficulty in keeping order. I well remember the strike committee, sitting around on the floor—we had no chairs—telling jokes and discussing sports. When things got dull, the fellows would make motions about certain things that are not fit for print.

"Mr. Chairman," one Irish boy was raising his arm for attention, as we used to do in school.

"Yes."

"I have a *notion* to make a *motion* to cause a *commotion!*"

A chorus of laughs greeted this announcement. One day, when they thought Bert was away, they acted on such a motion. All that could climbed upon an old heavy dining room table. I protested that it would collapse under their weight. But they only laughed and said there was always room for one more. As was to be expected, the table wabbled, then crashed to the floor, carrying with it the human cargo. They scrambled up and war-whooped, in Indian fashion, around the broken remains. I looked on helplessly. They paid little attention to me. Then one of the boys spied Emsley through the window coming up the street.

"Hey, fellows, Bert's coming!"

Silence. Then, "Quick, get a hammer and nails."

Hammer and nails were secured and before Bert arrived the table was standing on its legs. And they stood around like naughty children.

"In order to be a leader," said Bert, after I told him about the affair, "you cannot mix with the masses and do everything they do. You've got to show them that *you* are master of the situation, that *you* know more than they. You've got to keep a little above them. You play cards with them and take part in all their games. You've become one of them, and now they don't respect you as a leader but just as a 'good fellow.'"

Bert said he learned this from Ben Legere. "You know, Ben never was on time at a meeting," he went on. "He always came late, kept the masses waiting and in suspense. Soon they'd be yelling, 'We Want Ben! We

Want Ben!' And Ben would make his entrance at just the right time. He'd never hang around with the boys. He would close himself in a room and make them come to him if they had any business to transact. Yet he is popular as well as respected."

But I was too much a rank and filer. I just could not keep away from the masses.

4

Most of the strikers were swinging over to our union. In fact, the whole city, including the business men, began rooting for the One Big Union. The business men wanted the strike over. They thought our organization with its militant policies would bring it to a quick end in favor of the strikers. The city newspaper was, of course, against us. The United Textile Workers' Union officials became panic-stricken. They wanted to control the strike, and now it was slipping out of their hands. Their speakers, Tom McMahon, Francis J. Gorman and others, were not liked, because they were not radical enough. So they imported some radicals to speak for them, radicals who wouldn't upset their craft-union ideas. They even produced an official Communist speaker, named Wicks. When Wicks spoke on the same platform as the U.T.W. officials and denounced the One Big Union, the strikers would not stand for this sort of double-dealing. They started a genuine commotion and broke up the meeting.

Harry Wicks, commanding a choice verbal arsenal of vituperation, is a typical Stalinist. He had begun his career as a patrioteer and Red-baiter. His talents in these capacities made him a valuable addition to the field staff of the American Communist Party.

Unfortunately for Wicks, the One Big Union organizers in the Dover strike were able to circulate a little-known chapter from his career. It was in the form of the following item, culled from the *Post,* of Gary, Indiana, for March 25, 1920:

"H. M. Wicks, of Chicago, a reformed Socialist, spoke on the revolutionary tendencies of the times to some forty Gary men last evening. Bill Haywood and his satellites should not be tolerated in this country, Mr. Wicks said. He advised American Legion members not to permit these vermin to talk to them, but to knock them down. That, he said, was the only language they understand.... He commended the deportation proceedings that have rid the country of many agitators and urged that other foreign troublemakers be given the same treatment. He urged an Americanization program for the foreign-speaking workers and he said the American Legion is the one organization in the country which is doing good Americanization work. . . . He told of attending the congress of the Communist Party in Chicago. By use of a caucus of about one-fourth of the delegates he controlled the meeting . . . Lenin is a dictator. . . . The speaker could not find words to describe his disgust for the I.W.W. He charged them with being cowards and the scum of the earth. . . . Wicks is preparing to tour the country in order to let the American people understand the true situation."

This missive had a deadly effect in Dover, but it did not prevent Harry Wicks from rising to positions of greater service in the cause of Stalinism.

Next morning Emsley and I were arrested while picketing in front of the mill agent's house. They took us to the police station situated in the City Hall and put Bert in one cell and me in another. This was my first time in a cell. Within two hours the strikers were massed outside, demanding our freedom. Soon nearly the whole town picketed the jail. A crowd stormed the police station door. At first Bert thought it was the Ku Klux Klan come to run us out of town.

The police opened up the door and pulled in a few of those trying to break it down. One of them was an Irish girl who gave the cops plenty of trouble. She kicked them and pulled their hair. They put her in a cell. Some nice old ladies came to bail us out. At first we were not permitted to go, but when the strikers became more violent they accepted the bail. The strikers carried us on their shoulders to a Greek lunchroom where they filled us with food. It was a great celebration.

The following day we faced the court. It was crowded. Machine guns were placed on the roof. There were all sorts of preparations for trouble. But the trial itself was tame enough. We were charged with disturbing the peace at the meeting and there was no proof on which to base such a charge. The judge gave me a scolding and turned me loose. He dismissed the charge against Emsley, too, without giving him the benefit of a lecture.

Although it was clearly a trivial affair, my arrest was featured in the Lawrence papers. I attached no more importance to the publicity than to the arrest itself, made on trumped-up charges. But it worried my father who thought it was a shameful thing for me to spend a night in jail. Among the workers, on the other hand, this was considered to my credit. From that time on I was regarded as one of the local labor leaders. In Dover, also, this incident helped us to carry on the strike. It was one of the last gestures made by the mill owners and the officials of the U.T.W. before the strike was settled with a victory for the workers.

Despite this success, the One Big Union was doomed. It could not continue as an effective organization when its own executive board was plotting its destruction. Gradually the leaders who opposed the Communists fell away. Bert Emsley married a weaver in one of the mills and she insisted on his going back to college teaching, which he did. Ben Legere, too, became tired of the unequal struggle. He returned to his home in Canada, then came back to the United States. Gradually he worked his way West till he came to California. There he remembered that in his youth he had been an actor and the last I heard of him, he was trying to land a job in the movies. The rest of us were too weak to save the union. Not being on the inside at that time, I could not understand why the Communists were so anxious to break up the radical textile unions and to strengthen the A. F. of L., which they hated. Later I learned. Word had come from Moscow: Work through the American Federation of Labor. And they did as they were told although the orders were given by people who did not know the facts and did not understand conditions in the United States.

The radicalism of my youth was not the radicalism of Moscow. It was American, growing out of American conditions and suited to the American temperament. Even in the Lawrence strike of 1912, where most of the strikers were of foreign birth, the I.W.W. leaders were natives. They were interested in direct benefits to the workers of the United States, not in world revolution. I had the feeling that an organization founded on these principles could still be successful but I knew that it would be impossible to bring the leaders of the various textile unions together. So I decided to go directly to the masses. I formed the Rank and File Committee of Textile Workers. It was my first step as an independent leader. But I was not independent for long. The effort at once attracted the attention of the national office of the Communist Party. They ordered Johnny Ballam, the Communist district organizer for New England, to attend the first conference and Ballam, in turn, ordered the Communists among the textile workers to pack the meeting.

Before the conference opened, Ballam and his followers went into a huddle in another room. This was called a "fraction" meeting, something in which all party members had to participate. In plain English, "fraction" is a caucus of party members, but the Communists were too ignorant of our political tradition to know the word and the fact that holding a caucus is one of the most common procedures of our parties. They still think that they have made a great political innovation in the use of "fraction" meetings. I must admit that this "fraction" was completely successful. It took control of the conference, changed the name I had chosen to the United Front Committee of Textile Workers, and elected its leaders to most of the executive posts. It arranged for a second conference which was to show the United Front to the masses. It did—except that all union representatives who were not Communists were conspicuous by their absence.

In spite of all this, I was gradually moving "left," toward the Communist Party. One thing that brought me closer to them was that they were workers in the mills. Then, also, they were always active in organizing the workers. The Socialists and other radicals in Lawrence were chiefly middle-class intellectuals who loved to theorize about Utopia and felt they were bringing it about when they voted, once a year, against the major parties. In 1924 the Socialist Party endorsed Senator

Robert M. La Follette who was running for President on the Progressive ticket. I worked day and night trying to win the masses to that platform although I realized how far it was from my ideals. The La Follette campaign offered the first concrete illustrations of united front tactics applied to the American scene by direction from Moscow. In many other ways it was an historic campaign. For the first time in the annals of the American Federation of Labor, the policy of neutrality in political campaigns was abandoned. The powerful Sampel Gompers himself endorsed La Follette.

John L. Lewis, who was later to father the united front Committee for Industrial Organization, was the outstanding exception in that campaign. John L. Lewis came out for Cal Coolidge. He served on the advisory board of the Republican Party together with such "friends of labor" as William Butler, textile czar of New England.

In June of that year, the Communists held a "Farmer-Labor" Convention at St. Paul and nominated Duncan McDonald for President and William Bouck for Vice-President. This was to be a united front ticket.

But on July 11, the Communist Party changed its mind. The "Farmer-Labor" ticket was thrown overboard, upon orders from the Communist International, and a Communist ticket headed by William Z. Foster and Ben Gitlow was put in the field. Foster even dared to scold Eugene Debs for supporting La Follette, to which Debs replied as follows:

"That my endorsement of La Follette under the circumstances seemed 'astounding' and 'shocking' to you appears not a little strange to me in the light of the fact that the St. Paul Convention dominated absolutely by the Communists intended, according to some of its chief spokesmen, including Mahoney and Ruthenberg, to do that very thing, that is to say, to endorse the nomination of La Follette for the Presidency (the nomination of McDonald being made 'conditional' with that end in view), and it would no doubt have done so had not La Follette, knowing the record of the Communists and understanding their game, publicly denounced them and positively refused their endorsement. Mahoney has since, according to a press despatch, declared that he had been 'double-crossed' by the Communists."

With the election of Calvin Coolidge to office I realized something of much more vital significance: that the American workers would never be won over on the political side. I decided to drop out of the Socialist Party and to devote all my energies to union work. And for three years I did what I could, through the One Big Union, through small local organizations, and through the United Front. Then I gave up.

VII.   THE ROAD TO COMMUNISM

1

I WAS somewhere in New Jersey, on the Lincoln Highway, on the first leg of a hitch-hiking trek to California. It was July, 1927. I was resting under a tree. A companion was to join me at Niagara Falls. At last I would have a real vacation. As a radical trade union leader, my wages had been largely theoretical. True, I was supposed to be getting fifteen dollars a week. Actually I received my pay only when a little extra money was available. This was in accordance with the unwritten law of the radical labor movement. It is a law that does not apply to radical political movements, such as the Communist and the Socialist Parties. A trade unionist belonging to either of these parties is assured of a regular wage. But I had long since quit the Socialist Party, and I was not a member of the Communist Party. Although I was active in the United Front campaign, I was not an insider and was chronically moneyless. It was still in the era in which the thumb-jerkers enjoyed the freedom of the highways. I decided to leave my post in Lawrence for a few months, and took to the road.

But the road to California became the road to the Communist Party. A telegram from the Sacco-Vanzetti Defense Committee in Boston had been forwarded to me by my folks. It was a desperate call for mass action to save those two noble Italian workers from the electric chair. It was an appeal which arrested my steps and agitated my mind. I sat down by the roadside to decide whether to proceed or go back. The morning was clear and beautiful. There was happiness in the air. But my thoughts kept reverting to the shoemaker and the fish-peddler who from behind bars were challenging the forces of reaction. It was the land and the day of Cal Coolidge. As I surveyed the procession of cars on the road, I wondered how many of these pleasure-bent or business-bent people felt the great tragedy being enacted in Boston. The people's apathy aroused me.

"If it had not been for these things I might have lived out my life, talking at street corners to scorning men . . . I might have died, unmarked, unknown, a failure . . ." These words of Vanzetti, thrown into the face of the vindictive Judge Thayer who denied them a new trial burned into my heart. I was convinced then that Sacco and Vanzetti had been "framed" for preaching their ideas just as I am convinced now that the State of Massachusetts put two innocent men to death when it electrocuted them. I decided to return home and to fight for their freedom to the limit of my resources. I dashed out to the open road; a big limousine gave me a "lift" to New York; and it was easy to make Boston.

2

"Why can't you leave Sacco and Vanzetti alone? Why can't you let them die in peace?" Secretary Moro of the Sacco-Vanzetti Defense Committee, greeted me with this bitter outburst when I reported at the Boston headquarters.

"Why, Comrade Moro, what do you mean?" I cried out, taken aback.

"You people don't care for Sacco and Vanzetti. Let them burn; it will be better for the cause."

I was stunned as if hit on the head with a baseball bat. For nearly seven years he and others had been fighting for Sacco and Vanzetti, organizing mass meetings and demonstrations, issuing millions of leaflets, going to jail. And now he cried: "Let them burn!"

"Take it easy, Red," Mary Donovan, another leading spirit of the Defense Committee, turned to me. There was a twinkle in her dark and beautiful Irish eyes. "He's tired, worn out, and has just been having a fight with the Communists who are out to organize another defense committee."

It became clear to me that Moro, an Anarchist, had taken me for a Communist. And the Communists were suspected of trying to make capital out of the Sacco-Vanzetti case for their cause. Many felt that the Communists were not interested in saving, the lives of the two men. In fact, Sacco and Vanzetti themselves were of this opinion.

The little headquarters in the North End section of Boston, in a dingy building at 256 Hanover Street, was in a state of high fever. The Sacco-Vanzetti case had, after seven years of smoldering, broken out into a world blaze. The committee was frantically trying to organize the protesting forces. But they could no longer be directed.

Overwhelming proof had been furnished that the two men were innocent; that Judge Thayer had shown his bias against them even before the trial; that the prosecution had presented perjured evidence. The best legal minds in America had gone on record with the statement that the sentence was a gross miscarriage of justice. Public opinion throughout the world was unanimously in favor of a new trial. Yet there was no resource in the peculiar judicial system of Massachusetts except to one man, the Governor of the State. As the day of the execution approached, however, it began to look as if Governor Alvin Fuller would heed the pleas and arguments of those who represented humanity and justice. A newspaper close to the state administration appeared on Wednesday, August 3rd, with a streamer headline:

NEW TRIAL INDICATED AS STEP FULLER WILL TAKE

Governor is Expected to Call For Reprieve of Men and Action by Legislature

Nicola Sacco and Bartolomeo Vanzetti will not die in the electric chair on the date set. Neither will they be pardoned. Further reprieve pending steps by the Massachusetts Legislature looking to a new trial was indicated at the State House today as the solution of the historic case of the Italian radicals which Governor Fuller will place before the Executive Council when it meets tomorrow. The Governor will make known the decision tomorrow night.

Friends of Sacco and Vanzetti slept better that night. The horrors of the electric chair did not seem so close. But they did not know that an ambitious man sat in the Governor's chair. They had not noticed particularly that the same newspaper carried another headline: COOLIDGE DOES NOT CHOOSE TO RUN IN 1928. It did not escape Fuller's eye. Coolidge had entered the White House by smashing the Boston policemen's strike. It was inevitable that the parallel of another reactionary gesture and its consequences should suggest itself to the politician in the State House. On the following day Fuller called in the reporters, among them the very men to whom he had confided his plans for a reprieve, and handed out a statement. "Sacco and Vanzetti are guilty," it read. "The date of their execution is set for August 23, 1927."

The shame of that action spread like a dark cloud over our heads. We stumbled around blindly, seeking some way out. Although the finest and noblest spirits in the country answered the challenge of that political gesture, they were impotent in the face of the indifference and cynicism of the millions. It is the millions who elect the President of the United States.

3

On Sunday morning, August 14, I stood in front of St. Patrick's Church in Lawrence and passed out leaflets to people coming from early mass. The leaflets, bearing my signature, read:

> The Sixth Commandment says: "Thou Shalt Not Kill!"
> But the State of Massachusetts is about to murder two workingmen—Sacco and Vanzetti.
> Come to the Protest Meeting, at Ideal Hall, Essex Street, Sunday, August 14.
> Speakers: Father Dorbene, Irish Catholic Priest; Captain Paxton Hibben, United States Army; Alfred Baker Lewis.

In a few minutes a police car appeared. I was arrested and taken to the station. Chief of Police O'Brien questioned me and held a conference with his lieutenants. "I've got you this time," the Chief announced gleefully after the conference. "You know what you've done? You have accused the State of Massachusetts of murder in this leaflet, and you signed it. You'll get five years for this."

I tried to keep my composure. Chief O'Brien wasn't a bad sort of a man. But he considered me a nuisance in Lawrence, and he hated a nuisance. He really was scared of any kind of political or labor disturbance. He knew how to handle petty thieves and drunks but anything which had a social angle was beyond him.

I decided to play upon his fear of a disturbance. "That's swell, Chief," I said. "My friends expect to hold the meeting in front of this police station if I'm held. There'll be thousands in front of here in an hour. It's all been arranged."

It worked. O'Brien was afraid that thousands of Italians, of which Lawrence has a big population, would swarm around the police station. He decided in the interests of peace to let me go. "But don't you dare give out any more leaflets," was his parting shot.

Once out, I took three hundred leaflets which remained hidden under my shirt and continued passing them out on the streets and on Lawrence Common.

A ringing call came from Boston for one hundred thousand Americans to come and watch the solemn crucifixion of justice in the Cradle of Liberty: "Let all the roads of the nation converge on Beacon Hill. Come armed with a black band on your sleeve. Come armed with inextinguishable faith that Sacco and Vanzetti must and shall live!"

I rushed to Boston. This time I reported to the Citizens' National Committee for Sacco and Vanzetti, a newly organized body of representative Americans with headquarters at the fashionable Hotel Bellevue. The place was full of excitement. Yards of telegrams were streaming in and out. The battle was being waged against overwhelming odds with desperate frenzy. The only thing left to do was for hundreds of thousands of sympathizers throughout America to march on Boston, and by their sheer numbers and protests save the two innocent men from death. I organized a group in Lawrence and we came to Boston to picket the State House. There was a crowd on hand to watch the procession, but only a few on the line itself. The police gave us seven minutes to picket. Then the entire line was arrested and taken to the Joy Street station. Here several prominent people were waiting with money to bail us out. We then went back to the picket line. This happened several times. John Dos Passos, the author, hit upon the plan of walking the seven minutes, and then going off and coming on again later for another seven minutes. But the police had their eye on him. He walked off towards the Boston Common, two policemen dashed after him, making an arrest. My comrade Murdoch and I were able to follow Dos Passos' tactics a few times. Then we were recognized.

"I've seen those two sons-of-bitches on the line more than once," said one of the Boston bulls. "C'mon youse two, hop in the wagon." But the wagon was full, so they forced us to the wall, taking away a placard I was carrying. We walked to the station again. And again we were bailed out. We decided this time to stay out of jail long enough to attend the meetings called for that night.

A crowd filled the Laborers' Union Hall and overflowed into the street. From the window above Ella Reeves Bloor addressed the overflow. She was a Connecticut Yankee. Many years ago, as a newspaper woman in Waterbury, she had espoused the workers' cause and she was known throughout New England as "Mother" Bloor. But this crowd of sensation-seekers did

not know her. One of the women in the mob yelled out
to her: "Go back to Russia!" The police arrested
"Mother" Bloor. Inside the meeting was divided as to
the next step. I was in favor of picketing the Charlestown Prison, hoping that perhaps the pressure of thousands might lead to some action on behalf of the two
doomed men. The majority finally voted to go to
Charlestown. I led a group from the hall. We put
placards under our coats because the police were confiscating them. Our group marched over the Charlestown
bridge.

I shall never forget that night on the bridge. Stars
were shining and boats were passing underneath just
as if nothing were happening. Two innocent men were
about to die but, with the exception of our marching
group, it did not even affect the traffic on the bridge.
Cars which had just gone by the Charlestown Prison
drove past us, the people in them looking unconcerned,
laughing even when we yelled, "Save Sacco and Vanzetti." It was horrible to think of the fate of these two
men, so near the end; it was more awful to see these
others, so callous, so unaffected by the tragedy.

We arrived at the City Square. The precinct station
was filled with police and hundreds of them were moving
around outside, brandishing their nightsticks. Thousands of people were in the Square. Most of them had
come "to see the fun."

There were cries: "The Reds are coming! The Reds
are coming!"

The police stampeded out of the station to stop what
they must have thought was a marching army of thousands of Reds. Some of our group got by, but most were
held back by the cops and their nightsticks. For blocks
around Charlestown Prison, where Sacco and Vanzetti

were waiting to take their last walk, the streets were roped off. Between these ropes and the prison was forbidden territory. Even those that lived in these streets could not come or go. About thirty of us managed to get through the crowds. Fifteen of us began to display the posters we had brought. I decided to lead the group under the ropes and to the prison. I lifted the ropes and went under. I was followed by a dozen more. The police arrested nine of us. They marched us down the forbidden street. A shot was fired from the elevated railroad above. Hundreds of police on horses came dashing along the street towards us and the great mass of people behind the ropes.

The cops taking us to the station were scared. "Are they going to run us down?" they yelled.

We made for the sidewalk. The mounted men drove into the crowd. There were screams and the crowd swayed like a wave.

We were taken to a police box while a wagon was called. The news photographers were taking pictures. The police then began fighting among themselves to get into the pictures with us. "Say," bawled one of the cops, "I'm the one that arrested this guy. If there is any mug to get in the papers with this Red, it's me."

We finally went to the station in the wagon. At this moment Sacco and Vanzetti were being prepared for the chair.

We sang songs. My comrades and I were taken to a cell. To reach the cell corridor it was necessary to pass through a guard room filled with policemen. On the way I was beaten by two of them, as were some of my other comrades. It was the first and only beating I ever received at the hands of the police.

As I sat in the cell, unable to do more for Sacco and

Vanzetti, a motherly woman who came to arrange for our bail walked in. She said softly: "They've done it. Sacco and Vanzetti are dead."

A cop stood behind her with a smirk on his face.

I never wanted to be alone so much as at that moment. When the motherly lady left, I lay down on the hard bench and cried.

I took a solemn vow to carry on the work of Sacco and Vanzetti, to fight against human suffering, against injustice, against the system that framed them and killed them.

But I never dreamed that night that I too would be facing the electric chair two years later.

Sacco and Vanzetti were dead, but their ideals will live. Of this I feel deeply convinced. Perhaps Horace Carr of Cleveland came closest to expressing my feelings when he wrote:

On the Twenty-third of August, 1927
Nicola Sacco
and
Bartolomeo Vanzetti
workingmen and dreamers of the Brotherhood of Man, who thought to find it in America, after seven tortured years in prison were done to a cruel death by the children of those Pilgrims who, long ago, fled to this land—for freedom.

They are at peace; but their voices are gone into the earth, and they will be remembered with gratitude and tears when the names of those who murdered them—Statesmen—Judges—Scholars—have gone down into everlasting shame.

4

The Sacco-Vanzetti tragedy brought me closer than ever to the Communist Party. It seemed the most effective radical organization in the field, almost the only one that was really active in behalf of the workers. I decided to put aside my dislike of some of their methods and principles and to coöperate with the Communists in their union efforts without joining the Party. After a brief period among the brass workers in Waterbury, Connecticut, I received a call from Alex Bail, Communist district organizer in Boston. He wanted me to get back into the textile field and promised to give me a free hand. William Murdoch, a wiry little Scotchman with a long nose and strong accent, who had long been active in the textile labor movement, joined me in this work. Together we planned an extensive campaign for all New England. We decided to create a new organization called the Textile Mill Committees which would attempt to gather up all the scattered radical forces that had become discouraged and downhearted. We organized each mill as a unit with a central committee in each city which would eventually grow into a national union.

One day, on the train to Manchester, New Hampshire, we read in a Boston paper that a 10 per cent wage cut would be put into effect in the New Bedford mills on April 16th.

"Murdoch," I exclaimed, "we shouldn't go to Manchester. Our place is in New Bedford. Let's go there and organize a strike."

Murdoch agreeing, we got off the train at the next stop and made for Boston. At the Communist headquarters Bail agreed with us and we set to work immediately. We drew up a leaflet urging the New Bedford workers to strike and then went to a print-shop where a handful of us worked all night and got out ten thousand copies. The next day we were in New Bedford and on Saturday morning we began distributing the leaflets at the mill gates.

Now one of the things we had put in that leaflet was a warning that the leaders of the New Bedford Textile Council, the A. F. of L. organization, would try to sell out the workers by refusing to call a strike. The method by which this was usually done was to hold a secret vote on the question. Then the leaders counted the ballots privately and announced that the majority had voted against striking. To avoid this we urged the workers to "demand that the votes be counted openly." As a result of our propaganda, the Council was forced to call a meeting of the union members the next day at the Bristol Arena, the largest hall in town, generally used for prize fights. At the conclusion of the meeting a vote was taken and, as usual, the leaders started off with the ballot-box to their private office. But there arose such a howl from the audience that they came back to the platform and held an open count. The vote was overwhelmingly for "Strike."

The mill owners and the newspapers announced that this vote was the result of long Communist activity by many organizations. The correspondent of the New York *Times* even went into an explanation of how the workers had been weaned away from the Textile Council by Communist agencies. The fact of the matter is that there had been no organization in New Bedford before Murdoch and I came there with the strike leaflets. All we had was a knowledge of what the workers wanted to do. But the day after the vote we got together, with the help of a handful of Portuguese syndicalists, a group sufficiently large to work for a mass meeting which we called at the same Bristol Arena. The place was packed and there we organized hundreds of workers into Textile Mill Committees. On the same day we opened an office in the heart of this beautiful old whaling city and the famous New Bedford strike of 1928 was on in full swing.

5

In the interest of the strike, it became necessary for me to join the Communist Party. But almost immediately I began to have trouble with the Comrades. The national headquarters insisted on sending droves of organizers, representing all its puppet subsidiaries, to New Bedford. They flocked in from Boston, New York, and points west. They came armed with documents, with authority. The host had to be fed and housed, their various proposed activities had to be financed. Since the Textile Mill Committees had no funds, the Communist Party ordered that its agents should draw upon the strikers' relief fund.

Ann Washington Craton, a gallant little soul who had done splendid work for the Sacco-Vanzetti committee, was in charge of the relief drive. She insisted that all the money collected for relief should be given to needy strikers and not a cent for any other purpose. Murdoch and I supported her in this stand. But when the Party compromised and asked that a small part be diverted to "organizing" purposes, I succumbed to the argument. Miss Craton continued to fight bitterly against the proposal and Murdoch was on the point of breaking with the Party when he was taken for a ride by some Boston comrades who threatened "to beat hell out of him" if he did not yield. It may have been a coincidence, but the day after Murdoch's ride, Roger Baldwin of the Civil Liberties' Union came to New Bedford with another man to see Ann and as a result of this visit she discovered that she had urgent business in New York. Like her most famous ancestor, she retreated across the Hudson. Some of the Portuguese strikers presented her with flowers as she took the train.

The Communist Party dug deep into the relief treasury thereafter. And they took more than money by that action, for the heart went out of that strike. Towards the end of June it began to lag and the Communist officials became quite desperate. They called a conference in Boston and Murdoch and I were ordered to attend an all-night session. Most of the time we slept in our chairs while the Comrades lectured each other on how to conduct a strike.

6

One rainy day I was on the picket line in front of the Wamsutta Mill thinking how to put new life into the strike. I felt that if we could have a demonstration like the one at Dover when Emsley and I were arrested, it would arouse the strikers. Police were all about as usual. Patrolman Andy McLeod gave me an idea. He seemed to be peeved because I was wearing a red flower and reading a book. He made nasty remarks about this. Then he shouted to one of the strikers to stop singing. Now, I couldn't see why any one should stop singing in America at the order of a policeman. But I knew that this cop would try to show his authority if challenged. Here was a chance to get arrested! So I began singing *Ramboia,* a folk song the Portuguese taught me. It went something like this:

O Ramboia! O Ramboia
Andas sempre a ramboiar;
Quem casar com o papa seco,
pas precisa trabalhar!

Andy McLeod yelled: "Cut it out or I'll run you in."

This was what I wanted. So I sang again, and the strikers sang with me. It was the "picket line" song made up by the strikers.

On the line, on the line,
Come and picket on the picket line.
If you want to win the strike
Get in upon the fight
Come and picket on the picket line.

McLeod seized me and the pickets with umbrellas crowded around him. Other policemen rushed the strikers and there was a free-for-all. Some of the women present cut the belts that held up the cops' trousers or tore off their suspender-buttons, and they were put out of the fight temporarily. There was fighting all over the street, mostly with fists. The New Bedford police never used guns. I had counted on that and knowing that our people were not armed, I felt that the most any one could get would be a bruised head or a black eye.

My captor looked around for me while I was shouting to the strikers, "Stay in the picket line."

"Here I am," I said to McLeod. He placed me in a police car in charge of two other policemen named Trudel and Hickey. The strikers got on one side of the car and tried to tip it over so the cops couldn't take me away. The police ran to the other side and kept the car upright until we got started for the station.

Two strikers, a woman and a man, were thrown in the car with me. When Hickey got in, the woman poked her umbrella in his eyes.

"For God's sake, Beal, stop that woman, will you?" he cried. Finally he got hold of the umbrella and broke it. This started another free-for-all within the car. The man striker in the car had good teeth. He bit Hickey in the arm, right through his uniform. Hickey stuck his fingers in the biter's eyes. I received a punch in the jaw.

The strikers meanwhile marched upon the station. Bessie Katsikaras, a pretty young Greek girl, and her father Louis, were also arrested. Bessie was yelling: "Come on! We'll get the cops before they get us!" Once inside the cell Bessie sang one of the strikers' favorites.

> *Strawberry shortcake,*
> *Huckleberry pie,*
> *Who gave the bosses a punch in the eye?*
> *We did, we did!*
> *Who are we?*
> *We are members of the T.M.C.*

Not even the cops could keep Bessie still. She went on for hours at a time. They gave her the name of "Strawberry Shortcake Bessie."

Nine of us were arrested that day, brought up before a judge, and the cases continued. Our arrests gave great impetus to the strike. It doubtless contributed to keeping the mills closed the next few weeks. Then Judge Milliken ruled that mass-picketing was illegal. The strikers thought otherwise. Due to this ruling the police made raids on picket lines, breaking them up.

I picketed every morning in front of some mill. Once, while on the way to the picket line, I saw the strikers scatter in front of the Whitman Mill as the police came up with big trucks to make mass arrests. I was furious. I felt we had a right to mass picketing. At the strikers' meeting that morning I challenged the police to try the same thing again in the evening. The press headlined it and the police took up the challenge.

We marched to the Whitman Mill again that evening. While we were picketing and singing songs, two large covered trucks and a moving van came around the corner. An order was given to arrest only the men. The police jumped out of the vans and rushed the strikers. To their surprise, we did not resist. On the contrary, every one, including the women, tried to get in vans. The cops had to fight the women back. The plan I had and which the strike committee accepted was to fill the jails with strikers and make the city feed the workers in jail. We were crowded, eight to a cell, 256 of us. A slogan was passed around: "Refuse bail, stay in jail."

That night over ten thousand people, friends of the strikers, massed outside of the prison, demanding our release. A company of the National Guard was called out and with fixed bayonets drove the crowd away. But the friends of the strikers insisted upon getting us out on bail. I tried in every way possible to stay in, but to no avail. Clerks worked all night bailing the strikers out.

Our cases were heard in the Third District Court. I was one of the group sentenced to six months. All the cases were appealed. A few days later Murdoch and I were arrested again. This time Murdoch received a two months' sentence and I one month in the House of Correction. We served it, during the strike. It was the first rest we had in months. Murdoch and I made chairs in the prison factory and won over the prisoners and guards to the union.

7

The great strike was rapidly drawing to an end in October, 1928. The officials of the New Bedford Textile

Council made every effort to get the strikers back to work. Our organization found itself attacked by a coalition of all the established interests. The mill owners, business men, church leaders and the press joined with the Textile Council in its fight against us. The merchants displayed signs that no more credit would be given to strikers. The mill owners threatened to blacklist the militant workers. The church leaders denounced the godless radical leaders of the Textile Mill Committees. The press carried false headlines that the workers were ready to compromise on a five per cent wage cut. The police raided our relief stores and arrested many of our leaders with the intention of keeping them in jail while a poll was taken among the strikers.

The Textile Council of New Bedford consisted of seven unions with a membership of over five thousand. There were thirty thousand workers out on strike. Yet when the Council called for a vote on the question of going back to work not more than two thousand voted. The others no longer wished to be counted among the members of the Council. Even so, in their three largest unions the vote read: 904 in favor of returning to work; 710 in favor of continuing the strike. Nevertheless, the strike was broken. It had lasted twenty-three weeks. The loss to the workers in wages was six hundred thousand dollars; the losses of the mills ran into millions. But the coalition was jubilant. The "radicals" had been licked. The police saw to it on the morning when the men began to return to work that our representatives were not within sight of the mill gates.

The New Bedford strike is a large milestone in my life. There I learned many things, important as well as trivial. Among the latter was the meaning of the word, proletariat. One of our Communist organizers flaunted that word before the workers. "We, proletariat, demand this . . ." he used to say, or "the dictatorship of the proletariat will achieve that . . ." One day an indignant worker came to me to protest against being called a proletariat.

"I've been looking up this word, proletariat, in the dictionary," he said belligerently, "and I don't think we ought to be called such names."

I explained that nothing wrong was meant by the word, that it referred to the wage-earning class. But he led me to his dictionary and showed me: *"The lowest class of the community in ancient Rome, regarded as contributing nothing to the State but offspring . . . applied to the lowest class in society."*

Recently memories of the strike and the various people who participated in it were evoked by a meeting with Jackson Wales. He was a Harvard student who led a group of his class-mates to New Bedford to find out what it was all about. Wales joined the picket line and was arrested several times for singing *America* and the *Star Spangled Banner*. He taught these songs to the foreign strikers who found the words quite ironical in the face of all the patrol cars that were constantly dragging them off to jail. After the strike Wales did not return to college. He became a member of the Communist Party, was disowned and disinherited by his family, lost his wife through divorce because of his devotion to the "cause," and finally was expelled from the Party for being too democratic. He is now working "on relief."

The strike affected many lives—and mine most of all. For it placed me in the forefront of the Communist labor organizers. And it pointed directly to the next field of activity—the textile mills of the South.

BOOK TWO

GASTONIA

VIII. DOWN SOUTH

1

"ALL these here good roads you sees spread all over Carolina is the doin's of chain-gangs. I put in six months myself slavin' like a nigger with a gang 'n Carabus County." A round-shouldered man, his face furrowed, his voice full of resentment, was speaking. He was leaning against a signpost which read: CHARLOTTE—20 Miles.

Mario Thumudo and I had stopped along the road to pick a conversation with him and I said something about the good roads of North Carolina. He let loose on the subject of the chain-gangs and their terrors.

"For what reason did they get you?" asked Mario, as he climbed into the seat of our motorcycle.

"Fer no reason a-tall," he shot back. "I was walkin' peaceful-like when the law jumps out of a car, grabs me 'n takes me to jail. On the way they makes out like they found liquor in the back pocket of my overalls. The jedge—he believed the law-men—gave me six months. I found out, after they starts puttin' chains on my leg, they needs a lot of extra people on the chain-gang so that's why they took me 'n seven more, fer doin' nothin'."

The motorcycle chugged and we were off. Gliding along in the sidecar over the ribbon-like road, I thought of the chain-gang labor that had gone into it. The tall buildings of Charlotte made their appearance. As we approached the city line I shouted to Mario, above the din of the motor, that the Mayor and the police were not on hand to bid us welcome.

"In their absence then," he shouted back, laughing, "I'll give you the key to the city in the name of the National Textile Workers' Union! Do you accept?"

"I certainly do, with pleasure!"

Then, in the face of the cool morning breeze, we burst into song, the song of the national union, "Solidarity."

> *"Solidarity forever,*
> *Solidarity forever,*
> *Solidarity forever,*
> *For the Union makes us strong!"*

It was January 1, 1929. We passed through a mill village. We entered Charlotte itself and made for the house of a Communist Party member, whom I shall call Tom King,[1] the only functioning member in Charlotte and one of a few in the entire South. Our motorcycle came to a halt. "So here I am, down South," flashed through my mind. "A new year and a new place. I wonder what the year will bring." But it was an idle thought. I really did not try to look into the future. If I had, could I ever have foreseen that before the year was over a district attorney would be picturing my arrival in Charlotte to a jury as "sweeping into the South like a cyclone, like a tornado, to sink his fangs into the heart and life-blood of the community"?

2

Tom King knew I was coming and greeted me with much warmth and enthusiasm. His two young daugh-

[1] This name is fictitious. This man is still a resident of the South. His life and liberty might very possibly be jeopardized were his real name divulged.

ters, Mary and Anne, and his son Henry, who were present in the large front room of the bungalow, treated me quite coldly. Later in the afternoon I found out the reason. Their father had, some years earlier, lost his business because of his Communist activities in one of the southern states. Then he started over again as a merchant in Charlotte and soon became a respected member of the community, in the accepted sense. His children now were afraid of his getting into trouble all over again.

Tom was greatly concerned about the exploited southern workers. He said he had spent much time trying to convince them that they ought to organize to improve their conditions, but without success. "Now it's up to you," he said. "With your experience you should be able to organize thousands of the mill-slaves within a short time providing they know you are sincere."

"But they're afraid to talk about unionism," broke in Henry, who had been listening with considerable interest to our discussion. "They're afraid of the company spies."

"True enough," said Tom. "That's something we'll have to overcome. I'll do everything within my power to help you with the work, Fred, because God knows these poor starving workers need organization. How do you propose going about it?"

"Frankly, Comrade King," I replied, "I don't know. I must talk to the textile workers themselves, first. Suppose your son takes Mario and me to one of the mill villages to-night? To-morrow we'll look for work in one of the mills."

"An excellent idea!" exclaimed Tom with enthusiasm. "Get information first-hand. By golly, *now* we are going to get somewhere. I'd go with you myself, only I can't see three feet away."

For the first time I realized that Comrade King was nearly blind.

"I'll take him in the car," volunteered Henry.

It was getting dusk. I inquired, "Where are the workers likely to be just now, those working in the mills? How can we tell them from the other workers?"

"Heavens," laughed young King, "you'll have no trouble picking out a textile worker from a human being."

"Hush, son, I don't like a hear you talk like that. They're not to blame for their ugly condition. It's the fault of our society in general. But let's get down to something concrete; you take Fred in the car to the Chadwick-Hoskins Mill Village in North Charlotte. That's about the average. And you might stop in some of the pool rooms. You'll find textile workers there. Most of them wear blue denim overalls."

On the way to the mill village young King informed us that he had never set foot in a textile mill, but for the sake of starting conversation he'd say he was looking for a job. In ten minutes we were off the good roads of Charlotte proper. Then came the usual red, muddy road of the mill village, for the chain-gangs paved only the highways. "No one with a good car travels through a mill village," complained Henry as our sedan drove through large muddy pools. Rivulets of red trickled over the black polished surface of the car. Now and then rickety Fords passed us, driven by men in overalls.

On either side of the street were rows of one-story houses, all alike. Their corners rested on bricks piled two feet high, giving an appearance of houses on stilts. On the front porch of every house burned a small electric light. Soon we came upon a group of young people standing and sitting in front of a store. Henry thought it wise to park his car some distance away and come to the group on foot. The three of us were not dressed for the occasion. It was at a much later date that I found out that southern workers seldom wore their "Sunday-meeting" clothes on weekdays. Mario was wearing his motorcycle costume and Henry a gray suit of fine texture and a black topcoat. I came nearer the requirements, my coat was frazzled, my trousers shiny, and baggy at the knees.

"Hello, fellows!" King greeted the group. "How's chances getting a job in that mill?" He pointed in the direction of the Chadwick-Hoskins Mill. Four youngsters in overalls surrounded us with inquisitive looks, examining us from head to foot and back again. Then they began winking at each other. A red-headed boy, hands dug deep into the front pockets of his jeans, feet spread far apart, and a mischievous look upon his face, answered: "I reckon you *can* get a job. Just t'other day three new hands were took on. Whats't you do, mister?"

"Er . . . er," stammered Henry, "I'm a weaver."

"What kind of a weaver?"

"Oh, I'm all kinds. I weave anything."

"Well," continued Red, with mock seriousness, while his companions snickered, "we have left-handed and right-handed looms, which kind do you run?"

"Left-handed ones," quickly responded King.

" 'Sthat so! Well, in that case you can get a job with J. C. here. He runs square looms, but he's left-handed; ain'tcha, J. C.?"

Mario whispered to me, "Get him away before they send him for a pail of steam or a glass hammer."

The group was fast swelling into the proportions of a mass meeting. One of the boys sized me up as coming from the North, but Mario, with his dark features, seemed to them a puzzle. With young King sinking deeper and deeper into the hole, it was useless to expect any serious discussion with the boys at this time. Besides, I did not want to be discovered as a union organizer until I had learned more about the life of the southern workers. I maneuvered an orderly but not very dignified retreat.

3

"Where is the overseer?" I asked, according to the best usage in the North, at noon, the following day, as I walked into one of the small mills located in North Charlotte to look for work. Mario went to another. The weave room was on the first floor of the two-story brick building. I addressed myself to the first man I saw.

"You mean the boss-man? There he be, over yonder, fixing that thar loom."

I looked in the indicated direction. An old man in overalls tinkered at a loom that lay dismantled on the floor. "Why," I said, thinking he misunderstood my question, "is he the boss-man, the one that does the hiring?"

"Guess I oughta know. Have worked fo' him nigh onter eighteen years. He owns this here mill." And the fellow went on sweeping the floor.

I walked over to the boss-man who at this time was cleaning his greasy hands with cotton waste. He was bald-headed, with a smattering of gray around his ears. We looked at each other.

"Well?"

"I'm looking for a job."

He drew a sigh of relief. "I thought you was another

one of those salesmen. But about a job...I dunno. Come up to the office."

There was a sink in the corner of the room. Into it he spat a lump of tobacco and rinsed out his mouth. Then we walked up a narrow stairway to his office. He picked up stray pieces of cotton waste on the way, which he deposited in a round can at the top of the stairs. The office was littered with various kinds of textile magazines and newspapers. Many were on the floor. The flat-top desk in one corner of the room was in the most chaotic condition imaginable. On it were samples of cotton yarn, bobbins, gears, a weighing machine, and papers and letters piled high. I was wondering how he could find anything in a hurry in such a disordered office when he surmised my thoughts.

"Suppose you think this office kind of messy, but 'tain't to me. I can put my finger on any paper I want any time."

I was standing but he invited me to sit down. "I wanta ask you about business in the North." The bossman opened a side drawer of the desk. He took out a mousetrap, put it to his nose and sniffed: "I'll have to put in fresh cheese. The mice are getting awful numerous round here lately. He then took out a package wrapped in a newspaper, held together by a thick rubber band. "My lunch," he said. "Haven't time to go home today, gotta get that loom fixed." He sat down in a swivel chair, stretching his feet, one over the other, across the open drawer. "Now tell me, how's the textile business up North?" He smiled. "How come you wanta job in a Southern mill; ain't a Yankee mill good enough fer yer?"

I told him I had a relative in Charlotte with whom I

wanted to stay for a while and for this reason I needed a job.

"No, suh, young man, I'd never take on a Yankee or any other ferriner in my mill, 'n' that thar goes I reckon fo' all the South. They'd put too many strange ideas in the heads of mill-hands—some nonsense lak workin' only eight hours a day. Why, I work nine hours every day 'n' I own this here mill. I guess my help should be willin' to work at least 'leven, 'n' by the Lord Jesus Christ, they will! Work never hurt no one. Read yer Bible! It condemned man to hard work forever because he sinned. But nowadays the ferriners, like those Rooshin Communists are tearin' down religion—but they'll never make headway in the South, because we are all God-fearin' people."

At this point we were interrupted by a tall, thin woman. She hesitated at the office threshold. She addressed the boss-man as "suh."

"Come in, Mrs. Wally. What you want?"

"I come to ask you, suh, can I go home right now? My baby has the colic 'n' I'm afraid Ted will forget to give the medicine. Pauline gets out of school about four 'n' I can come back 'n' work to-night to make up time."

"That girl of yours is big enough to leave school. Why doesn't she stay home 'n' take care of your baby?"

"But, suh, Pauline is only fourteen, 'n' I want her to get educated 'n' not be ignorant like me."

"Sorry, Mrs. Wally, I can't let you go home now. You should take Pauline out of school if you want to work here. Education is the snare of the devil. What do mill-hands want with education nohow? Pauline should be workin' and give you a rest."

Mrs. Wally's body stiffened. Her hands clenched the sides of her black cotton dress. "I'll die 'fore I let her become a mill-hand!" She walked straight out the door.

Here was the smoldering fire of revolt.

"Gol-darn-it," scowled the boss-man, "these mill-hands are gettin' more like children every day. Guess they'll never grow up. The young people 'specially, think they know it all. Even my son wants to change everything in this mill since he came back from that darn school in New England. He's in the spinnin' room now tryin' to speedup the hands." His lunch over, he began cutting into a plug of tobacco.

"Why did you send him to school in New England?" I ventured to ask. "Ain't a Southern school good enough for *him?*"

"Well, competition is strong in my business to-day and in order to stay in it, my boy just naturally had to learn Northern business methods to compete with those smart Yankees 'n' Jews 'n' other ferriners up in that country."

"Say, isn't this part of America?" I put to him.

"Darn tootin' it is. This is the *real* America. We don't go-a-messin' up with ferriners from across the water. . . . Say, young man, you are not one of those Union organizers from the North, are you?" He stood up and I stood up. His face was red.

"I belong to the Union there," I said. "Sorry you can't give me a job."

The boss-man said good-by, pleasantly enough.

4

During the few years that I had been actively engaged in union work, I had never been paid a regular wage. I just lived, from day to day, on whatever expense money the national office sent or whatever money my father could afford. In the South, Comrade King helped me quite a lot financially. My clothes were torn and I was practically barefooted. I was ashamed to walk on the streets. I wrote to Jim Reid, our union president, about it, threatening to hitch-hike home and find a "master," and he wrote:

"... For Christ's sake, don't let me hear you talk any more about that hitch-hike home stuff. You will come back on cushions when you do come home, but that must not be until you have built a union base that will stay."

When I wrote to Jay Lovestone about my seedy clothes, he sent me one of his castaway suits, which I promptly returned. That was considered a great joke in the Party. Alex Bail closed a letter to me, saying: "What's this I hear about Lovestone sending you his suit? This is the most interesting international development. Everybody here is awaiting a reply. Pete will send in his application as soon as he hears about your suit." But it was no joke for me; I was destined to carry on with my torn suit all through the strike because I couldn't buy clothes while the strikers needed food. Despite my financial worries, I made progress in unionizing the workers. Mario and I worked hard to bring in new union members. We issued leaflets explaining the new union and personally distributed them through the villages. After a few weeks, Mario had to return North because the union could not support two people in the southern field.

I made it my business to spend whole evenings with families. In this way I was to find out whether they really wanted a union. If they didn't, then I was wasting my time: back to New England I would go. But I found out that almost every worker wanted some sort of organization that would unite them and demand from the bosses more wages, fewer hours, and better living conditions. Night after night I traveled alone from one mill village to another. I had been warned by workers that the bosses were on the lookout for the northern union man so I wasn't surprised when a high-powered car breezed by me one night in the Highland Park village, so close that I was thrown into the gutter. The act was deliberate because I was walking on the left side of the road, close to the gutter, and the car came up on my right and swerved to the left with the aim of picking me off. I watched every car thereafter.

North Charlotte contained a number of mill villages, of which Chadwick-Hoskins, Highland Park, Calvine and Veritas were the largest. One typical family I visited had eight grown-ups and two babies living in three rooms—two bedrooms and a kitchen. The beds were of the old-fashioned wooden type, always unmade because, as one of the workers expressed it, "they never get cold." For when the day-shift worker rose, his place was taken by the night worker. In this particular family the grandmother stayed home and looked after the two babies while the mother worked on the day-shift. She also did much of the general housework. The father had run away, leaving the burden of bringing up the children on the women. The rest of the family included three children from fourteen to twenty years old and three boarders—all working in the mill. We sat in a semicircle around a fireplace burning soft coal. One of the boarders, O. D. Martins, nervously paced the room, like an animal in a cage, giving vent now and then to his feelings against union organizers from the North who had run out on them in the past. The last big strike they had was fought under the United Textile Workers' Union with John Dean as one of the leaders.

"All they wanted was our money and what money they could get from the mill-men to sell us out," complained Martins. "How can we be sure you won't do the same thing?"

"The mill people won't stick together," said the mother. She stared sadly into the burning coals.

"No, it's no use, we've tried it before. I've spun, and spun and spun. I guess I've spun in every village in the South, and now, what have I got to show for it—nothing. The people in the city looks down on us mill-folks. They can always tell us mill-folks from other folks because we's chalky-faced and skinny."

It was the grandmother's opinion that they ought to return to the mountains but the children were for organizing and fighting for better conditions.

I won Martins over to our union and he gave me the name of his brother, working at the Loray Mill in Gastonia. "Go to him," he said, "and he'll help you organize the workers there. If you succeed in organizing the workers at Loray, you'll organize the South," he added.

I had heard this many times from workers and I made up my mind to tackle the job there. But I did not want to leave Charlotte without having obtained any results. Finally my work in this neighborhood was rewarded. To my surprise and delight I was able to organize the Chadwick-Hoskins Mill at Pineville practically one hundred per cent. This was not due to my eloquence, however, nearly as much as to the fact that the bosses in this village had tried the experiment of working Negroes instead of whites. The experiment was a failure in all respects but one; it succeeded in antagonizing the white mill-hands to such a point that they flocked into our union.

These southern workers were more interested in protecting their prejudices than their interests. They did not complain about such low wages and long hours as would never be tolerated in the mills of New England but they hated what they called the "stretch-out," which was accepted as inevitable by the northern workers. When the loom was first invented, it took as many as two or three weavers to run one. Then, as the workers became more expert and the machine was technically improved, one man was able to attend to as many as thirty looms. At that time the weaver still removed the finished cloth from the machine and carried it to a receiving station. He had to truck bobbins of yarn to the loom and place them in the shuttle. He oiled and cleaned the machines and mended broken threads in the warps. But soon it was found advisable to take these tasks off the hands of the weaver. A group of specially trained workers, called loomfixers, repaired the machines and installed the warps. Another body of assistants, known as battery hands, attended to other details, leaving the weavers more time for their special work. Finally the automatic loom was invented which now does the weaving mechanically so that to-day a weaver can take care of from eighty to one hundred looms. The old-fashioned weaver who was justly proud of his skill hates the new system which has made him a cog in the machine. The new men hate the "stretch-out" because it keeps them keyed up to a high point of efficiency at a tiresome and routine job. Yet the increased production has not brought with it shorter hours and better pay. On the contrary, in the South wages decreased. The profits from the new inventions went to the bosses; their hardships were added to the lot of the workers. The southern mill-hands, like most other Southerners, are temperamentally easy-going and inefficient. They do not mind long hours so much if they can dawdle along through the day. But under the "stretch-out" system of the new machines they had both the speed of the North and the long hours, wretched working conditions, and low wages of the South. No wonder they hated their work.

IX. GASTONIA SEES RED

1

Gastonia. It was just another name to me, another dot on the industrial map of the South. I had heard of the Manville-Jenckes Mill at Loray village as a keg of dynamite, but who could have foretold that the great explosion would take place there? I went down to Gastonia in the middle of March, 1929, and found conditions among the Loray workers even worse than in Charlotte. Trouble was brewing and the seething mass was ripe for organization. A local worker, Will Truet, who later proved a most efficient organizer, was itching for action. We launched a union local at the Manville-Jenckes Mill. It was a secret unit, with Will as its secretary-treasurer. We limited membership to a small number in the beginning. I was afraid that the situation might run away with us.

I made a flying trip to New York where I urged the need of sending more organizers to the South. Upon getting assurances that this would be done, I returned to Charlotte. Shortly afterwards a wire from Will Truet, from Gastonia, reached me. It read: "Fired today. What will I do about it?" I wired back that I would come to him immediately. When I arrived in Gastonia, Will told me that the bosses had fired him for organizing the workers. Moreover, they were ferreting out other members of the union to fire. To Truet I said: "This is a declaration of war from the bosses, a challenge to us. Unless we take action at once, our union will be smashed to smithereens before it's hardly started." Truet agreed, and suggested calling a secret meeting of the members working on the day-shift that very night at the house of Valentine.

So it was. A capable fellow, this Will Truet; in one hour he somehow managed to notify all the membership of the day-shift about the meeting without going near the mill. The house of Valentine was one of the many company houses belonging to Manville-Jenckes. It had three large rooms, kitchen, bedroom and parlor. Between seven and eight o'clock the three rooms were filled with men and women. Many who were not members of our secret union had responded to the call. I spoke to them for more than an hour, presenting as simply as possible the case of the southern mill-workers, the need of organization, and the difference between the Communist National Textile Workers' Union and the A. F. of L. group which they distrusted and disliked. I sat down, quite exhausted, as I had put all my strength and feeling into the talk. I had spoken in a conversational manner, as one person to another, but the reply I received was more like a mass-meeting. The room turned into a bedlam of shouts and whoops. There were cries of "Strike Now! Strike Now! We've Suffered Enough!" There followed a discussion as to the possibility of getting fired for attending this meeting. The men were not afraid but wanted to know what to do about it. For the moment I felt uplifted by the response of the workers, a response which with my help might achieve on this backward southern soil, a great resounding victory for the American working class.

Finally one tall bony-looking man succeeded in gaining the floor and there was a sudden hush. Out of the silence this man was pointing a finger at me: "Now,

look a-here, young man, what you said to-night is the
gospel truth. You got to tell the same story to all the
mill-folks of this here Loray Mill. No more of this
sneakin' round holdin' meetings behind closed doors.
We'll hold 'em in God's own sunshine and if the boss-
men fire nary a hand they'll be mighty sorry, because
we'll strike the whole mill from top to bottom. That's
all I want to say, young man. We know you won't run
out on us."

Every one was up at once acclaiming his speech and
the place got so noisy with yells that the meeting could
no longer be considered a secret one. Women were crying. Men were shouting. Children were dancing. Will
Truet sat at my right, calm, pleading for help in regis-
tering new union members. Two young men and a girl
volunteered. One fellow, about sixteen, said, his face
aglow: "I can't write, but I'm agoin' out now and bring
in new members." Out the door he ran.

"Brother Beal," queried an old woman with knotted
hands, "you won't go away from us, will you? There be
one of those union men from the North once who ran
away." On having my assurance that I would stay, she
said, "God bless you," and turned, trying to get out of
the way of young folks scrambling about with questions
as to the strikes in the North. My blood tingled and
raced through my veins. I was overcome with the joy
of working among these people, unspoiled and uncor-
rupted by forces that split the northern workers. What
confidence they placed in me. A confidence I must never
betray!

While the joy of this seemingly religious revival was
spending itself, I was thinking: "How will the mill
owners answer the challenge of this union? ... Will these
people carry out their threats to strike if the bosses

prove contrary?... What will happen after the strike starts?... Where can the money be raised to feed the hungry strikers?... How about new leaders?... I must look around for the best type of leaders from the ranks of the workers here in this room...."

They were voting, voting to hold an open meeting on the morrow, Saturday afternoon, "behind the mill," voting to strike if any workers got fired for attending. The die was cast. I was pledged to a new struggle.

A few young workers insisted that I stay with them that night so as to be on the job for the speaking next day, but I told them it would be necessary for me to journey to Charlotte to get in touch with national headquarters of the union. Also I wanted to spend the night with my good comrade Tom King and receive the comfort of his advice on the coming struggle. I had to wait until the greater part of my audience went home before departing, because most of them dreaded the thought of my leaving the village.

2

Saturday, March 30, 1929! The day of the first open meeting of textile workers held in the South under the auspices of our union and of a recognized Communist speaker. Fortunately, the national office of the union heeded my request, made a few days before, for another organizer. Nellie Dawson, a wee bit of a girl hailing from Scotland but an experienced organizer in New England, made her début in the South this day. Nellie and I waited with Will Truet at the house of Valentine until there were several thousand workers at the meeting-ground. Then we walked up the reddish muddy road, so often trod by the workers to and from the mill, a road that the heavy rains could not entirely obliterate. The great mass of workers met us with silence.

A girl came near us and whispered as she passed by: "The boss-men are all here, taking the names of those at the meeting!" "Boss-men" applied not only to mill owners but to the mill-agents, overseers and all straw-bosses.

"Well," I said, "they'll certainly have a tough time taking down the names of all these people."

Nellie Dawson spoke first. I delivered practically the same speech as on the previous night. I stood on a hump in the ground, up on the bank of the road. During my talk, I noticed two well-dressed men close to me. I took them for detectives, but soon discovered that they were village preachers, the kind paid by the mill owners to console workers in the belief of heavenly rewards after death—"pie in the sky," as the Wobblies aptly put it. When I finished, one of them began to yell: "Fellow Citizens, what you are doing here is wrong. It's the wrong way to go about this thing. This man is a Communist from the North. . . ."

Some of the workers began to heckle him with embarrassing questions: "What about us mothers working nights?" . . . "What about the stretch-out?" . . . "How about God and the bathtubs?" (It seems that this preacher, in order to save Manville-Jenckes the expense of furnishing bathtubs in their houses, said that God was opposed to people taking baths.) Fists were dangerously near the preachers' noses. I thought it time to call a halt for fear that the workers might beat them up. They seemed gratified that I saved them from such humiliation and staged a hasty retreat. The workers sensed a victory. The straw-bosses also made an inglorious retreat, though the workers said little to them.

"Will," I said to the quiet secretary-organizer of this mill local, "you can just bet there will be a strike on Monday. The bosses will force the issue, whether we want it or not. We must prepare at once for a big struggle. Where can we get union headquarters in this section of town?"

He said he knew a place, an old building once used for a post-office, on Franklin Street, about seven minutes' walk from the mill. It could be rented for very little and we quickly decided to take it. At that time it seemed an unimportant detail, but now it represents to me the stage where the first act of the tragedy of my life took place.

I left for Charlotte again, confident that Will Truet would carry on. I wanted to spend all Sunday mimeographing leaflets and making special preparations for the following Monday.

Once in Charlotte I rushed to Tom King's house. "As sure as you're born, Tom," I ventured to prophesy, "the bosses will pick a fight on Monday."

"Good, good," yelled Tom, and began dancing around. "You've done it, my boy, you've done it! At last the mill-slaves are coming to their senses. The revolution is on its way. Yes, yes, the 'white-trash' are on the offensive. Glory, Glory, Glory, this is a great day for me, for all of us." How happy this grand old man was. His blindness forgotten in the thought that at last the underdog would have his day. I felt cheerful with him. Yet I also worried, because of the responsibility that fell upon my shoulders. I did not feel that I had a united organization behind me. The union was national in scope, but the Communist Party leaders controlled its every policy so much so that it might well have been another Communist branch. And I did not trust the Party to think only of the interests of these workers. I feared that other plans, different interests might take precedence here as they did in New Bedford which would make these people cat's-paws for the world-revolution which every Communist sees just around the corner. But I hoped for the best.

3

In the conduct of its strikes the Communist Party sees to it that they do not become straight, out-and-out struggles for unionization. Its chief aim is to bring out the political nature of the conflict. A horde of organizers sweeps into the field and before the local union leader realizes what is happening, he finds himself surrounded by a flock of political enthusiasts bent upon accomplishing something usually foreign to the strike itself. The following Communist organizations dispatch their representatives to the battleground: the Communist Party itself, the Young Communist League, the Young Pioneers, the International Labor Defense, the Workers' International Relief. Each of these organizers gets busy recruiting members for his particular organization and disseminating propaganda. It is also customary for the Communist Party to send a "women's organizer," on the theory that women are more backward politically than men. These various organizers are often shuffled around so as to make them fit the community and the struggle to which they are assigned. I knew many products of this system. There was Johnny Ballam, for instance, who was a cigarmaker forty years ago. During one period, he was a district organizer for the Communist Party in Boston; on another occasion he acted as organizer of textile workers in Lawrence. Later he was switched to New York to run for the office of United States Senator on the Communist ticket; again he was shifted to serve as general organizer for the "Friends of Soviet Russia."

I was therefore not surprised to find George Pershing bobbing up in Gastonia. I had never met George, but I had heard and read that he was a cousin of General Pershing; at least, the *Daily Worker* played this up to the limit. George was a handsome fellow with a pleasing personality and a real American. I hoped that he was sent by the national headquarters, and said so to him.

"No," he replied, "the League sent me," meaning the Young Communist League.

"But we don't need League organizers now," I protested. "What we need is union organizers and that's what you must be."

"I would rather do work for the union, but I was sent with instructions to do work for the League and that's what I've got to do. Of course, I'll have to get in with the workers first."

"Well, there is only one way to do that, and that is to help me with union work. Do you agree to this?"

He did. We made plans for the next day. During our conversation he told me that he had spent a few months in brig while in the army for a fight that took place in a house of prostitution which he and half a dozen other soldiers were visiting. "The capitalist papers use this against me now at every possible chance. I tell you this, so as to warn you what the press will write about me here."

"That's all right, George," I said. "It's an ordinary thing for soldiers to go to brothels, so I think the workers will understand. The capitalist press, of course, expects revolutionists to be pure and lead practically a sexless life, while the class they represent wallows in all kinds of filth. The bosses also send experienced prostitutes into our midst to frame up organizers, so be on your guard. Declare yourself a sexless holiday for the duration of the strike."

4

In the heart of Gaston County lies Gastonia, twenty miles west of Charlotte. The Gastonia Chamber of Commerce calls Gaston County the "Combed Yarn Center of the South—with 112 mills." About six miles west of Gastonia is Loray Village. The lords and masters of Loray Village, as well as of Gastonia proper, are Manville and Jenckes, Northern mill owners. Gastonia politics are Manville-Jenckes politics. The Mayor, police, school teachers, preachers, and press are part and parcel of the Manville-Jenckes profit-making machine.

To this village went George Pershing and I Monday morning, April 1, 1929. We arrived in a "jitney" bus, right in front of our new union headquarters on Franklin Street. Will Truet, the union's secretary, met us at the door with a hammer in one hand and a box of nails in the other. He showed us round the hall. It was an old wooden shack fifteen feet wide and thirty-five feet long, one story high. There were two windows, one on either side of the double door which opened in the center. The room was badly in need of repairs and about six men were trying to make things presentable. With all his outward calmness, Truet seemed to be agitated over something. Fear was in his eyes, but he went about his work of repairing chairs as if he were attending a Sunday-school picnic.

About ten o'clock two workers came hurrying to the hall and announced that they had been fired because they attended "the speakin' on Saturday." Within ten more minutes three more discharged workers joined the others. They got together in a corner and sang hymns.

"You don't seem to be sorry that they fired you—in fact, you seem well pleased," I remarked to one of the men.

"Yeah," he replied, "yeah, that's because I quit before they fired me." We all laughed at this. Another said that there would be many more out shortly, because old Jenckes had ordered all union folks fired. As discharged workers kept arriving, it occurred to me that the night workers had not had a chance to vote on a strike. I asked those already in the hall to round up the night workers for an immediate mass meeting in back of the union's hall where there was a large open space, about one hundred feet square, extending to a railroad track. While the lot was filling up I had workers in the hall practice picket duty. They marched around the side of the hall singing whatever songs came to their minds. From experience I knew the tremendous value of singing the right songs on a picket line. These workers knew none of the union's strike songs. To overcome this, I typed a number of copies of *Solidarity* and told them to sing it to the tune of *Glory, Glory Hallelujah*. It comes to me only now that it is also the tune of *John Brown's Body* and was perhaps somewhat inappropriate for Southerners.

By three o'clock the lot was filled with anxious and excited workers. There were cries, "Beal! Beal!" I went out on the bank of the railroad track and spoke to the assembled workers. I reviewed the situation and told them that the workers of the day shift had voted to strike if the bosses fired any people for attending Saturday's meeting or for belonging to the union. Since the bosses had already fired a large number of workers, I asked the night workers, at the conclusion of my speech, for a strike vote. The vote was unanimous, many putting up both hands. There was great enthusiasm, whoops and mountaineers' yells, the like of which I had never heard. I spoke for an hour, putting every ounce of energy into my speech. My voice cracked, I strained my throat, and my mouth filled with blood. At the sight of that there was great excitement, but as soon as order was restored at the meeting, I announced dramatically: "I now declare a strike in the Manville-Jenckes Mill in the name of the National Textile Workers' Union, local of Gastonia."

For purposes of publicity, I had a picture taken of the strike vote, with its accompanying enthusiasm. Later I gave it to a reporter and it was published all over the world. Obscure Gastonia was leaping into the limelight.

The strikers then proceeded to form their picket line, two by two, and march to the mill. I jumped down from the railroad tracks and led the line. At the mill gate one of the strikers pointed out old man Jenckes to me and each time I passed him on the picket line one of his straw-bosses would say to Jenckes, "There he is— there's the cause of the trouble!"

The bosses were not caught wholly unprepared. They passed out leaflets, too. They read:

> "Beal Says He Has a Million Dollars in the Amalgamated Bank of New York. There Is No Such Bank!... Here Is a List of Organizers of the National Textile Workers Union. Do You Want Foreigners to Lead You?"

Listed were seven or eight foreign names, but they failed to mention the American organizers—Reid,

Bush, Pershing, and myself. Still another leaflet warned that after I got the workers' money, I would fold up my tent and go away. Just inside the wire fence that surrounded the mill, the bosses put up a red cloth sign reading: BE A MAN—DON'T BE DRIVEN. What a fitting slogan for the strikers, I thought. The same idea evidently occurred to an old woman striker. She appeared with a similar sign roughly drawn on a large piece of cardboard. We cheered her and put her at the head of our line.

As the day wore on, however, the cheers and enthusiasm seemed to peter out and subdued murmurs were taking their place. What was worse, the number of pickets began to diminish. At first there were between 150 and 200 persons on the line; gradually they dwindled down to about thirty-five. This was due to the activities of the boss-men on the side lines who were jotting down the names of the pickets. I realized that fear, the great enemy of the workers, would end this strike before it was really begun unless something drastic was done immediately. Fear of being singled out, of being blacklisted as leaders, this was driving the men off the line. I ordered Truet to send out every man and woman he could. Then Pershing and I harangued the backsliders and shamed a few of them back. We formed a solid group and began to yell, "To hell with the bosses. Come on the line. Stick together and win this time."

"Sing," I cried, "sing *Solidarity.*"

As the song rang out, the workers on the side lines began to draw nearer to our group. Their lips began to move; soon they were singing. Then we started to march again, two by two, two by two, the line growing longer and longer. The timid ones had been swayed by the militants; the revival spirit again gripped the crowd.

From a window of one of the mills a worker shouted that the bosses had locked them in until quitting time but that they were coming out to join us. We answered with a cheer and sang louder, more sincerely than ever, *For the Union makes us strong.*

The strike was on.

X. BREAD AND PROFIT

1

MINIMUM WEEKLY WAGE OF $20.

40-HOUR 5-DAY WORKING WEEK.

BETTER SANITARY CONDITIONS.

NO MORE HANK CLOCKS.

NO MORE PIECE WORK.

COMPANY HOUSES TO BE REPAIRED, SCREENS AND BATH-
TUBS ADDED.

CHEAPER RENTS AND LIGHTS.

RECOGNITION OF THE UNION.

These demands were presented to Superintendent
J. A. Baugh of the Manville-Jenckes Mills by the Strike
Committee.

"Now that I have read these demands," Mr. Baugh
replied, "you realize that if we should comply with them
it would mean that we would virtually give you the
plant. You surely don't expect us to do that."

I considered the demands very moderate. But the
manufacturers did not intend to let the strikers win even
a few crumbs. As one of the mill owners put it: "Give in
an inch and they'll demand the works." The Gaston
County manufacturers met immediately in Gastonia
and raised a huge fund to fight the strikers. The fund,
it was reported, was to be used to pay off thugs, gunmen, newspaper editors, and other flunkeys of the mill
owners.

George Pershing, representing the Young Communist League, thought it his Communist duty to give

out red-hot statements. "I am here," he said to the anxious reporters, "for the purpose of organizing the Young Communist Workers' League. The principal view of the Communists is control of the country by the workers. Under Communist control the Loray Mill and every other mill would be operated by a general committee made up of one representative worker from each department, and they would elect a manager who would be responsible to this general committee." At this point, I broke in. I took George aside and told him that the struggle in Gastonia was to win the strike for its immediate benefits and not for forming Soviets. Hereafter I would give out all press reports. But the damage had been done. It was the sort of material the mill owners had been looking for. They made the most of it. It was not Pershing's fault. It was the fault of the Communist Party's theory-ridden leaders. They appear to think when a strike takes place, that it is the first step of a revolution. They have been rebuffed time and again. But that does not disillusion them; it seems to add fuel to the fire of their fanaticism.

On the second day of the strike one of the strikers ran to me and said, "The boss-men have strung a rope across the street in front of the mill gate so we can't picket. What shall we do?"

"Is it on public property?" I asked.

"Yes."

"Then," I ordered, "cut the rope."

A few hours later a cable was used instead of the rope. A tug of war took place! The police and deputies on one end and the strikers on the other. The strikers won the pull. A few of them galloped up the street victoriously clinging to their hard-won trophy.

The police and deputies were doing everything within

their power to antagonize the strikers. The minor skirmish with the cable was the excuse used by the mill owners for calling out the militia. Governor Max Gardner, himself a mill owner, ordered the Gastonia Howitzer Company mobilized. Later in the day, Adjt. Gen. Metts ordered the Shelby Infantry and the Lincoln Cavalry to the rescue of the mill owners. When they arrived, the streets were cleared to the accompaniment of nagging cries from the workers. One of the soldiers started to push back a woman who stood her ground. She told him to stop pushing. She was willing to go away, but not to be driven. The soldier was not smart enough to take the hint. So Mrs. Bertha Tompkins cracked him over the head with a stick. It required four soldier boys to carry her from the field and deposit her in the calaboose. She was the mother of four children under five and earned only four dollars for three nights' work of eleven hours each. Small wonder certain unconventional ideas got into her head!

The public, in general, sympathized with the strikers. They were startled, on the third day of the strike, to witness such a display of military force. Some of them inquired whether the Germans were on their way to make an attack. These jokes did not improve the temper of the troops and I began to fear a serious incident was in the making. But then General Metts honored me with a social call at union headquarters, our meeting was quite cordial. We chatted freely, even jokingly.

"I hope," he said, "you will warn the strikers not to commit violence."

"There's no need of the militia," I replied. "The strikers have committed no violence. The police were to blame for the scuffle that took place yesterday when they roped off a public street."

"The strikers must not commit violence," he repeated.

"I hope you will protect the lives and property of the strikers as well as of the mill owners," I retorted.

"That's what we're here for," he said.

I had a hunch he didn't mean it. He was there on the call of the mill owners and to protect their interests, not those of the workers. This feeling was confirmed the next day when I saw the interview which this impartial warrior gave to the newspapers. He called the situation at Gastonia dangerous and said that Pershing and I were true types of the Red variety.

"These men are enemies of our Government, for they regard the Russian Government as ideal."—When General Metts spoke of *our* government, he meant Manville and Jenckes.

The bringing in of the militia served one good purpose. It advertised our strike throughout the country, especially in the South. Workers came from every southern state. By foot, horse, and ramshackle car, they came to join the union.

2

During this time I received letters from the national office of the Union and the headquarters of the Communist Party. Albert Weisbord, a typical dogmatic Communist, was the national secretary of the Union. He had been the young leader of the great Passaic strike in 1926. I received most of my letters from him. He transmitted orders and decisions as fast as they were made. The factional differences of the Lovestone and Fosterites still complicated the situation in the Party. There were orders and counter-orders. I disregarded them all and answered with counter-demands for more organizers and relief. But Comrade Weisbord was not the kind to be sidetracked. He made a special trip to the South with special documents from the Communist Party and even the Moscow Comintern. We faced each other at Charlotte in another comrade's house. Phrase-mongering, mechanical-minded Weisbord insisted that workers be called out in all mills. If they couldn't find means of support they could return, work a week, receive more money, and strike again. In this way there would be a rolling wave of strikes. I tried to explain to him my plan of using the Gastonia strike as a basis for organizing the South. But he couldn't see that. He produced a paper from the Party Central Committee demanding that I, as a loyal disciplined Party member, put the general textile strike into practice at once. He brought orders from the Comintern and from the Central Committee that I emphasize the Negro Question. I explained that there had been only two Negroes working in the mill and they had fled when the strike started. But Weisbord argued that this situation involved other things than a mere strike.

"It is not just a skirmish. We must prepare the workers for the coming revolution. We must look ahead and smash all feeling of inequality," he insisted.

I failed to understand how it was possible to bring into the strike the question of Negro rights when there were no Negroes involved. It reminded me of the time when the Party made the idiotic mistake in the miners' strike of placing in the demands the "recognition of Soviet Russia."

Every strike that Communists have anything to do with has to have a REP (Representative of the Central Committee of the Communist Party) close at hand to see that the Comrades are hewing to the given line. I had been expecting a REP for several days. I didn't know who it was to be. At noon, one day, in the doorway of the Union Hall, I was interrupted by a few strikers who claimed that there was a spy hanging around the head-quarters.

"How do you know that?" I asked.

"Well, he's hanging 'round posts and corners near the Union Hall. He's not one of us. He must be a spy."

"Where is he?"

They pointed him out, skulking for all the world like a movie comic behind a post. I recognized his face. Ex-plaining he wasn't a spy, I walked over to him. "Hello, Comrade Johnstone," I greeted him.

"Sh-h-h. Don't recognize me. I'm not supposed to be known."

"But you certainly are known. They're saying you're a spy."

Johnstone, a little man with a Scotch accent, now changed his rôle from a movie detective to the Great Conspirator. He spoke in an undertone, very mysteri-ously. "Come down the street."

My guards skipped around, looking askance, while I went along.

He continued in an undertone: "For Christ's sake, didn't you know I was coming? I'm the REP."

"I knew some kind of a REP was coming, but this is a deuce of a way to appear to the workers—like a stool-pigeon."

"We've got to get together, we Party members, and straighten out matters of policy," he said, ignoring my criticism.

At the get-together of Party members then in the field, Johnstone took up the question of emphasizing the Negroes in our work. He said it was a decision of the

Comintern to make this the paramount issue. I again argued against such a procedure.

"When they make a decision, it's final. You have no right even to discuss it," said Johnstone categorically.

The mighty had spoken. I had only to obey.

3

Gastonia was, and still is, afflicted with a man who puts out a sheet called "The Gastonia *Gazette.*" Disguised as a newspaper, in reality it speaks only the language of the mill owners. Editor Atkins filled its four to eight pages daily with statements calculated to incite the public against the strike and its leaders. Two days after the strike was declared the paper published a full-page advertisement announced as "paid for by the Citizens of Gaston County." This fooled no one. The payment came from the fund raised by the mill owners to defeat the strike. The advertisement was a clear invitation to violence.

> Men and women of Gaston County, are you willing to permit men of the type of Beal and his associates to continue to preach the doctrines of Bolshevism anywhere in America and especially in Gaston County?
>
> Before the troops arrived yesterday the mob was rampant at and near the Loray Mill in all its seething hideousness, ready to kill, ready to destroy property. The troops arrived, men uniformed and armed, men true and loyal to their country, and all became quiet and the mob disappeared.
>
> Let every man and woman in Gaston County ask the question: Am I willing to allow the mob to control Gaston County? The

mob whose leaders do not believe in God and who would destroy the Government?

The strike at the Loray is something more than merely a few men striking for better wages. It was not inaugurated for that purpose. It was started simply for the purpose of overthrowing this Government and destroying property and to kill, kill, kill.

The time is at hand for every American to do his duty.

We had no newspaper through which to win over the citizens of Gastonia but we countered this propaganda by means of leaflets which were distributed on the streets. We set down some of the facts which were responsible for the strike: that the average wage paid by the Manville-Jenckes Company to the men, women and children employed in the Loray Mill was less than nine dollars for a full week of sixty-six hours; that the men, heads of families, on the day shift averaged eleven dollars a week, on the night shift twelve; that women were forced to work on the night shift; that the Loray Mill village was notorious even throughout the South for the overcrowded and unsanitary conditions of its shacks; that the workers were intimidated by the mill-bosses to trade at the high-priced company store and that they were kept perpetually in debt there. We told them the story of Binney Green who was one of our fourteen-year-old strikers. Binney worked in the spinning room eleven hours a day, six days a week for the magnificent wage of $4.95. She had been employed for two years and as an experienced worker had to run two spinning frames with four sides, which compelled her to stand on her feet all day. She and her young brother were the

sole support of a family of five. Binney was no exception. Other children replaced their parents at the mill,
doing the same work at half the wage. "Most of the
children," Binney explained, "never get beyond the
fourth grade in school. That's when the mill-bosses think
they are old enough to leave studying and start work."

As the propaganda of Manville-Jenckes constantly
played upon southern prejudice by emphasizing that the
leaders of the strike were Yankees and foreigners, we
pointed out that all the mills around Gastonia were
owned or controlled by northern bankers and capitalists,
a telling argument. But what turned out to be our
trump card was a letter we managed to get from the
office of the Loray Mill, which proved the truth of our
statements.

Member of the Cotton Textile Institute, Inc.,
Manville-Jenckes Company,
Pawtucket, R. I.

November 8, 1927.

Mr. G. A. Johnstone, Resident Agent,
Manville-Jenckes Company,
Loray Division,
Gastonia, N. C.
Dear Mr. Johnstone:

I have been keeping close tab on your
payroll and production at Loray division and I
am glad to say, it is very gratifying to see your
payroll come down and your production go up.
I am frank to say I was skeptical about your
being able to cut $500,000 a year on the Loray
payroll and keep your production up. I want
to apologize now for this skepticism. Now I
think you can cut out $1,000,000 a year and
still keep your production up.

I am in hopes of getting South but you are

making such a good job of it that I am only
afraid I will upset things rather than help.

Yours very truly,

F.L.J./E.V.G.   (*Signed*) *F. L. Jenckes.*

This was written two years before the strike. In
the interval the half-million cut in the payroll had been
increased to a million. A million dollars, which represented bread and meat and clothes, had been taken from
the workers by means of the "stretch-out," by replacing
men with women and children, by ruthlessly slashing the
low wages far beneath the meanest subsistence level.
And Mr. F. L. Jenckes, writing smugly from Pawtucket, congratulates his manager that he has taken this
bread from the workers and increased the profits of his
company. He takes it as a matter of course that he has
a right to do so. But when the workers seek to increase
their portion of bread and to decrease the margin of
profit, this same Mr. Jenckes and his servant, Agent
Johnstone, and his other servants, Superintendent
Baugh and Editor Atkins, cry to the public that the
strike "was started simply for the purpose of overthrowing this Government and destroying property and to
kill, kill, kill."

Yet our efforts to combat this propaganda achieved
but a limited success. We made converts among the reasonable and peaceable citizens of Gastonia but we
gained little besides their sympathy. Manville-Jenckes,
on the other hand, organized the "Committee of One
Hundred," a band of ruffians and vandals whose ranks
were enlarged by the company's hired strong-arm men.
Under cover of this so-called Committee and with the
support of the law-enforcement officials, the mill bosses
began a reign of violence and terrorism which has had
few equals in the annals of American labor troubles.

XI. PORTENTS

1

I DID not realize that my life was constantly in danger. True, I had received threats almost from the first, but I thought this the work of cranks or a bluff on the part of the boss-men. In the North one does not face death merely because one is a labor organizer. The murders of union officials that are announced in the papers occasionally are not due to their activities on behalf of the workers; they are the results of participation in the labor rackets, which like all other rackets have their gang feuds and gun play. The most I ever expected was to feel the weight of a policeman's club as the cops rushed the picket line or broke up a strikers' meeting.

But Gastonia was different. In so far as the Bill of Rights was concerned, it was not part of America. The Fourth Amendment to the Constitution is as much a dead letter law there as the Fourteenth. The strikers knew this if I didn't. They insisted on providing me with a personal bodyguard of several armed men and, after some argument, I yielded to their anxiety.

I still recall vividly my embarrassment the first night with the guard. Five of us were in a little bedroom. The first thing my guards did was to take out their guns. One of the boys—and they were all barely out of their 'teens—had an extra gun. "Here's a '32' for you," he said off-handedly as he handed it to me. "You'll find the bullets up on the shelf," said another helpfully. Some one had dumped a double-handful of cartridges there.

The lads broke open their guns and proceeded to load them. I looked blankly at the weapon in my hand, embarrassed by my helplessness, annoyed at the dilemma I was in.

How could I tell these boys that I did not know how to load a revolver? How explain that I had never held a gun in my hand before, that in the North the people felt "secure in their persons, houses, papers, and effects," as the Constitution has it, without the need of arms to protect them? Through long usage and custom these men had come to regard a gun as much a part of man's attire as his trousers. Would they continue to respect as their leader one who was so ignorant as I of this "manly" weapon? And yet, this was the least difficult part of my dilemma. For besides my ignorance there was my distaste for fire-arms and bloodshed. I had experienced in my life no personal fear. So far as I could judge by those things which tested me and other men, I was no coward. But inwardly I had always recoiled from violence, its cruelty and its futility. Could I explain this to my bodyguard? Was this the time to preach pacificism? In the bitter strike struggle upon which we had entered the presence of arms on either side was a source of danger to our cause. But the boss-men and their gangs were already armed and ready to use their guns. How, in the face of this fact, could I persuade my people to adopt an attitude of non-resistance when, despite their deep religious feeling, they had not learned non-resistance from their Christian doctrine?

I decided that I must accept their way of life rather than to try to force mine—for the while. And as I did so, the means of solving my immediate difficulty flashed across my mind. "Here," I said, thrusting the gun at one of the boys, "load this for me. I'm dead tired and I'm going to sleep." He never questioned the excuse but took the gun, broke it open, and slipped the cartridges into the revolving section. As I undressed, I watched him out of the corner of my eye so that I would know next time the way it was done. He came up and slipped the gun under my pillow. I lay awake until they had all dropped off to sleep; then I hid it in a box of papers under the bed, hoping that no one would find it there. Strangely enough, I felt much more secure without its protection.

2

The publicity given the Gastonia strike in the southern newspapers, unfavorable though it was, enabled me to make contacts with workers throughout the South. Letters came pouring into our headquarters from surrounding mill villages begging for organizers and I spent all the time I could spare from Gastonia in establishing union locals elsewhere. But neither I nor the northern men who were helping me could attend to the work on hand in anything like adequate style as more and more mills went out on strike. Besides, I felt that the time had come when the southern worker must do his own leading. I began to hold trade union classes each morning for at least an hour and out of the group that gathered earnestly each day to discuss the problems of the workers have come the best union leaders of the South: "Red" Hendricks, Dewey Martin, Ella May, Russell Knight, Delmar Hampton, Gladys Wallace, Louis McLaughlin, William McGinnis, Ruby McMahon, Robert Allen and a number of others. They had plenty of practical work to illustrate their studies for soon the strikes had spread to Bessemer City, Pineville,

Charlotte, Lexington, to Elizabethton, Tennessee, and to mills in South Carolina.

It was after my return from Pineville, where I had distributed food to the strikers, on April 19th, that we had the first portent of the coming storm in Gastonia. I drove in about one o'clock in the morning and, too tired to stop at our headquarters, went directly to my lodging and promptly fell asleep with the comfortable feeling that things were generally going well—our men in good spirit, our relief stores holding out, and the union growing stronger every day. Shortly after dawn, however, there was a commotion at the house and soon my hostess and my guard came running into the room.

"They've smashed our headquarters," they cried together.

I was heavy with sleep. "Who's they?" I asked drowsily.

"They, the boss-men," exclaimed Mrs. Lodge. "We've just heard that they tore down Union Hall and destroyed the food. The militia didn't do a thing about it." She stood by my bed wringing her hands.

I dressed quickly and hurried to the scene. There I learned that at two in the morning a mob of more than fifty masked men, armed with shot-guns and rifles, had surprised the five or six strikers who were on guard at the Union Hall. At the point of their guns they forced the guard to go across the street and then with crowbars and axes proceeded to demolish the furniture, mimeograph machine, and the office supplies. The helpless guards prayed that the police or the militia who were camped within a short distance of our headquarters would be attracted by the noise of destruction. But, for some reason, the guardians of law and order could not be roused that night though people from many blocks away came running to see what was happening. After they had finished with the Union Hall, the masked men moved on to the relief store next door. Before the horrified eyes of the watching crowd, the vandals smashed the large plate glass windows and entered the store. They seized the flour, sugar, potatoes, and other foodstuffs meant for the hungry strikers and dumped them into the street; then they poured kerosene over everything. As if at some given signal, when the last car of the masked mob drove off, Major Dolly and his militiamen came rushing to the scene. And they promptly arrested our guards for tearing down the union headquarters! This was such a barefaced fraud that even Gastonia would not stand for it. The men were soon released, but the deputy sheriffs who boasted openly in town that they had raided the Union Hall were not even questioned by the special grand jury called to investigate the crime. It was freely rumored that more than one man on the grand jury had taken part in the raid and it surprised no one when these good men and true dismissed the case.

This dramatic act, which the Committee of One Hundred proudly claimed as its work, began a campaign of terrorism against strikers and organizers, equally flagrant and equally unpunished. Apart from the increasing roughness of the militia toward the people on the picket line, individual acts of brutality began to multiply. Both Mrs. Ida Howell's eyes were blackened by loud defenders of southern womanhood because she dared to speak against the attack on union hall. "Red" Hendricks was arrested without a warrant and beaten into unconsciousness at the city jail. Russell Knight was bayonetted, clubbed with rifles, and thrown into jail. Carl Reeve and I were twice arrested, taken for a ride, and told to get out of the country. On another occasion, when I was in a restaurant, I was called to the 'phone. A peremptory voice at the other end of the wire said threateningly: "Beal, get out of Gastonia within forty-eight hours or you'll leave in a wooden box. This is a warning." A few minutes later I was again summoned to the telephone. A different voice repeated the same message: "Out of Gastonia, Beal, or you'll be carried out." Needless to say, this had no effect on me so that another means was taken for my removal. I was arrested on charges of abduction. I had sent Violet Jones to New York to collect relief funds. She was an active striker and a good natural speaker, but she happened to be the wife of Troy Jones, one of the few scabs who actually tried to harm the cause of the strikers. The abduction case was laughed out of court but, ostensibly for the same reason, Jones tried to throw a stick of dynamite at George Pershing while he was on the speakers' stand. Jones was caught just in time and taken to the authorities. He gave his excuse and was dismissed with a reprimand and a warning!

Pershing had another narrow escape. He had gone alone to address a small group of workers from the Armstrong Mill. In the midst of his talk a car drove up and several armed men jumped out. They cowed the workers with their guns and threatened to break George's neck. Whether they would have lynched him or not, I cannot say; they never had a chance. A striker in Gastonia had casually mentioned to me that Pershing had gone out alone. I called my bodyguard and we broke the speed limit getting to that mill. As we came up to the automobile of the boss-men, the workers took heart and with a menacing murmur began to surround the men who had threatened George. They retreated towards their car. One of them created a diversion by starting a joking argument with some of the workers during which Pershing joined us. Now that we had him safe, we wanted no further trouble with the boss-men. We knew by bitter experience in the courts who would get the blame and the punishment. We drove off leaving the thugs of the bosses to explain away their joke and to put a good face on their failure to go through with it.

The increasing brutality on the picket line reached such a point that the American Civil Liberties Union brought suit against the Manville-Jenckes Company, the Mayor, and Chief of Police Aderholt. This was a form of strike-publicity which these interests did not relish and for a time they held back the bullies of the militia. Instead they chose a more legal means to oppress the strikers by evicting them from the company houses. Over one hundred families were turned out of their homes in a few days. The evictions began one afternoon without warning. Thirteen of the mill-shacks were entered by the deputies, the people forced outside, the humble furnishings and cherished possessions thrown out into the street. The strikers offered no resistance but stood passively by, some women weeping, some speaking bitter words. For two families these evictions were a very grave matter since a member of each was seriously ill; but the officers' hands were not stayed by any considerations of illness or possible death.—And we were supposed to be the people whose purpose it was to "kill, kill, kill!"

3

This last act of the mill owners gave us a brave and happy inspiration. We decided to build a union headquarters which could take care of the evicted strikers. After some negotiations we got a plot of ground from a sympathizer by the name of Jenkins. As usual, Tom King was of the greatest help in bringing this about. He offered Jenkins some of his own real estate in Charlotte in exchange for this piece of property in order that it might be used by the strikers. The deal never went through but it prompted Jenkins to equal generosity and he allowed us to use his land. It was large enough for a union hall and relief store, a group of guards' tents, a speaking-ground, as the workers called our place for mass-meetings, and an entire tent colony for the evicted strikers. Although we had great difficulty in obtaining material from the lumber mills in Gastonia, which did not want to do business with us for fear of displeasing the mill-bosses, the union hall went up in record time. The entire structure was built by the strikers themselves. And I never saw a happier or more industrious lot of people than these volunteer builders. Here was something that was really theirs; something that did not belong to the bosses. And love and care and joy of good workmanship went into it. The building was one story high, made of plain boards, unfinished on the inside. It had a front door facing North Loray Street and a rear door which overlooked the guards' tents and the tent colony. Two windows on each side gave us a clear view of the entire grounds and, from the first, we had guards posted at the windows.

For threats of destruction had come to us from the "Committee of One Hundred" both directly and by roundabout means. We were told that the union hall would be burned to the ground with all that was in it. This caused us a great deal of anxiety but we decided to meet the challenge boldly. The Strike Committee sent

off the following letter to Governor Gardner which
warned him of the impending trouble and clearly set
forth the attitude of the workers.

NATIONAL TEXTILE WORKERS UNION OF AMERICA

GASTONIA LOCALS

May 16, 1929.

Max Gardner,
Governor of the State of North Carolina,
Raleigh, N. C.
Sir:

The textile strikers of Gastonia are building
with their own hands new union headquarters
to take the place of the one demolished by
thugs while the state militiamen were looking
on. The new building is about to be finished
and the dedication will take place next Saturday evening, May 18th, before thousands of
workers.

It is rumored around Gastonia that enemies
of the workers, inspired by the mill owners,
are plotting to wreck our new headquarters
within three days after completion.

The Strike Committee took the matter up
today and decided that it is useless to expect
the one-sided Manville-Jenckes law to protect
the life and property of the many striking
workers of Gastonia. Every striker is determined to defend the new union headquarters at
all costs.

Very truly yours,
Roy Stroud,
Chairman of the Strike Committee.

At the dedication we presented this letter to the assembled workers and they unanimously approved its sentiments. As the cheers that greeted the vote died down,

Tom Gilbert, one of the three police officers who attended the dedication, turned to Dewey Martin and said good-naturedly, "You'd better make the most of it now, big boy, because it won't stand a week."

4

At this time, when the local situation was most critical, my old troubles with the Communist Party—in the matter of money and of what I called remote control—again returned to plague me. Thus, just when George Pershing was most urgently needed at Bessemer City, he was ordered by the leaders of the Young Communist League to go to New York and report to the convention of the League, then in progress. I pleaded with him to ignore these orders, but he left hurriedly and did not show up again in the South. His zeal as a Communist organizer did not last long, however; he soon quit the Party and became a business man of some sort. In time, I think, he will make a successful Babbitt. Like Pershing, others who were helping me were shuffled around like pieces on a chess-board by the dictators in New York who were indeed making a political game of what to the people in Gastonia was a struggle for existence. My pleas and protests went unheeded because our objectives were not the same. I was all for winning the strike; they were intent on making a good impression on Moscow.

The difficulty over money was not unlike the trouble I had in New Bedford, but much worse. These southern strikers had the support of unions throughout the country. In the first place, it was to their own interest to help the workers of the South. American labor felt justly that it was the industrial situation there which was low-

ering the workers' standard of living everywhere. So
long as child and woman labor, long hours and low
wages existed below the Mason-Dixon line, so long
would the exploiting capitalists defeat organized workers in the North and East by moving their plants to the
land of cheap labor. Besides this consideration was the
fact that these simple mountain-folk had won the sympathy of their fellow workers by their brave and cheerful conduct under adversity, by their home-made poets
and lay-preachers who made something of a spiritual
revival of the strike. And the persecutions of the authorities who were under the thumb of the mill owners,
widely reported in the press, had aroused liberal public
opinion in favor of the Gastonia strikers. The result was
that money literally poured into the New York headquarters of the Workers' International Relief and there
were sufficient funds to carry on the strike indefinitely.
But the old Communist trick of diverting these funds to
other purposes soon left us only a trickle of the original
source spring. I learned that the back wages of not
only the W. I. R. office force, but of the International
Labor Defense, the Party, and other organizations were
paid out of this money. On top of this I discovered that
relief funds were being used to pay the expenses of
Party members traveling to Moscow. Backed by this
information I made my protest to Alfred Wagenknecht, head of the relief organization. I did not like
the fact that Wagenknecht was receiving a salary of
sixty-five dollars a week out of the money which was to
feed the strikers. A. F. of L. leaders are notoriously
well paid but it has been the boast of Communists that
they work as organizers for next to nothing. That is
what we rank and file leaders got—nothing. I made this

clear in my protest and Wagenknecht himself hurried South to deal with me.

When he walked into our relief store, the shelves were bare. This did not perturb him. Fitting a cigarette into a long holder, he lighted it and surveyed the scene. Then with the air of a business executive or efficiency expert, he offered his solution to our problem. "The thing to do," he said, "is to stop giving relief for a few days until the shelves are stocked up again. Then the strikers will feel that they have got something and it will keep up their morale."

My boys, who had expected great things from the big man in New York, looked at him sourly, then at me. The order was ridiculous. The strikers were living from hand to mouth and to stop relief even for a day meant exactly twenty-four hours of starvation. When I finally impressed this upon him, Wagenknecht rose to the situation. He got us some available cash and agreed to have future relief funds come directly to Gastonia. In addition the W. I. R. did a splendid job in securing a large number of tents for the evicted strikers. About fifty families were taken care of in this way and our little community in the valley back of the union hall, with its guards and its flood lights shining through the trees, took on the aspect of a military camp.

5

It was impossible to hide from the strikers the many failures of the Communist Party to be of help in their crisis. They realized, too, that I was constantly at war with the C. P. leaders and they wondered at my loyalty to Communism in the face of these disagreements. Then I explained to them what was so clear to me in those days—the difference between the Party and the *cause*. I knew that many of our leaders were what the wobblies used to call, "pie card artists"; that they were incompetent and untrue to the best interests of labor; that they came into the movement not because they were inspired by humanitarian ideals but because they were social misfits and neurotics who found expression for their warped souls in a radical opposition party. But I could not condemn the cause because it attracted these characters. I also knew that many members of the Party were unselfish idealists who were sacrificing themselves for what they believed to be the best interests of humanity. And I pointed out to my listeners that such men were in control in Russia. In Soviet Russia everything was different. I was sure of that. There the workers were in complete control. What a happy land it must be! No child labor, no overworked men and women; no need for strikes; no police, soldiers, and gunmen to beat up the workers. Short hours; cheerful working conditions; plenty to eat. Security for the future. No drones; neither capitalist nor union exploiters and betrayers of labor. The Workers' Fatherland. I passed on these glowing beliefs to the Gastonia strikers and they always greeted with a spasm of joy this new religion of Communism. To be sure, what I knew about Soviet Russia came only through the *Daily Worker* and from the reports of some of these very leaders whom I despised. But I believed that in Soviet Russia lay the hope of a bright future for the workers of the world. I felt like some Moses come to lead these southern slaves out of the wilderness of despair and to them I seemed like a delegate from a new world, from the Kingdom of Heaven.

These talks about Russia and other topics were generally held in the evenings as a sort of relief from the regular mass-meetings. They were interspersed with songs, reports from other strike areas, and tales of local incidents between the strikers and the boss-men. No evening passed without getting a new song from our Ella May, the minstrel of our strike. She would stand somewhere in a corner, chewing tobacco or snuff and fumbling over notes of a new poem scribbled on the back of a union leaflet. Suddenly some one would call for her to sing and other voices would take up the suggestion. Then in a deep, resonant voice she would give us a simple ballad like the following:

> *How it grieves the heart of a mother*
> *You every one must know,*
> *For we can't buy for our children*
> *Our wages are too low.*

The crowd would join in with an old refrain and Ella May would add verse after verse to her song. From these the singers would drift into spirituals or hymns and many a "praise-the-Lord" would resound through the quiet night. Although most of the local ministers held against them, the strikers had faith that a Superior Court would reverse their verdict on the great Judgment Day.

But the decision was long in coming and the scales swung up and down. At first practically the entire force of 2,500 employees went out on strike. Then, due to meager relief, many drifted back. Within a few weeks they came out again. So that the scab of to-day was the striker of to-morrow. This, and the fact that most of the workers were related to each other, established a unique attitude on the part of the strikers towards the scabs. Elsewhere the scab or strike-breaker is regarded by the workers as the most contemptible of creatures; in Gastonia the scab was considered merely as a potential striker. Those that worked on the day shift attended union meetings on the lot in the evening; night shift workers argued strike issues with the strikers in the daytime. At mass-meetings I always spoke to a mixed audience of strikers, scabs, a few police officers, undercover men, members of the Committee of One Hundred, and press reporters. On Saturday evenings the lot was crowded with workers from other mills where no strike was in progress.

The situation called for a different type of strategy from that usually practiced in strikes. I began to organize the scabs in order to have periodic walkouts to support the regular strike. Sometimes this succeeded. More often it failed because the plans would be betrayed to the bosses and at the crucial moment the mill doors would be locked, armed men would force the workers to remain at their machines, the militant scabs would be beaten up and fired. The rest would be cowed into submission. But not for long. Soon another attempt would be under way.

So it went for weeks until we finally decided to organize a mass walkout on a grand scale. I sent back to work a few of the most trusted strikers. Some were rejected with threats by the bosses; others were received with open arms. Enough were placed in strategic positions to carry on organizing activities and we began to hold secret meetings to plan our campaign.

On Saturday night, the first of June, word came that twenty scabs were gathered at the secret meeting place, each one representing a department or section of the mill, and that these men were ready to set the date for the mass walk-out. One of the scabs led me to the place.

I did not go there with any great show of heroics. In fact, I was scared, scared that the majority might turn out to be members of the Committee of One Hundred who had laid the trap. But it was something which had to be faced if the work was to be done. We were the last to arrive at a hut on the outskirts of the village. A few candles were burning. My guide reported that he could see a ray of light through a crack under the window and the place was covered up with a coat.

The meeting began. Every one talked in whispers. The scabs from the spinning rooms reported that armed guards walked up and down the aisles between the spinning frames, keeping an eye on the workers. The latter were not permitted to talk with each other. They were even watched at the toilets. The doors were locked most of the time. Similar conditions were reported for other departments. Nevertheless, the men felt that they could communicate with the workers and would get a great majority to walk out if all the departments would take action at the same moment.

It was decided, therefore, to start the strike on Friday night, June 7th, at nine o'clock. Friday night was chosen because it was "pay night." The company had not scrupled to withhold the pay of the strikers before and this time we planned to get these needed funds in our hands before we took action. The walk-out was to begin on the top floor. As soon as the workers there received their pay, they were to march down and call out the people on the floor below, and so on till every one left the mill. Once out of the mill, they were to march to union headquarters where a mass meeting would be held. In order to draw off the armed guards and the Committee of One Hundred, who would try to keep them in by force, I promised to have all the strikers at the gate before nine. The mill bosses had been attacking the picket-line again and I knew that they would send their thugs out to attend to us if we showed up at the gate. The scabs promised that they would break the doors down if these were locked. They seemed cheerful and confident and I left the meeting with the feeling that on June 7th the strike would take on a new lease of life.

We had pledged each other to secrecy. But during the week at Elizabethton, Tenn., one of the strike leaders heard the report that "Beal will be taken care of at Gastonia on June seventh."

6

Another portent. On the night of June sixth the guards brought into the office a man caught pouring something into the brook running in the hollow of the strikers' colony. They searched him and found a few small bottles of liquid and a black-jack.

"We want to beat hell out of him," said one of the boys. "He's the one who's been poisoning Ella May's well."

The man was defiant. He brazenly admitted that the fluid was poison.

"Go and call the police," I said.

"Call the police? What for?" asked a guard, angered by the attitude of the man. "The law will turn him loose, the way they did every one else."

"I know you're right." I agreed. "But I want to have it proved. The more evidence we have about this matter the better. Hold the man and get the police."

In about ten minutes Chief Aderholt and Constable Adam Hord made their appearance at the union hall.

The Chief wore a large black slouch hat and black suit, the kind usually worn by sheriffs in the South. When we explained why he was called, he took the black-jack and poison from the accused man.

"You oughtn't be cahrryin' these, son," he said.

Meanwhile Hord was more interested in the guns stacked in one of the corners of the room. He took each one up and examined it. "These guns are pretty rusty," he sneered. Then, looking carefully through the barrel of one gun, he put it aside with the question, "Does it shoot?"

"Well, why don't you pull the trigger and find out?" said a red-headed guard who couldn't keep his temper any longer.

Chief Aderholt turned to the prisoner. "Well, boy, guess you'll have to come with me." They left together.

The red-headed boy said: "Betwixt you and I, they'll turn him loose as soon as they get out of sight."

They did. The man was seen again a few hours later at the Loray Village bragging that Manville-Jenckes had bailed him out.

XII. LYNCH LAW

1

JUNE SEVENTH, the fatal Friday. All through the day there was something electric in the air of Gastonia. It was clear to me that the mill bosses knew about our plans and were taking steps against them. What these steps were, none of us knew. But we were not long in the dark.

After supper the strikers began to gather on the union lot. We had not yet made public our scheme to march everybody down in a picket line to the gates, but the Strike Committee was getting every one out to the speaking grounds with the message that something very important was going on.

It was about eight o'clock when Paul Shepherd, a young divinity student who had become an active leader in the strike, began the speaking. He was allowed to finish unmolested while he told the crowd that a great test awaited them that night and cautioned them to listen attentively to the instructions which they would receive and to obey their orders. But when Vera Bush started to tell the strikers how they were to form the picket line, eggs came flying through the air, splashing against the wall of the union building behind the speakers' stand. Then came bottles and rocks. A great disturbance was created and Vera was forced down by the guards although she wanted to stand up against the missiles. I jumped upon the stand in an effort to quiet things. Above the noise of the disturbance I shouted to the strikers why they had been specially called together

Chief O. Aderholt (right), of whose death Beal and his comrades were accused. Major Dolley is pictured with him.

that night. I was about to go on and give them the instructions regarding the march to the mill gates when from the rear I saw a pistol pointing straight at me. Before I had time to duck or do anything else, some one in the crowd pulled the arm of the gunman. The shot went into the ground. Then bedlam broke loose.

When some sort of order was finally obtained, Guard McLaughlin dragged a fellow by the name of Hanna before Police Officer Jackson and asked him to arrest the man for firing the shot and causing the disturbance. Jackson refused. Then the union guards took matters in their own hands and started to throw the disturbers off the lot. This caused more fighting but at last the speaking ground was cleared. It was getting close to nine o'clock.

"The bosses have sent down their stool-pigeons and thugs," I shouted as soon as I could make myself heard, "to smash our meeting here and keep us from picketing the mill. Don't let them win. Go, fellow-workers, go to the mill gates and greet the workers in the mill when they come out to strike."

The picket-line formed and started out of the union grounds. At the railroad track the marchers were met by Chief Aderholt, Adam Hord and Ferguson.

2

Meanwhile Officers Gilbert and Roach of Gastonia had participated in a little incident far from our union headquarters. About sundown they drove up to a general store near the Catawba River in Mecklenburg County and asked Pedro Melton to sell them liquor.

"I don't know where there is any liquor," Melton replied.

"Where's Mr. Hensley?" the officers demanded.

"I can't tell you that either." returned Melton.

"You're a liar, you God-damned bootlegging son-of-a-bitch," said Officer Gilbert.

Melton turned away and started into the store.

Whereupon Officer Roach drew a pistol and pointed it at him. "Don't you go in, you son-of-a-bitch, or I'll kill you," he snarled.

Gilbert got out a blackjack and both he and Roach started for Melton. They were so menacing that Melton ran to the river and jumped in. He was swimming out when Gilbert grabbed the pistol from Roach. He shot twice at Melton while the latter was in the water. Hensley took to the woods. Roach took the gun back and emptied it at the fleeing man. He missed, too. Then they threw rocks at Melton, cursing him and calling him vile names, threatening to kill him if he got out of the water. This went on until Officers Ervine and Mosley of the Mecklenburg rural police arrived and disarmed the Gastonia officers.

As Melton did not dare to make charges, the Gastonia officers were ordered back home. It was obvious to every one that they were drunk. These vicious drunks reached the railroad tracks at the same time the other police officers and the strikers did.

At the crossing the pickets were turned back toward union headquarters. They had a brutal mauling by the police. Grannie McGinnis had her glasses knocked off and while she was on the ground looking for them, Officer Gilbert stamped them into the ground.

"Get up or I'll blow your brains out," snarled another of the officers at her.

Sophie Melvin and Vera Bush at the head of the line

were choked. Earle Tompkins was beaten and thrown to the ground and kicked.

"Let's go down and kill them all," shouted the drunken Gilbert. "This is the best chance we'll ever get." The officers all got into their car and started for the union headquarters.

3

I was sitting at my desk in the inner office, trying to type a report. I felt that I had to occupy my mind some way until the pickets and the new strikers came back to our mass meeting, but my thoughts were not on the report. I was wishing that some one else could stay behind to talk to the strikers and leave me free to join the crowd at the gates. It was the first time in my life as organizer that the responsibility of being the chief leader kept me from sharing the work and the danger which fell to the rank and file. I hated it. I did not know then that the greater danger lay in staying where I was.

Suddenly there was a commotion in the hall outside the office. I heard raised voices and the steps of people rushing into the room. As I stepped out into the hall, the girls came in. "They've smashed the picket line. They're mad, crazy mad and drunk. Look at us They choked us." Some of the girls were crying. The men were tending to their wounds. Strikers and guards milled about in the hall and through the crowd I remember noticing Clarence Miller standing quietly in a corner and bathing his eye in cold water. It was already black and swollen.

Just then some one shouted, "The Committee of One Hundred is coming!" I turned and looked out of the window. Some cars had driven up inside the union grounds and in their light two men were walking toward our front door. First came Officer Roach, pistol in hand, lurching forward in an unsteady, drunken gait; behind him walked Chief Aderholt. Roach started to come into the hall. Bill McGinnis, one of the guards at the door, armed with a rifle, demanded his right to enter.

"Don't you go in there," Chief Aderholt cautioned Roach.

"You yellow son-of-a-bitch, you wouldn't dare fire that firecracker," Roach taunted McGinnis. But the guard kept his temper and didn't say a word. Aderholt took Roach by the arm and led him back onto the union lot. The headlights of the officers' cars shone over the grounds like a spotlight on a stage. And in the spotlight, near the door, stood Tom Gilbert and George Carter.

"Where's your warrant?" We heard Carter's calm voice.

"We don't need any goddam warrant," yelled the drunken officer. He slapped the gun in his holster. "This is all the warrant we need."

Carter still barred his way. Gilbert pulled out his gun with one hand and grabbed Carter's rifle with the other. They grappled for it. Suddenly Gilbert let it go and struck George over the head with the butt of his revolver. Carter fell to the ground and Gilbert pointed his gun at him.

"Let him go, Tom Gilbert, let him go," shouted Bill McGinnis as he opened the door and rushed to Carter's aid.

From the direction of the officers' cars came a shot and Bill's hat fell to the ground, a bullet clean through it. Then a volley of shots rang out, followed by the sound of smashed glass and splintering wood as the bullets struck the windows and the door.

"Lie down on the floor," some one cried. "You-all as ain't got guns, lie down."

We threw ourselves down. But our guards stood at their posts and began to answer the shots of the officers. The room filled with rifle smoke. Above the noise of the guns I heard a voice cry out, "The boys outside are shooting too." Forgetting the danger I ran to the window where I could see that while some of the officers were shooting in our direction, others were firing at the outside guards and drawing an answering fire.

Suddenly it was quiet. The officers' cars had turned off their lights and pulled out of the yard. The whole affair had not lasted five minutes.

Edith Miller joined me at the window. "Look," she cried, "Joe Harrison is shot. They are bringing him in."

Paul Shepherd brought Joe in. He was shot in the arm and the side. "We must get him to the hospital right away," said Paul.

Ruby McMahon ran up. "I've got a car in the street," she said. She led the way and Paul and I carried Joe out. We expected to be shot at any moment but no one of the gathering crowd on the street made any threatening gesture.

The driver was at the wheel of the car. Ruby got in beside him and K. O. Byers, my personal guard, squeezed in on the front seat too. Paul and I held up Joe between us in the rear. A few blocks on our way to the hospital we passed a group of men with white handkerchiefs tied round their arms and guns in their hands. It was the bosses' Committee of One Hundred gathering for the hunt. They did not recognize us.

As soon as we arrived at the Gastonia hospital, I placed Joe in charge of a nurse. Ruby followed me into the room. Two officers carried in a wounded man and when they saw me, one of them said: "There's the son-of-a-bitch, now. We'll get him after."

"Let's get out of here, Fred, quick," Ruby urged anxiously. We hurried out to our waiting car.

"Chief Aderholt has been wounded," the driver greeted us.

"Take me to Mrs. Lodge's," I ordered. I wanted to return there and telephone Miller to arrange the gathering up of our forces. When we reached there Byers and I got out. Ruby McMahon and Shepherd went on with the driver.

A little ways up the road from the house I saw a parked car. I was suspicious. "Let's pretend we're going into the house by the back way," I suggested to Byers, "and see who gets out of that car." From a clump of bushes we watched five men jump out of the parked car. They were all armed with rifles and pistols. They made a dash for the front of the house. Simultaneously Byers and I ran for the woods in the rear.

I knew if these gunmen of the bosses found me, I would be either lynched or shot. It was different with Byers. He wasn't known by the bosses. They weren't after him. They wanted me. Once he parted from me he would be safe. I told him so and advised him to set off in another direction.

"Oh, hell, Fred, I'll stick with you," he said, "I'm not running away now."

"Then we'll have to get away from Gastonia tonight or we'll both be lynched," I said, still making my way through the brush. "Let's get to Charlotte and see Lawyer Jimison."

With difficulty we made our way out of the woods on to the main street of Gastonia. This was no place for us. We went into a store and called a taxi. The owner of the store had evidently not heard of the shooting. "Hello, Beal," he greeted me pleasantly, "how's the strike getting along? Expect to win?"

"We expect to win," I answered.

While I was 'phoning Byers stood quietly by, constantly watching the door. The cab arrived in a few minutes; it seemed like several hours. We jumped in and leaned back against the cushions. I told the taxi-driver I had to make a train in Charlotte. We got there after midnight and paid off the cab at the station.

4

Tom Jimison, the union's lawyer, had volunteered his services early in the strike. He stuck faithfully to the strikers throughout the struggle. He was tall and thin. He always carried a cane and wore a fresh flower in his lapel. Before becoming a lawyer he had been a preacher. This may account for his love of speech-making.

He was in bed when Byers and I knocked at his door. "Waal," he drawled, after letting us in, "what seems to be the trouble?"

I was excited. He was calm and unruffled as I poured out my version of the shooting.

"Now don't get upset." He spoke slowly, choosing his words. "It's serious, all right. I'm afraid for your life if that Loray crowd gets you. I advise you to take the next train to New York and stay there until things calm down."

"No, I'll not leave the South," I insisted. "I was not the cause of the shooting. I will not run away."

"We might go to my uncle's house near Spartanburg, South Carolina," suggested Byers. "We could stay there a few days, if Mr. Jimison thinks we'd better."

There was some discussion. I decided to take up Byers' suggestion. Both of us were exhausted. We took showers and went to bed.

At the time Byers and I were driving to Spartanburg my picture was on the front page of every newspaper. The headlines announced that the police were searching everywhere for Beal. They thought I had fled to New York. To "the dives of Passaic, Hoboken and New York," as the Gastonia *Gazette* put it. In Spartanburg we learned that Chief Aderholt was dead and that Roach, Gilbert and Ferguson had been wounded, but not seriously. We walked about the streets in our natural way. I was bareheaded as usual. I sent a telegram to the national office of the Union asking for instructions. Then Byers and I went into a lunch room for dinner. We were eating peacefully when Byers suddenly nudged me.

"We've been recognized, Fred. See that fellow over there? He's from Gastonia."

The man indicated left in great haste. Within an hour, when Byers and I went into the Western Union office for an answer to our telegram, we were arrested by the Spartanburg police. They took us to the police station. Then to the county jail. Byers and I were separated.

A flock of reporters visited me. They wanted statements. I referred them to my lawyer.

"Aren't you sorry for Chief Aderholt who was killed?" one asked me.

"I'm sorry for any man who is shot," I replied. "Especially one who is shot fighting for a bad cause."

I was in a cell with ten other prisoners. They were all young boys wearing denim trousers. They were in for petty stealing or drinking. The boys didn't seem to mind their predicament. They played checkers and cards, told dirty stories, and discussed the probable length of their sentences. When they found out who I was, they became interested in my story.

About nine o'clock that night City Councilman Craig and two policemen from Gastonia came to take me back on the charge of "complicity in the murder of Aderholt." The Chief had died that day as a result of his wounds. They handcuffed Byers and me together and hustled us into the rear seat. The car couldn't go over thirty miles an hour. The driver and policeman who sat in front were agitated about something. It seemed as if there was a conspiracy in the making. They kept whispering to each other. We were spoken to only once or twice. Once they stopped. They bought us coca-cola at a drug store in King's Mountain. Here they used the telephone. Later I heard them say: "I wonder who let it out that Beal would come through tonight." We drove past the Loray Mill in Gastonia. Then down a side street. On into a yard. Officer Rankin who rode in front dashed into a dimly-lighted house. In the shadows I could make out men moving. Could the jail be crowded with arrested strikers? Was that why they were bringing us here? Was it the headquarters of the Committee of One Hundred? That would mean the end for us!

When Rankin had dashed into the house he had said, "I'm going to telephone for a faster car."

A car approached us. It was filled with men carrying shotguns and pistols. Some were on the running boards. It drew up close to our car. Two men jumped out. One had on a dress suit. It looked as if he had just left a party. He opened the door to our car and pointed a pistol straight at Byers and me.

"Come out, Beal, or I'll shoot you where you are," he demanded.

The driver of our car grabbed his arm. He pleaded with him. Finally he took him to one side. I heard the driver say, "We'll take him to Church Street. Have the gang there." This seemed to satisfy the man in the dress suit. He hurriedly jumped in the car and they drove off.

Rankin who had come out and talked to the man in the dress suit, too, said, "We must get to Charlotte as quickly as possible."

We drove miles and miles through the woods with the headlights out. Hours later we arrived at the Charlotte jail. Here Byers and I were hustled into a high-powered car and driven to the Monroe jail, miles from Gastonia and Charlotte.

We had escaped lynching by a hair's breadth.

5

I was instantly won over by the fatherly manner of Cliff Fowler, the Sheriff. He told me, "You're being kept here in secret. Don't let any one suspect who you are. Take the name of Anderson."

There was some prospect of the Loray gang nosing us out here. The Sheriff said, "They'll get you only over my dead body." It was a tense night. But nothing untoward happened.

Then one morning I was returned to Charlotte. A writ of habeas corpus was served on the Gaston County authorities. I and the other striker leaders were brought before Judge Harding for a preliminary hearing. It was soon evident that we were to be tried, not for murder, but for our political and religious beliefs. The following colloquy took place between Prosecutor Hoey, the

silver-tongued brother-in-law of Governor Gardner, and
Amy Schechter:

Q. Do you believe in God?

Amy hesitated. Jimison, our lawyer, objected.
Judge Harding overruled the objection.

A. I don't believe I can answer in one word.

Q. Yes or No.

A. Well, then, No.

Q. Then you don't regard the oath you have taken
on the Bible?

A. Yes, I regard it as part of the court procedure
and an obligation to tell the truth.

Later she was questioned about a telephone call
she made to New York after the shooting.

Q. Were you telephoning for more gunmen?

A. No. I was telling headquarters about the police
attack on defenseless women.

The political angle was brought in.

Q. You are opposed to government as far as you
are concerned?

A. I speak for the Workers' International Relief.

Q. So far as you are personally concerned, you do
not believe in the American form of government?

A. In what sense do you mean?

Q. You are opposed to it. You don't like its ideals.
You know what form of government we have in this
country.

A. You mean the form or the method by which it is
carried out?

Q. You are an objector to both the form and the
method?

A. I don't think this is a question of belief.

Q. Which do you like the best? You know what sort

of government we have. You know the type and character of our government. You know we have a Constitution?

A. Oh, yes.

Q. You know we have laws passed under that Constitution? Or would you like to change it and adopt the Russian form? Which do you want to do? You believe in the protection of property? Or in taking it away, confiscating it? You believe in the Russian government? You know what sort of government that is, the Soviet Government.

A. I believe in government by the majority of the population who happen to be farmers and workers.

Edith Miller was subjected to political and religious questioning which reminded me of the days of the Spanish Inquisition.

Q. What do *you* believe? Do you believe there is a God? That there is no God?

A. I do not believe that there is an all-powerful spirit that rules. I believe that man rules his own destiny.

Q. Do you mean to say that you believe that there is no God?

A. I told you that I believe that man controls his own destiny.

Q. Do you believe in the Bible?

A. What do you mean?

Q. Do you believe in the inspired Word of God?

A. No.

As an outcome of this sort of hearing sixteen of us—strikers and leaders—were remanded to Gastonia common jail on the charges: "Conspiracy to murder and secret assault with deadly weapons with intent to kill."

Three were women: Vera Bush, Amy Schechter, and nineteen-year-old Sophie Melvin, all from the North. Of the thirteen men, four were from the North: Clarence Miller, Joseph Harrison, George Carter and myself. The nine Southern boys were: seventeen-year-old J. C. Heffner, Dell Hampton, N. F. Gibson, Louis McLaughlin, Russell Knight, K. O. Byers, William McGinnis, Robert Allen, and K. Y. Hendricks.

Not one of the sixteen was indicted for firing the shot which killed Aderholt.

Major Bulwinkle, the attorney for the Loray Mills, announced to his friends: "We are out to get Beal. And we'll get him even if we have to electrocute the whole damned lot of strikers."

Since there was no way of manufacturing evidence that I actually fired the shot which killed Chief Aderholt, or any shot whatever, the people who were "out to get Beal" could not quite put me in the class of such union martyrs as Mooney and Billings, Sacco and Vanzetti. The prosecution could do no better than resort to a charge of conspiracy to murder. But they bolstered up their weak case with a campaign of propaganda meant to reach every possible juror in the county. Almost every newspaper poured out a venomous stream of calumny against the characters and beliefs of the defendants. In a typical editorial, the Charlotte *News* incited its readers against us, then tried to save face by seeming to urge "a fair trial" while it was really recommending a death sentence to the jury: "The leaders of the National Textile Workers' Union are Communists and are a menace to all that we hold most sacred. They believe in violence, arson, murder. They want to destroy our institutions, our traditions. They are undermining all morality, all religion. But nevertheless they must be given a fair trial, although every one knows that they deserve to be shot at sunrise."

To the credit of the community it must be said that occasionally a voice was lifted in our defense. One Charlotte reporter wrote in his flamboyant style: "Gaston County is desperately near the mood to try and condemn them by what they think about God, marriage, and the nigger question. The history of the world has shown that on the first and last of these subjects the human race, when it has tried to think, has invariably gone insane."

Before the propaganda campaign against the defendants had achieved its effect, a prominent Gaston County official, whose name I cannot use for obvious reasons, said: "If Beal were to walk down the street in Gastonia this morning, he'd find only about two hundred people in the whole community who might try to shoot him. Outside of this group, no one would lay a hand on him. The people here on the whole are with the strikers. I'll tell you something. The night of the shooting, when a crowd of more than a thousand persons was gathered around the City Hall, volunteers were asked to go after the strikers. There were just three who volunteered."

This naïve statement about two hundred men in a small town who would take the law into their own hands will seem fantastic to northern readers. Nevertheless, it was made in all innocence and good faith to our lawyers and is probably a correct estimate of the sadistic group of thugs who went under the name of Committee of One Hundred.—By the time we came to trial the campaign of hate had done its work. The attitude of Gastonia was changed and two hundred would have been an exaggerated number of those who were *not* incited to the point of shooting Beal and his codefendants.

XIII. GENTLEMEN ALL

1

FROM the middle of June to the latter part of August, 1929, the sixteen of us were confined in the County jail in Gastonia. This jail was not of the modern type. It was more suited for the many bugs of various kinds that it harbored than for human beings. The thirteen men were caged, like the wild animals of a circus, in one large room entirely surrounded by iron bars erected four feet from the walls. The room was divided by bars into four smaller rooms, seven feet by six, called cells. Each cell had four bunks, attached by chains, which could be hung up during the day. A door led out to a central room about eight feet by six. At one end of this room was an open toilet; at the opposite end was the exit.

The first thing we did was to demand from Sheriff Tom Hanna clean bedclothing and mattresses. These were obtained. But before we used the clean bedding we built fires under the iron bunks to kill the bugs. The floor was made of steel, so there was no danger. After the fire, we thoroughly scoured the place with soap and water. This was to be our home for many weeks to come, so we settled down to make the best of it.

Heffner, the blue-eyed, sandy-haired boy, the youngest of the group, was born on May Day, 1912. J. C., as he was affectionately called, joined the union only one day before the shooting. He'd found work in the Loray Mill after the strike. Then he decided that he would rather not be a scab, and dropped 'round to the union "to help out the boys." They put him on guard duty. When the Loray Committee of One Hundred raided the union colony on the night of the shooting, he took to the woods and to the railroad track, resting under a water tank. He intended to hop the first freighter that came along. But the day had been an unusually hard one, and J. C. fell asleep. The train went by without him. His rifle lay beside him. But not for long. The Loray crowd was arresting every striker on sight. They found them scattered in all directions, up on trees and under haystacks. They found J. C. beside the water tank and dragged him to the city jail. Here he was interrogated by Major Bulwinkle: "You heard Beal say, 'Shoot and shoot to kill,' didn't you, now?"

"I never heard Beal use such words," replied young Heffner.

"I can promise you freedom, my boy, if you can remember those words," said the Major. "Otherwise you may get the electric chair. And you're so young to die now."

"I never heard Beal use such words," repeated J. C.

If the Major was not guilty of what the lawyers call subornation of perjury, it was due to the fact this boy preferred to face the electric chair himself than tell the lie which would surely have sent me to one. So he joined the rest of us in jail.

Heffner's scrupulous honesty came from a deeply religious background although he himself was neither very pious nor particularly interested in organized religion. One of the things that troubled him on being thrown with our group of sophisticates is that he had promised his mother, a kindly woman and a lay-preacher, that he would read the Bible she had sent him

The Gastonia defendants: left to right, Louis McLaughlin, William McGinnis, George Carter, K. Y. Hendricks, Fred E. Beal, Joseph Harrison and Clarence Miller.

Fred E. Beal on the shoulders of his comrades after his return to Boston from Charlotte, N. C.

every day. He was shy and the boys were rather cynical in their comments. He came to me and asked whether I thought he was offending them by this practice. I realized that going on within him was the struggle between conformity and conscience and I threw my weight on the side of conscience. "Read it, J. C., read it," I urged. "It won't do any harm." Sometimes we'd lie down on the bunk and read passages to each other, and soon Bible-reading was an accepted diversion in our crowd.

George Carter, twenty-three years old, was the eccentric fellow of our group. He, like Heffner, was a newcomer, having hitch-hiked to Gastonia from his home town of Mispah, New Jersey, about two weeks before the night of the shooting. He had read a great deal about the strike in the newspapers, but George never believed what he read. So he came South to find out for himself. Since he was a textile worker, and had a credential from the Communist Party of Atlantic City, I thought it would be a good idea to send him into the mill to help organize the scabs. But his northern accent betrayed him. The boss-men were not hiring any northern workers who did not have credentials from scab agencies. However, George offered to do anything at all to help out and, as he had had some experience in carpentry work, I sent him to the tent colony to make floors for the tents. That job and the fact that a drunken officer hit him over the head with a gun earned for him the sentence of twenty years in the chain-gang.

George was a nature lover. One day during the strike the police saw him climb a tree and sit there looking at a bird's nest. They thought he was robbing the nest of its eggs and when he came down, they searched him from head to foot. Finding no eggs, they cursed him out for being "a queer nut" and causing them trouble. But whatever eccentricities he had were on the right side. We received special food every day, sent to us by the International Labor Defense. George would seldom touch any of it, preferring to diet on the jail food of hard cornbread and red beans and to turn over the special food to prisoners not of our group. Candy, cigarettes, and other things we received in the mail he would give away, too. He rather enjoyed the rôle of martyr. During playful moments he would put his fingers into an electric socket just to show us how it feels to receive a shock. He was well-educated and spent hour after hour teaching the illiterate Bill McGinnis to read and write.

The most colorful and interesting character among the defendants was fiery, quick-tempered K. Y. Hendricks, commonly known as "Red" for his flaming thatch of hair. "Red" had started to work in the mill at the age of eleven as gear-wiper. He worked on a twelve-hour night shift. Like many southern workers, he had spent some time on a chain gang. This and the long hours in the mill had undermined his health. He contracted tuberculosis. "Red" became the strikers' best speaker. He was a member of the Strike Committee and was one of the natural leaders of our group. His first-born was named Lenin Hendricks, the first child in the South to be named after the Soviet leader.

Louis McLaughlin was a "Georgia cracker." He started to work when he was thirteen as a sweeper in the Augusta cotton mills. In 1928, when he was twenty-two, he got a job in the Manville-Jenckes Mill. He was among the first to come out on strike under the banner of the National Textile Workers' Union. He sometimes spoke in public, but usually acted as a guard. On the night of that fatal Friday he was horribly beaten up, and he hasn't been right, mentally, since.

Clarence Miller came to Gastonia from Passaic about a month before the shooting to help with the strike leadership. He was arrested on June seventh, but the authorities at first did not think him important enough to put in our group. Hence he was simply charged with assault and freed on bail. But as soon as he got out, he began to tour the North to raise money for our defense. When he returned South for his hearing, the charge was changed to murder.

These men and others among the defendants were to be my companions for the next five years. They played their parts in this narrative of proletarian adventure—and not all were heroic parts.

Tom Hanna, the sheriff, was very decent to us during our stay at the Gastonia jail. He was not a southerner. He had been a prize-fighter at one time, and through political maneuvers obtained the job of sheriff of Gastonia County Jail. Sometimes he would come into our cells and talk to us. He permitted us to examine his pistol and his jail keys. We used to "kid" him about escaping. We could easily have tied him to one of our bunks. He always laughed it off. Could it be that he wanted us to escape? It often seemed so.

"They'll never convict you, boys," he'd often say. Yet at the trial he did his bit for the other side. He had his job to hold.

The Gastonia *Gazette,* of course, was still howling for our blood. But the thing had its humorous side. For instance, to prove my radicalism, it reported that on the night of my arrest I had with me a copy of "Mencken's Magazine" (*The American Mercury*). This association was enough to burn any one in the chair!

2

We were innocent. We had committed no crime. But in the eyes of the bosses and the courts they controlled, we were guilty of something far more serious than murder. We were guilty of organizing workers to resist starvation wages. I was an organizer; therefore a criminal. It was legal to organize unions in America in 1929. But Gastonia was not part of America. Not the America I had been brought up to love and revere.

On August 26, our trial began.

With the eyes of the nation focused on North Carolina, it was necessary for the ruling powers to make a pretense of giving us a fair trial. The biggest job was to find a "fair" judge. Governor Gardner had settled this by appointing Judge M. V. Barnhill, who was considered a liberal. At least he had the reputation of being fair. He had just handed down a decision that the North Carolina Bus Company must provide decent accommodations for Negroes; a progressive step for that State. Judge Barnhill was young, lean and good-looking, very unlike the usual type of judge that infests our courts. Unlike that one at Dover, N. H., with a "puss like a pig." Unlike the one in New Bedford with a "mug like a gorilla."

After Judge Barnhill had granted the change of venue from Gaston to Mecklenburg County, Norman Thomas, the Socialist Party leader, wrote: "It looks as if North Carolina was spared the disgrace of furnishing the United States with another Judge Thayer (of the Sacco-Vanzetti case). Judge Barnhill, by granting to the Gastonia defendants the change of venue, and by admitting the women defendants to reasonable bail, lives up to his former reputation for fairness."

This was great publicity. Reporters flocked to the trial.

In New York a bitter controversy took place among the Communist Party leaders on the policy to be pursued by the defense. The so-called Right-wingers insisted that the charges should be fought as a "frame-up." The Dunne-Foster group demanded that we stand on our right to defend the union headquarters. The International Labor Defense, a Communist organization, had charge of our case and until the day of trial it did not know whether to obey the Right or Left Wing.

We discarded our overalls for freshly pressed trousers, starched shirts, and new ties. We polished our shoes and slicked our hair. When we marched into the courtroom we resembled, as one writer put it, "a college fraternity more than a gang of murderers."

The Judge sat upon the usual raised platform. On both right and left were jury boxes, also raised from the floor. The left jury box was reserved for special writers. Radio instruments were installed on a table below the Judge.

The attorneys for the prosecution included: Solicitor John Carpenter, Major Bulwinkle, regular Manville-Jenckes lawyer, Clyde Hoey, brother-in-law of Governor Gardner,[1] T. Cansler, leading corporation lawyer, A. G. Mangum, Major Cherry, A. Wolty, George Mason, R. Whitaker, and J. Newell. The defense counsel were: Thomas P. Jimison. J. Frank Flowers, Thaddeus Adams, S. Abernathy, and J. D. McCall, all from Charlotte; Leon Josephson of Trenton, N. J., Arthur Garfield Hays of New York and John R. Neal of Knoxville, Tenn. The last two were representatives of

[1] Now Governor of North Carolina.

the American Civil Liberties Union and had volunteered their services.

The veniremen sat in the rear of the large courtroom, waiting to be called. Save for the twelve peremptory challenges which were our right, we were at the mercy of these men. We watched them eagerly, trying to learn how they were disposed. A little girl came up to the side of the judge and began to draw their names out of a hat. The trial was on.

A dark, sullen fellow is in the box, being questioned by the defense. Has he formed an opinion of the case, Jimison asks him?

"They're all guilty!" shouts the prospective juror.

Quick as a flash, Arthur Hays is on his feet: "Sophie Melvin, stand up."

Sophie, a pretty girl, rises, shaking back her long, wavy hair.

"Do you think she is guilty?" Hays challenges the venireman.

Solicitor Carpenter jumps up from his seat. "I object, if your Honor please. Attorney Jimison is questioning now for the defense, your Honor, if you please, and not Mr. Hays, if you please."

Sophie and Mr. Hays sit down. The prospective juror is excused but the prosecution beams. That opinion has made an impression on the rest. However, they are not happy long. C. H. James, a young mechanic, now answers the same question. "I believe all the defendants are innocent. I believe they were exercising their constitutional rights. I believe they were intimidated and interfered with and had a perfect right to shoot in self-defense."

There is a stir in the courtroom. Carpenter looks

crestfallen; Major Bulwinkle is wringing his pudgy
hands. One of the prosecution lawyers mutters, "Ten'e·
'im."

The clerk rises and sings out: "Ju-roar, look upon
the prisoner. . . . Prisoner, look upon the ju-roar. . . .
D'y like 'im?"

"Nuh," grunts the lawyer, and this venireman, too,
is excused.

It took nine days and three panels of veniremen, total-
ing 650, to find twelve men considered fit to listen to
the evidence and return a fair verdict.

My friend, Bill Rollins, author of "Shadow Before,"
described the atmosphere and conduct of the trial in
this way:

> This trial was a gentleman's game, and all
> of North Carolina was damned proud of it.
> Instead of a sour-faced, snarling Thayer on the
> bench, there was the slim, keen-eyed Barnhill
> with his winning smile, a paragon of im-
> partiality. The sheriffs were friendly to all
> concerned. There was no roughhousing the
> prisoners. The lawyers, for the most part, were
> courteous, soft-voiced southern gentlemen.
> They would appear in the morning, with their
> arms intertwined; virgin rose buds, still fresh
> with dew, graced the lapels of their carefully
> tailored linen coats.
>
> And the town itself joined in the game.
> The Chamber of Commerce spread itself at a
> luncheon. All were invited to make whoopee
> over the industrial disruption of the State of
> North Carolina, the shooting of their chief of
> police, and the resulting imprisonment of six-
> teen men and women. Every representative of
> the press was invited to rise and name his
> paper, conservative or subversive, and assured

of a delightful welcome. Charlotte is no
Dedham!

"Here we're going to play the game like
sports," the Community Spirit seemed to be
saying. "And when the cleverest battery of
lawyers has succeeded in twisting twelve confused minds to suit our purpose, we'll all shake
hands. And call it a day!"

What could one do with such Civic Virtue?
How could you, even if you had the nerve, get
up in that well-mannered courtroom and tell
them it was all a goddam farce; that thirteen
lives were at stake; that they were sitting there
and playing tiddledywinks for the corpses;
that if Judge, lawyers, sheriffs and all suddenly rose up in passionate anger and black-
jacked, stabbed and shot the prisoners, it
would at least have a certain human dignity
which was lacking in this solemn questioning
of veniremen as to their ancestry, and this
weighty consideration of the evidence that the
prisoner Hendricks had jumped on a soapbox
and crowed like a rooster?

One could not do it. One had to be a good
sport—even on the way to the electric chair.
For this was a gentleman's game!

Day after day the prosecution tried to show that a
great conspiracy had existed to kill Chief Aderholt.
One State witness after another made an appearance
on the stand without proving anything. The trial was
becoming monotonous. Workers in overalls packed the
courtroom, giving us prisoners signs of encouragement.
We were beginning to take heart. We did not realize
that the prosecution was merely marking time, waiting
for a "break." This "break" came from a wholly unex-
pected source. It was a moving picture, "The Trial of
Mary Dugan," which was being shown in the South

at this time. The dramatic part of the picture is the closing scene where a dummy, a perfect likeness of the murdered policeman, is wheeled into the courtroom. In the picture it created a sensation, causing the conviction of the criminal.

Solicitor Carpenter and his force of gentlemen hit upon a brilliant idea: "Just the thing to make our trial spectacular, to put life in our cause!" With great secrecy they had a dummy made of the dead Chief Aderholt. The cost was one thousand dollars.

We prisoners learned about the dummy the night before it was wheeled into the courtroom when a negro "trustee" came running to us saying he had seen the ghost of Chief Aderholt. But we did not know what he was talking about until, during a dull moment, Solicitor Carpenter dramatically signaled to a court flunkey and the sheriff. They wheeled into the courtroom a tall, black-shrouded *thing*. Carpenter rushed up and unpinned the shroud. The image of the late officer in his last bloody uniform was revealed.

Aderholt's widow and daughter, carefully placed near the jury, began to cry. Reporters laughed. Jurors stared wild-eyed.

"Remove that model," ordered Judge Barnhill.

"I'm so sorry. I don't know why it was done," said Carpenter, pretending to straighten out a crease in the dummy's coat.

"Take it out!" snapped the Judge.

"I just wanted to . . ." Carpenter gained time by fussing with the Chief's collar and lifting his hat until Aderholt's eyes stared at the jury.

"I said, *Take That Out!*" the Judge yelled at the top of his voice.

At last, it went, wobbling on its wheels.

The result of dragging in this ghastly life-sized effigy of the dead Chief was to drive one of the jurors mad. That night he broke away from the sheriff and it took five men to place him in a padded cell.

The following day Judge Barnhill declared a mistrial.

3

The mistrial and the favorable statements of the jurors whipped the lynch gang into a frenzy. One of the jurors, speaking for the twelve, had said to a reporter: "We were so far solid for acquittal. If the State had no stronger evidence than that so far presented, we would never have voted to convict the defendants of any crime." Were the hounds about to lose their quarry? Major Bulwinkle, Carpenter and the Loray boss-gang were frustrated at the first trial. But vengeance would be theirs!

That night a mob lined up in front of Carpenter's office in Gastonia. In an affidavit Cliff Saylors, one of the mob victims, swore he saw Major Bulwinkle leading the pack and that his assistant was no other than Solicitor Carpenter, erstwhile prosecutor of the sixteen strike prisoners. The mob took to cars. Ferguson and Tom Gilbert, the two policemen that accompanied Aderholt to the union lot on that fatal June Seventh, led the parade. The Charlotte *Observer* wrote that the mob was accompanied by two carloads of "Gaston peace officers."

At nine in the evening the cars pulled up in front of Mrs. Lodge's house on Airline Avenue, where I had been living at the time of the shooting. She continued to rent rooms to strikers and strike leaders. A few of the men walked up on the porch. Suddenly the front door banged open. About a hundred men rushed in. They were all singing *Praise God From Whom All Blessings Flow.* C. M. Lell, Cliff Saylors, and Ben Wells, union organizers, were in the room. Mrs. Lodge recognized Major Bulwinkle and Solicitor Carpenter in the yard. The Major lost his glasses. A union member of Bessemer City still has them!

"You got any statement you want to make?" a leader of the group asked Wells.

Wells started to reply when one of the super-patriots ordered him to kiss a small American flag and denounce trade unionism.

Wells started making a speech on unionism, when the leader interrupted:—"That's enough. Let's go."

With these words, Wells was attacked by the mob. Then they put the three organizers in the cars and started for Charlotte.

"Now we'll get that damned red-headed Beal out of jail and lynch him!" one man shouted. "We'll take every damned organizer and lynch them."

About half way to Charlotte, Wells was pulled out of the car and was told to telephone Hugo Oehler, another organizer, to meet him in a quiet spot. Two men stood beside Wells with revolvers against his ribs. Oehler became suspicious and before Wells could say any more, one of the mob cut the telephone wire. Then Wells was taken out and put into a separate car. Lell and Saylors followed in another car. The rest of the caravan drove on to Charlotte. While in the car, Wells was smashed on the head with a blackjack. Then they showed him the rope with which they intended to lynch him.

On a lonely road the cars stopped. Wells, Saylor and Lell were dragged to the road. "We'll beat him up first, then do the next job," said the leader, taking Wells by the arm. They removed Wells' clothes. The mob ordered Saylors to whip him with a strap. Saylors refused and was knocked to the ground. The strap looked too delicate to the mob. They took branches and sticks. Wells was whipped into unconsciousness.

An automobile approached from the opposite direction. "It's the law," cried one of the mob. They left the three organizers on the roadside and made a hasty retreat into Gaston County. They had feared the "law," because they were in a neighboring county. But the "law" from which they fled turned out to be just two possum hunters. They assisted the beaten trio to Concord for medical aid.

The other part of the mob had ridden on to Charlotte. Here they tried to get defense lawyer Jimison and the union organizers living in Charlotte. Oehler, who had become suspicious, notified his comrades. They made their escape. Jimison was not at home. And the Charlotte jail is too modern for a mob to break into, if the sheriff makes any pretense of defending it. The jail is so constructed that one man can hold back a mob. This is what saved me and the others from being lynched.

Of course, nothing was done to these mobsters. But three days later a raiding party searched the rooms of union organizers and arrested seven of them, charging them with "insurrection to overthrow the government of North Carolina."

In the face of this mob activity, the union made plans for a mass meeting to be held for the afternoon of September 14, near Loray Mill. The organizers for the meeting sent out calls to workers in neighboring villages. The Bessemer City members were especially urged to attend. An armed mob mobilized to prevent it. On the day of the meeting they blocked all roads leading into Gastonia, and turned back every truckload of workers.

Ella May Wiggins—we had always known her as Ella May—got the Bessemer City group together. Some of the men wanted to carry guns for self-defense but she protested. The workers went unarmed. At the border line they were met by the Gastonia outlaws and turned back. They obeyed. A carload of the gangsters followed and forced the truck off the road. Most of the people in the truck jumped out and scampered across the cotton fields. Ella May remained on the truck. The mob recognized her as one of the union leaders. How they hated her! They fired straight at her unprotected breast. She gasped: "My God, they have shot me," and dropped to the bottom of the truck—dead.

In our cells we knew very little of what was going on. Late in the afternoon Sheriff Hanna came to our cells to tell us that he had been called to Gastonia because more shooting had taken place there. "They say the wife of one of the mill bosses has been shot by union men," he announced angrily. "God help you prisoners if this is so. They'll tear down the jail and lynch you all."

That night the jail was strangely silent.

The next morning we received the Sunday papers as usual. Spread out on the front page was the story of the shooting of Ella May. There were pictures of her family of five small children. This was the saddest thing that happened while we were in jail. We were speechless. We knew no one would be punished. She was not a boss's wife. She was only a workingwoman. It's no crime in the South to kill a mill worker.

I can still hear her speaking at a union meeting: "I'm the mother of nine. Four of them died with whooping cough, all at once. I was working nights and nobody to do for them, only Myrtle. She's eleven and a sight of help. I asked the super to put me on day shift so's I could tend 'em, but he refused. I don't know why. So I had to quit my job and then there wasn't any money for medicines, so they just died. I never could do anything for my children. Not even keep 'em alive, it seems. That's why I'm for the union. So's I can do better for them."

I can still hear her singing one of her best songs. When the first red earth fell on her coffin, Katie Barrett sang it:

We leave our homes in the morning,
We kiss our children good-by,
While we slave for the bosses,
Our children scream and cry.

It is for our little children
That seem to us so dear,
But for them nor us, dear workers,
The bosses do not care.

But listen to me, workers,
A union they do fear;
Let's stand together, workers,
And have a union here.

XIV. "GUILTY"

1

OUR second trial began on the thirtieth of September
with Judge Barnhill again presiding. The attorneys on
both sides were virtually the same except that Arthur
Garfield Hays was no longer with us. The Communist pressure on the International Labor Defense had
crowded out the American Civil Liberties Union. During the three weeks that the trial lasted, we sorely missed
the ability and resourcefulness of this man.

The prosecution was no longer playing the gentle-
manly game. This time it was not taking any chances.
Having realized some of the weaknesses of their position in the first attempt, the lawyers proceeded to revise
their tactics. They withdrew the indictment of first degree murder and they freed nine of the defendants.
Carter, Harrison, Hendricks, McGinnis, McLaughlin,
Miller, and I were then again charged with conspiracy
to murder Chief Aderholt. The reduced number of defendants deprived us of the greater part of our challenges and the effect was immediately apparent in the
jury, which consisted of one reputed millionaire, nine
farmers, and only two industrial workers. As the trial
progressed, the political and religious views of the defendants were continually paraded before these men.
We were to be convicted, the prosecution seemed to insist, not so much for what we did as because our religion
was not that of Solicitor Carpenter, because our economic ideas were not those of Major Bulwinkle, because

we did not profess the same social ethics as Hoey, the Governor's brother-in-law.

The Communist Party had anticipated these tactics and the leaders had debated whether to use the courtroom as a rostrum for propagating Communist principles or to avoid propaganda in order not to antagonize the jury. It was decided, so the defendants were informed, to take the latter course. We were instructed not to discuss the issues of the strike, not to attack the mill bosses, the Committee of One Hundred, and the police for their violence and acts of provocation. Our testimony was to be merely one of defense against the charges and was to be given in a way which would win the sympathy of the jury for all of us. But we were not told that exactly the opposite instructions had been issued to Edith Miller who, though no longer one of the defendants, was still to appear as a witness. The result of this brilliant "compromise" between the factions, which held different views on what should be the Communist policy at the trial, was to discredit the defendants. If we denied our beliefs for fear of the consequences, would we not, therefore, deny the facts?

2

I took the stand on Monday, October 14. E. T. Cansler, an old and experienced Charlotte lawyer, rigorously cross-examined me for the prosecution. All the hate and rage of the mill bosses seemed to be stored up in that old man. I felt it as I faced his hostile glare from the witness stand. But this did not unnerve me. On my shoulders rested the lives of six other men and the case of thousands of enslaved textile workers. Cansler's opening question was: "Do you know what this magazine is I hand you?"

"Yes," I replied, "that is the official magazine of the I.L.D."

"Did you," continued Cansler, waving the magazine, "prior to September of this year, give any facts or statements to the officials of this magazine concerning a sketch of your life?"

Objection. Overruled by Judge Barnhill.

"I gave them a history of my life that I wrote myself."

"Is this it?"

Objection. Overruled.

"Yes. That is it."

Cansler read from my life story. "Now you say you joined the Socialist Party?"

Objection. Sustained. The jury was excused.

A conflict now took place over the admissibility of evidence as to my affiliation with the Communist Party and my beliefs.

CANSLER: "If you will read this article carefully, you will find that he states in here why he left the Socialist Party and joined the Communist Party. We propose to develop in this case the reason he left the Socialist Party was because it was a party of peace, and the reason he joined the Communist Party was because it was a party of war. We propose to prove that the Communist Party of America is a branch of the Soviet Union of Russia, that the cardinal principle of that party is the overthrow by force and violence of the Constitution of the United States of America. That we will prove by the declarations in the *Daily Worker,* the organ of the Communist Party.... Now with reference to the question that is going to come up regarding his views on the Negro question. *Social equality* is what he advocates. I wish to call Your Honor's attention to the fact

that Your Honor very well knows in this country
no high-class respectable white man advocates social
equality. Neither will any high class Negro advocate it.
Take, for instance, Booker T. Washington and his suc-
cessors who founded that Institution in Alabama. They
held there ought not to be social equality. That both
races should work out their own salvation among their
own people. I submit if there is any question in the
world which ought to impeach this man's testimony it is
his notorious advocacy of social equality among the
races.

COURT: "There would be a great deal of force to your
argument if the man were a native of North Carolina.
But as a Northern man ... But I believe a man who advocates doctrines of Communism and advocates the overthrowing of the government would be impeached anywhere."

Shades of Abraham Lincoln! I was thinking of his
forgotten words: "This country and its institutions belong to the people who inhabit it. Whenever they shall
grow weary of the existing government, they can exer-
cise their constitutional right of amending it, or their
revolutionary right to dismember or overthrow it."

LAWYER JIMISON: "Saint Peter and Saint John were
not overthrowing the Government when they advised
Ananias to join the Communist union. The minute you
put in that jury box the notion and arguments about
Communism, it's just simply so highly prejudicial to
the defendants that it is not worth arguing about."

COURT: "If he is a Communist, you cannot complain
about it. If he is a Communist, he ought to be considered
such when tried by loyal citizens of America."

The jury was readmitted. The question was settled.
I was branded by a word which was not understood,

which I was not allowed to explain, and which impeached whatever I might say. Was it possible to win
against these odds? I watched the members of the jury.
They were not looking at me. What were they thinking
about? My own thoughts rambled on while I was being
cross-examined: "Cansler, old man with tired gray eyes,
represents the putrid order of things. What had I said
to the workers on the night of June Seventh? Cansler
wants to know. What a joke! It is *I* who should be
asking *him* questions, him and the other flunkeys of the
mill owners behind him.... To hell with Communism...
To hell with Capitalism... To hell· with the Court!
What about the workers in the mills, slaving and starving? Answer *me* that question, you Cansler and you
Carpenter and you Judge Barnhill...."

CANSLER: "I ask you again, Mr. Beal, do you believe
in violence?"

"No."

(*To myself: Ask Mr. Carpenter or Major Bulwinkle,
please!*)

CANSLER: "I ask you, Mr. Beal, do you believe in the
overthrow of the United States Government by force
and violence?"

"No."

(*To myself: Ask Mr. Manville and Jenckes, please.
...And shall I rise and shout that the workers in the
rear of the courtroom would like to know if I believe in
shorter hours and higher wages and better housing?*)

The reaction in the courtroom at the close of my testimony seemed to be favorable. The other defendants
were well pleased. But the witness called after me was
Edith Saunders Miller, wife of Clarence Miller. From
her very first words we, defendants, sat dumbfounded.
Blood, thunder, and fireworks! She flaunted the revolu-

tionary ideas of the Communist Party, and stretched its most rabid principles until they seemed to cover this very incident of the strike. Proudly she defined that it was striving by violence to bring about a Soviet régime in Gastonia and the rest of the United States.

The lackeys of the mill owners had dragged the political issue of Communism into the court. And the Communist Party at the last minute decided to make political capital out of it for the Cause. It no longer mattered that seven lives were at stake. Comrade Edith Miller was addressing the Court, but she was anticipating the commendation of Stalin's lackeys in New York and Moscow. When she descended from the witness stand, the courtroom was in somber silence. Only Newell smiled at his associates as if to say: "This finishes them."

3

I shall always believe that the testimony of Edith Miller weighed more heavily against us than all the other matter presented before the jury. The evidence of their witnesses as to the killing of Aderholt was so flimsy, so contradictory that it is doubtful whether even the most prejudiced jury could possibly have accepted it without Mrs. Miller's admission that violence was a recognized policy and method of Communism and, therefore, by implication that it was part of our policy at Gastonia.

Policeman Gilbert, one of the men wounded with Aderholt, testified as follows: "We went on a little further and a black-headed fellow standing on the outside, three or four steps from the door, jumped up and down and said, 'Turn him loose, turn him loose.' Then he just squatted down and shot. I know who that was.

Two of the cartoons which appeared
in the *Labor Defender*, 1929.

Solicitor Carpenter, Prosecuting
Attorney at the Gastonia trial.

Major Bulwinkle, attorney for
the Loray Mills.

It was that black-headed fellow, McGinnis. When he shot me, I said, 'Chief, I'm shot.' The Chief turned loose the fellow he had hold of and came around. About that time the fellow in the door fired a shot. That was Mc-Laughlin. He fired. At that time they began to shoot from all directions. I don't much think that shot hit any one."

It is in evidence by the State's witness, therefore, that Aderholt was shot after Gilbert. Gilbert claimed that McGinnis shot him and that the shot fired by McLaughlin, the second shot, did not hit any one. These first and second shots were the only shots identified by any of the witnesses as having been fired by any one of the defendants.

Policeman H. C. Jackson often attended the union's mass meetings. There was nothing unusual in his presence at the affair of June Seventh. He testified that he heard me say: "Go on the picket line. Go to the mill and into the mill. If any one stops you, *Shoot and Shoot to Kill.*" But Jackson could not explain why he did not arrest me immediately, or why he did not report at once my "shoot-to-kill" order to Chief Aderholt. He declared that he had entered my statement verbatim in a "little red book."

In summing up, the defense pointed out to the jury that:

1. There was no direct testimony that any of the defendants shot Aderholt or any one of the other wounded officers.

2. There was absolutely no evidence that Miller ever had a gun in his hands or uttered a single word before or during the affray.

3. No one testified that Harrison did any shooting.

4. No one identified Hendricks as one of the strikers'

guards. The only evidence that Hendricks did any shooting was testimony alleged to have been made by him three or four minutes after the shooting at a place several blocks away.

5. Only one witness, Roach, claimed that he saw Beal with a gun. No witness claimed that Beal did any shooting.

6. Except Gilbert, all the witnesses who testified that McGinnis fired the first shot, also said he had shot into the ground.

7. Gilbert, who credited McLaughlin with the second shot, said that this shot hit no one.

8. The testimony was unanimous that no one fell, though Police Officer Gilbert claimed to have been hit, until at least the third shot or subsequent volleys of shots, with only circumstantial evidence as to the sources of any of these latter shots.

9. The State's evidence affirmatively showed that Carter did no shooting.

Our first defense witness was Henry Strange, a middle-aged carpenter. He was at the railroad crossing where the police officers attacked the picket line and broke it up. As the strikers fled, he heard the drunken Gilbert cry out to Chief Aderholt: "Let's go down and kill them all off. This is the best time we'll ever get."

Clyde Hoey took up the cross-examination of this witness for the State. Try as he might, he could not shake Strange's statement in any way. However, he did make the man admit having had intercourse with a prostitute.

"Was the woman white?"

"Yes."

"How many women at her house?"

"It was not at her house."

"Where was it?"

"On the train."

"On the train? In the coach?" asked Mr. Hoey, mouth wide open in prurient curiosity. *"Right there in the coach?"*

At this point Judge Barnhill intervened. "The details of it are not material."

But Hoey was too far under the spell. "Did you say, right there in the coach?"

"That's where it was."

"Go on ... what else?" panted the attorney.

"That is all."

Mr. Hoey brushed back his long gray locks and straightened out his cutaway coat. He looked like a cheated man. He had missed an important event.

The State had tried to prove that on the night of June seventh I had ordered the strikers to go to the mill, get inside, and drag out the workers there—even to shoot them, if it was necessary. More than a hundred men and women had heard my instructions, given openly from the platform of our speaking grounds. Gladys Wallace, who was on the scene all of the time, was called as the second defense witness.

"He told us to form a picket line," she testified, "to go down in front of the mill gate and stand out there in front of the mill gate. He said that a crowd in the mill wanted to come out and that they would meet us at the mill gate."

Attorney Newell, who cross-examined Mrs. Wallace, had not the suave and eloquent manner of Clyde Hoey but in his blustering way he tried to impugn her veracity and to cast aspersions on her virtue. But no amount of bullying confused or intimidated her. In response to questions over and over again as to her whereabouts at various times in her life, she flashed back the answer, "I spun."

4

While we were in the midst of our trial, the country was shocked by an event which occurred within one hundred miles of Charlotte. Seven textile workers were deliberately killed and twenty-four others wounded in Marion, N. C.

About a thousand were out on strike there, under the United Textile Workers of the A. F. of L. Some compromise was made and they went back to work. The bosses did not keep their promises. The men walked out again on the night of October second. They picketed in front of the mill. The day shift joined them.

Sheriff Adkins and fifteen of his men, who had arrived early, suddenly released tear gas into the strikers' ranks. The latter turned and fled, their eyes stinging. Old man Jonas couldn't run fast enough. He was struck over the head with the butt of a sheriff's gun and handcuffed. The sheriff's men then opened fire on the fleeing strikers, shooting them in the back. Not one of the sheriff's men or mill officials suffered a scratch; not one was punished for the murder of the unarmed and defenseless strikers.

The shooting of these workers came a short time after the killing of Ella May. It seemed to us, locked up in the Charlotte jail for the act of defending ourselves against such gunmen, that fair-minded people would understand our position; it was cruel proof of our plight and our danger when Aderholt and his drunken officers invaded the union grounds. But not a single newspaper in the State, of all those that had cried for our blood, drew this conclusion from the events. As for the jury . . .

Let me record here the infamous remarks of T. P. Baldwin, the owner of the striking plant, the Marion Manufacturing Company, as they were reported by the Asheville *Citizen*. Mr. Baldwin rails publicly and often at the Communist theories of violence, which I have always abhorred and denounced, but nothing I have ever experienced did so much to incite and justify violence as his humorous remarks at the expense of the victims of this wanton slaughter.

"I understand there were sixty or seventy shots fired in the Wednesday fight. There are thirty or so bullets accounted for. If this is true, I think the officers are damn good marksmen. If I ever organize an army, they can have jobs with me. I've read that the death of each soldier in the World War consumed more than five tons of lead. Here we have less than five pounds and these casualties. A good average, I call it!"

As the murdered strikers were laid out in a row, an old mountain preacher stepped forth and prayed. "Oh, Lord Jesus Christ, here are men in their coffins, blood of my blood, bone of my bone. I trust, Oh God, that these friends will go to a place better than this village or any other place in North Carolina. Oh, God, we know we are not in high society, but we know Jesus Christ loves us. The poor people have their rights too. For the work we do in this world, is this what we get if we demand our rights? Jesus Christ, your Son, Oh God, was a workingman. If He were to pass under these trees to-day, He would see these cold bodies lying here before us ... Dear God, what would Jesus Christ do if He were to come to Carolina?"

Yes, what would Christ do? Would he give His blessings to the Adkinses, Baldwins, Carpenters, and Bulwinkles?

5

If we had not had so much at stake, we should have enjoyed the comedy of the summations to the jury by which the prosecution closed its case. Clyde Hoey, looking for all the world like a quack medicine-barker, with his winged collar and chocolate-brown swallow-tailed coat, orated for hours. Pointing an accusing finger at me, he said: *"He* fired through the knot holes with the walls of the union building as his breastworks. That was also what Clarence Miller, his compatriot from the North, did." But later he accused me of being a coward to let other people do the shooting while I lay on the floor.

But the real clowning came when Solicitor Carpenter took the ring. The breezy, dapper, incomparable showman Carpenter! He painted us as Red Revolutionists, atheists and murderers. He described us as "devils with hoofs and horns, who threw away their pitchforks for shotguns. . . . Mine is a holy gang, a God-serving gang," he shouted, his arms taking in with a sweep all of the prosecuting staff and its witnesses. "Gentlemen, gentlemen of the jury, do you believe in the Flag? Do you believe in North Carolina? Do you believe in Good Roads?" He paced before the jury box painting the supposed havoc wrought by the Communists. As the New York *Times* reported, "He impersonated every actor in the drama, changing with protean skill from male to female. He sank to his knees for the moment in which the wounded policeman was returning the enemy's fire."

"They came into peaceful, contented Gastonia, with its flowers, birds and churches," he grew lyrical. "They came sweeping like a cyclone, like a tornado, to sink their fangs into the heart and life-blood of *my* community, *your* community. Men, do your duty. Do your duty, in the Name of God!"

He made tatters of rhetoric, none worse than the above. He tore into shreds the emotions of the jury. To emphasize his plea, he knelt and prayed before the jury box. Mrs. Aderholt was conveniently near, attired in deep mourning, wiping her eyes. He seized her hand. "Moses paid for his act by wandering and doing penance for forty years. Do your duty, men. Make these men do penance for their crime by thirty years in the penitentiary."

Then he threw the gunshot-riddled coat at Aderholt's widow. *"Take It Home! Take It Home!"*

At the height of this emotional appeal to the jury, in which he had rolled on the floor like a man with delirium tremens, Carpenter was finally called to order by Judge Barnhill. The spectators looked on with amazement. Reporters tittered. The jury gazed open-mouthed. They were going through another revival.

Carpenter concluded with the following bit of oratory: "They stood it till the Great God looked down from the very battlements of heaven and broke the chains and traces of their patience, and caused them to call the officers to the lot and stop the infernal scenes that came sweeping down from the wild plains of Soviet Russia into the peaceful community of Gastonia, bringing bloodshed and death, creeping like the hellish serpent crept into the Garden of Eden. *Do Your Duty, Men!"*

When this outburst was over and the echoes still, Judge Barnhill adjourned the court over the week-end. He said he wanted to think over the charge. He left those men with the words of Carpenter ringing in their ears—words that any intelligent mind would dismiss as hysterical ranting signifying nothing. But Carpenter knew his jury—and so did Judge Barnhill.

On Monday the court was packed to the doors, mostly with mill hands. The police were instructed to guard against a demonstration. The jury was sent out and returned in about forty-five minutes.

"Gentlemen, have you arrived at a verdict?"

"We have. *We Find the Defendants Guilty of Murder in the First Degree.*"

The surprised judge swung around in his chair and looked in silence at the jury, then he informed them that the defendants were only charged with murder in the second degree. The foreman then explained that the jury had confused the first, second, third, and fourth counts with the various degrees of murder. The jury was directed to retire and consider these charges. In a few minutes they returned with a verdict of "Guilty"— against all defendants, on all counts.

The courtroom was deathly in silence. From the elevation of our box I looked at the upturned faces. Major Bulwinkle wore a leery look; on Hoey's face there was a self-righteous expression; Solicitor Carpenter, the bellicose revivalist, smiled triumphantly. My strike guard, hard-boiled K. O. Byers, was weeping. The reporters scanned our faces for signs of emotion.

Then I heard the judge say: "Beal, Miller, Harrison, and Carter, I sentence you to from seventeen to twenty years in the Raleigh penitentiary at hard labor. McGinnis and McLaughlin from twelve to fifteen years in the Raleigh penitentiary. K. Y. Hendricks, though I think he is NOT guilty, from five to seven years at the same place. Sheriff, the prisoners are in your custody!"

Back to our cells—the inevitable abiding place for rebels.

XV. TO "SKIP" OR NOT TO "SKIP"

1

WE paced our cells. We paced the "bull-pen." The International Labor Defense raised $5,000 bail for each of us while the case was appealed to the State Supreme Court. Five thousand dollars was extremely low bail under the circumstances. What was the reason for this sudden laxity? Did the authorities want us to "skip" our bail? They had won a technical victory. They were less anxious to fight years of propaganda for our release. At any rate, it was significant that one of our local lawyers suggested that we "skip" to Soviet Russia. And soon after that, as we paced the bull pen, "Bill" Dunne visited us with Juliet Stuart Poyntz.

"Take it easy, fellas," said Dunne, "you'll leave for over there as soon as you're out of here on bail."

"Over there" meant Soviet Russia. "Bill" Dunne was on the highest committee of the American Communist Party, so we regarded his views as authoritative. Later we found out this was not so. "Bill" was speaking for himself.

My reaction to this was one of intense joy. To live and work in the Workers' Fatherland instead of serving twenty years in a southern Bastille! For the moment I forgot all about my duty to the union and the promise I had made to the southern workers not to run away. I was so pleased with the prospect of seeing Soviet Russia that all else left my mind. Clarence Miller, usually noncommittal, was positively enraptured. He rose to ecstatic heights as he led prisoners in a march round and round the bull-pen, singing the *International*. Only George Carter protested against the idea of "skipping." He was angry at "Bill" Dunne for putting forward the proposition. We laid this to his martyr complex.

Within a few weeks I was out on bail, speaking before a crowd of loyal union members in front of the Charlotte courthouse. The union immediately made arrangements for a speaking tour for me in the Eastern cities. My first stop was New York City. I arrived at the Pennsylvania Station. The huge crowd on hand was kept back by ropes. Some one recognized me coming up the stairs, and yelled: "Beal! Beal!"

A policeman ran after me. I thought to myself: arrested again! But, to my surprise, the cop was very gentle. He seemed to know about the case. While putting me into a taxi, he said, "Aren't you glad to be back in civilization again, away from that hell?"

I mumbled something in reply. I was too astonished to thank him.

It was in New Bedford, my old stamping grounds, that I received the greatest reception. There were so many at the station that the train was unable to drive through. To my inner satisfaction, there were no policemen in sight. I was carried all the way to the meeting place. Here I was presented with a watch, engraved: New Bedford South End Workers to Fred Beal, 11-17-'29, which I still wear. After the meeting, the North End of the town took me to one of the clothing stores and fitted me out with a much needed suit of clothes, shirts, shoes, etc.

At Woonsocket, R. I., however, the police acted as of old. They prohibited our meeting. Jim Reed, the union's president, and I protested this arbitrary decision to the mayor, whose office was situated in a bank. We also protested to one of the editors of the Providence *Journal*. But of no avail.

My tour included dozens of New England cities. The meetings were enthusiastic, orderly, and uneventful until I returned for a second time to New Bedford. There I was arrested. It was rather a futile affair, made all the more distasteful to me because I felt the police were right. Martin Russek, Communist leader and district organizer for the union, forced me into the situation. His theory of organizing workers was to create some sort of sensational incident and depend on the publicity to get sympathizers for his cause. He could always rely on the police for assistance. What actually happened was that Russek succeeded only in organizing occasions where workers got their skulls cracked. The membership of the union did not increase; it merely grew to look more and more like the casualty ward of a hospital.

This time Russek decided it would be a fine publicity stunt to have me arrested at one of the mill gates. Unbeknown to me, he planned a gala demonstration of head-cracking. There are any number of places in New Bedford where any one can yell himself hoarse without being molested. These places Martin carefully avoided. He announced that I would speak at the gate of the mill and he deliberately failed to get a permit. When I arrived in New Bedford and learned the truth of the situation, I tried to have the meeting called off. But it was too late. The announcements were out; the crowd was waiting. I made the best of it. So did the police— with their clubs. About fifteen workers with bandaged heads appeared in court with me. I was fined five dollars.

Probably the judge thought one twenty-year sentence was enough.

This was but a mild foretaste of my experience in the Middle West. When I arrived in Detroit, I was informed at the district headquarters of the Communist Party that twelve members had been arrested in Pontiac for distributing leaflets announcing my meeting. The police had declared I would be arrested on sight.

What to do? My idea was to get out of the town and go on to Chicago. But Jack Statchel, the district organizer, insisted that I speak at Pontiac. He said: "We need the publicity for organizing the automobile workers."

The Party had failed completely in its efforts to organize the automobile workers into a union. My arrest, they thought, would bring the issue before the public. Again the meeting was well advertised. I felt I had to go. But none of these leaders who were so insistent on my duty would go along with me! Statchel suddenly had an important meeting elsewhere. Philip Raymond, rank-and-file leader, was then in jail with his teeth knocked out.

Despite threats by the police against any one attending my meeting, the hall was crowded to the doors. Police lined the walls. I spoke for two hours, mostly about the South and what took place at Gastonia. But I devoted part of my talk to an attack on General Motors for discharging local workers at the same time that the company was bringing in outside help to create a labor surplus. I had found this out in a talk with local workers just before the meeting.

When I stepped down from the platform an officer, in plain clothes, approached me and laid his hand on my shoulder, saying, "Beal, you're under arrest."

"What for?" I asked.

"Ask the District Attorney downstairs."

Workers in the hall began to shout: "Let him go! Let him go!" Police drew their pistols. I was afraid of another shooting, so I advised the workers to let me go in peace. The next day I was fingerprinted and "mugged" for the first time in my life. Not even the Gastonia police did this. I was charged with "trying to overthrow the State of Michigan by force and violence." My bail was set at $25,000.

Seven years later John L. Lewis held up the entire sovereign State of Michigan in nearby Flint. But this time the great State and the powerful General Motors Corporation yielded to "force and violence." What a difference these seven years have made in the attitude of the law towards labor!

"Fresh meat," cried a prisoner, as I was put into the Pontiac County jail bull-pen. "Fresh meat, boys."

The same steel bars, the same table and benches, as in Charlotte. It made me feel at home! About eight or ten Bulgarian Communists had preceded me.

When I stood before the "Kangaroo Court," surrounded by about twenty-five prisoners who were there for various causes, such as bootlegging, adultery, hold-ups, and robbery, the "Kangaroo Judge" asked: "Why did you break in jail?"

"I'm here for trying to overthrow the State by force and violence."

The "Judge," who was there for holding-up a gasoline station, looked at me incredulously. "All by yourself?"

"All by myself," I assured him.

"I'd start with the banks," offered one of the boys.

"What's the bail?" asked the "Judge."

"Twenty-five thousand dollars."

"Wow!" cried a Negro prisoner, in for bootlegging. "Man, what youse do? Hold up the United States mint?"

The "Judge" thought I was bluffing. "I'm accused of shooting a man and I'm held for only three thousand," he said.

When they found out how true it was, they treated me with great respect. I was made District Attorney of the "Court"!

A few weeks later the bail was reduced to ten thousand dollars and I again walked out of jail into the free air.

The remainder of my tour was canceled.

2

I had received a telegram from Clarence Miller in New York urging me to avoid further arrests and to come immediately to New York for a conference among the seven Gastonia men. I knew what that conference would discuss and in the train on the way to New York I made my decision: not to "skip" bail, but to see the Soviet Union at any cost before going to prison. It would be months before the Supreme Court made a decision in our case. Why shouldn't I take a few months' vacation?

I knew what Clarence Miller thought about the matter. He had declared to me many times that he would not serve. The other boys, especially Carter, were for returning to prison. After I arrived in New York, we, seven, met with all the members of the Central Committee of the Communist Party. Every one of them was against our "skipping" bail. Not only this, they were against our paying a visit to Soviet Russia. They feared

that the Comintern—the Communist International—
would keep us there. But soon after the meeting with
the Central Committee, five of us (Miller, Hendricks,
McGinnis, Harrison and I), and Edith Miller, met
secretly and made plans for a visit to Soviet Russia.
Carter and McLaughlin were not present because they
had been sent out of New York on Party business.

Miller said he had a very good friend in the Bronx
who would help us escape to Soviet Russia. But when
the friend made his appearance, I learned that Clarence
had been doing some double-dealing. He had told this
friend of his that the Party was unanimous for our
"skipping" and that he was delegated very quietly to
raise the money. But the friend was a loyal Party member. He made a private investigation. When he discovered the Party did not want us to go, he turned
Miller down. He even tried to persuade Clarence not to
leave the country. But the latter was determined on his
course. He proposed taking our case to the Comintern
over the heads of the American Party. He was convinced
that this organization would want us to "skip" bail and
remain in the Soviet Union. I was just as sure that they
would insist we serve. "Red" Hendricks was against going at all. But Miller prevailed upon him to at least visit
the Soviet Union. Bill McGinnis was indifferent. He'd
"skip" or return to prison, whichever the rest did. Joe
Harrison was definitely for "skipping."

Edith Miller volunteered to raise the fare and to
secure the much needed passports.

3

The first to cross were Clarence Miller and "Red"
Hendricks. They planned to wait in Berlin for us.

I was the third. I traveled alone under the passport of Jacob Katz.[1] I haven't the slightest idea who the real Jacob Katz is. I never met the gentleman. His name, age and birthplace were given to me by Edith Miller. At first, I objected to this passport. Those for Miller and Hendricks had Anglo-Saxon names and I wanted the same. I argued that this was too definitely Jewish and that it would be quite difficult, with my face, to pass as a Jew. But Edith assured me that the passport customs officials would not take notice of this detail and everything would be all right. She proved to be correct. I made four trips as Jacob Katz without any trouble!

On the night of my departure, I checked my suitcases at the Grand Central Station and went to see a movie at the Paramount Theater in Times Square. I was too excited to enjoy the picture. Was it possible that I should actually be leaving for Russia in a few hours? What would it look like? What would it be like? I felt the watch on my wrist, given me by the New Bedford workers. Would the workers think I was running away from the fight?

I'd be back. This was to be only a short vacation. Nevertheless, I could hear an inner voice saying: "Don't go . . . don't go . . . don't go . . ."

I looked at my watch. Eleven o'clock. I seemed paralyzed. Suddenly the theater seemed alive with policemen and detectives. The moving figures on the curtain were saying: "Get him! Shoot him!" Perhaps a "dick" had actually followed me into the theater. I looked into the face of the man next to me. He had come in after me. Was he a "dick"? Yes, he must be. I got up and almost ran out of the theater. I raced to the station and got my suitcases and hurried up the Grand Central runway.

[1] This name, for obvious reasons, is fictitious.

"Hey, there!" some one yelled in back of me.

I nearly dropped in my tracks. Should I surrender? Should I drop the suitcases and run?

"Taxi, mister! Taxi!"

I looked over my shoulder. The fellow was a taxi driver. A policeman saw me trying to make a crosstown car. He kept it waiting until I got on. I thanked him.

At the pier I fumbled in my pockets for the horned-rimmed glasses. This was to be my only disguise.

It took some time to find my cabin in the tourist section. I had never been on a liner before. Two young German-Americans shared my cabin. One of them was unpacking when I entered. "Are you Mr. Katz?" he asked.

"Yes," I said. How strange it seemed to be called Jacob Katz.

"There's a letter up there for you."

Stuck in the frame of the mirror was a letter. Inside was a note: "Bon Voyage," with no signature. I never found out who sent it. No one except Edith Miller knew I was leaving, not even my own folks. This was not in Edith's handwriting.

When the boat moved out I was on deck to bid America farewell. It was foggy and gray. The skyscrapers and passing boats were almost hidden. The Statue of Liberty, like liberty itself, was hidden in the fog. I could see the light, and barely make out the line of the uplifted arm.

I was thinking about Bill Haywood and his escape to Soviet Russia. Of how he felt when he left America. I worried and fretted throughout the crossing for fear the newspapers would find out about my trip. They would say I was running away. How pleased the forces of reaction in the South would be! I could hardly sleep at night. I lay on my back listening to the throb of the engine. "Go ... back. Don't run. Go ... back. Don't ... run," it cried articulately.

This maddening torture by my conscience went on until I decided to take the next boat back to America. I wrote about this to Louis Engdahl, then National Secretary of the International Labor Defense. In the letter I admitted the error of even wanting to see the Soviet Union when the Party objected. In fact, I confessed everything as if Louis were my father confessor. I almost apologized for being born. I asked him for my fare back. I mailed this letter on the boat the day before landing. But I never heard from Engdahl.

4

Clarence Miller had provided me with an address of a German comrade high up in the circles of the German Communist Party. His name was Eugene Schonhaar. The address was 62, Weser Strasse, Neuköln, Berlin. Clarence had become acquainted with Schonhaar during his visit to America. Miller's strategy was to throw himself completely on Schonhaar's mercy with the hope that through him and the German Communist Party a way could be found to enter Soviet Russia with the Comintern's permission. On the day before landing I asked a few fellow-passengers the whereabouts of Neuköln. I had no idea that right behind me was a man whom I suspected of being a detective.

"Why do you want to go to Neuköln?" he interrupted.

"Because I have a friend there," I replied.

"Is he a Communist?"

"What's that? A new religion?"

"No. Neuköln is lousy with these Communists.

There's shooting going on there every day. You'd better keep away from that place."

"I hope my friend hasn't been hurt," I said, trying not to show too much interest. "I'm expecting to have a good vacation."

He seemed satisfied with my answers and told me how to get to Neuköln.

Eugene Schonhaar was not at home when I finally reached the suburb, so I waited on the steps in front of his door for three hours. Neighbors passing up and down the stairs became suspicious. Heads kept popping out of doors. When I looked at them, they hurriedly withdrew. Soon they were at the railing above and below. Since they spoke German, I didn't understand one word of what they said. After a while I hit upon the notion of drawing a hammer and sickle on a piece of paper. Then I wrote the words *"Rote Fahne."* It was the name of the Communist paper. At first they were surprised. Then one of the fellows shook his head up and down. The result was that I was taken to the central headquarters of the German Communist Party, known as the Carl Liebknecht House. It stood on the corner of Bülow Square, six stories high and taking up almost a block. It was plastered with German Communist slogans and large pictures of Lenin and Thaelman. There was a large gate for trucks and a small one for people. Both gates were guarded by armed men and no one could get in without a pass stamped by the Communist Party. I was led through a narrow subterranean place to a lunchroom used by those who worked in the building. And there at one of the tables were "Red" Hendricks and Clarence Miller!

Later, when Miller was treating Hendricks and me to dinner at a restaurant in the center of Berlin, "Red" and I told him that we had sent a letter to the American Party that we were returning as soon as they sent our fare. We had decided to accept the decision of the Party and give up seeing Soviet Russia.

Miller's face turned scarlet. "What do you guys mean by writing to the American Party about this?" he demanded. "They'll wire the Comintern not to let us in. You damn fools! When did you write? I'll have to work fast with the German and Russian Parties."

"What about party discipline?" Hendricks wanted to know.

"You should have thought about that before you left," Clarence replied.

"Yes," I said, "we should have. But we can rectify our mistake now before it is too late. Before the Supreme Court makes a decision. If they ever hear about us over here, they'll make a decision immediately."

"Well, there's one thing about it," said Clarence firmly. "You fellows can serve if you want to. I never will. No matter what decision the Comintern makes. I know German and I can make my escape in Germany." Miller insisted that "Red" and I keep away from the Carl Liebknecht House. He gave as his reason for this that it would be too dangerous for us to be seen in the neighborhood. The real reason, I later found out, was to keep us from receiving incoming mail. As it was, we never received any reply from the American Party.

Clarence and high members of the German Party told me they considered the American Party a joke, the leaders either fools or careerists. The German Party would ignore their wishes. This was the first taste I had of Communist Nationalism. I was to see more of this in Russia.

The day came, shortly after the arrival of McGinnis

and Harrison from America, when Clarence excitedly
announced permission had been granted for the five of
us to enter the Soviet Union. I was excited, too. At last
I was to see the country which was governed entirely by
the working class. No more exploitation. "All for One
and One for All." Whatever merit there was in returning to America to serve the labor movement, Hendricks
and I temporarily put aside all thought of it in our
great joy at the fact that we would soon see the wonders
of the Workers' Fatherland.

How naïve I was! I do not blame Clarence Miller for
misrepresenting "Red" and McGinnis and me to the
Comintern. He knew that the Russian authorities would
listen only if he said we were unanimous in our desire to
"skip" bail and remain in Soviet Russia. And to achieve
his ends, he told them just that. He also said that the
American Party was out of touch with the American
workers who were unanimously in favor of our "skipping." All this I learned only later. I put almost child-
like trust in the representatives of the German and Russian Parties. Miller felt one way. I another. His view
was that we could better serve the labor movement by
"skipping" than by rotting for twenty years in prison.
"We'd be forgotten in two years," he said.

There was much truth in this. But I held that the
leaders of a revolutionary movement must take prison
sentences as a matter of course. Besides, I did not relish
the idea of being pushed out of America for organizing
workers.

"Martyr complex!" flung Clarence.

"Maybe so. But every change for the better in this
world is brought about through martyrs. Isn't there
something about the blood of the martyrs being the seed
of the church?"

BOOK THREE

MOSCOW

XVI. THE PROMISED LAND

1

CARRYING a cargo of mysterious passengers, the German boat, *Preussen,* quietly sailed from Stettin for Leningrad on June 28, 1930. In addition to a number of legitimate tourists, there were many others who were traveling "incognito," as we were. Some were political fugitives from Germany and Hungary, seeking to escape prison sentences for revolutionary activities. Others were secret couriers working for the Comintern, carrying important documents from various countries to Moscow. One of these couriers, whom I'll name Beth, was a young woman from England. Clarence Miller met her at the Karl Liebknecht House in Berlin just before we left. She had in her possession documents from the English and German Communist Parties which could not be trusted to the mails. Beth taught me a few words of Russian: *zavtra* (to-morrow), *niet* (no), and *seichass* (immediately). These three words, she said, were used very often by the Russians.

Beth also informed us that some of the tourists were spies, going into Russia to carry on some sort of counter-revolutionary propaganda. This provided Miller with a chance to play detective. For the remainder of the trip he shadowed a Polish-American whom he suspected of being the ring-leader of a gang of spies. He drank and got drunk with his suspect in the hope of drawing out of him damaging information. But, alas, Miller couldn't hold his liquor and the *tête-à-têtes* usually ended by the

Polish "spy" putting Clarence to bed. Hendricks and I also had our suspects whom we trailed from deck to deck, but we gave up the game when we could not find evidence of a plot against the Soviet Union.

As each day brought us nearer and nearer to the promised land our spirits rose to a higher pitch. And when our boat steamed past the historic Kronstadt Fortress we were almost hysterical. Our first great thrill came when a freighter named after Sacco and Vanzetti passed us. We waved greetings and shouted cheers for Sacco and Vanzetti. New thrills. . . . The Red Flag flying over factories—big, huge, giant factories owned by *workers*. . . . Clouds of smoke coming out of chimneys— sign of employment, of clothes, food and comfort. We had just left Germany where the factories were dead. In the Soviet Union they were alive. Happy, happy land! How silly of America not to have a revolution and put the Red Flag on the White House, we thought in our brief enthusiasm.

"All the more reason why we should return to America," said "Red" Hendricks. "We must return and fight for a Soviet America."

How exhilarating the Red Flag was to us! It was the symbol of all that we held dear, of all our beliefs in a new society. It could wave only over a free people. Its folds were dyed in workers' blood. Like the cross to the devout Catholic was the Red Flag to us. And just before the boat entered the Leningrad harbor the Red Flag was raised to the masthead and the German flag taken down. A German sailor did this work, a little nonchalantly, I thought, but perhaps he had to be careful not to expose himself to the captain.

We sang the *International*.

A small launch maneuvered around our boat. Two

uniformed men climbed aboard. They were inspectors calling on the captain to see our passports. They proudly strutted past us, keenly aware that all eyes were on them. One stopped close to me. I examined the brass buttons on his blue coat. On each one was the Communist emblem, the Hammer and Sickle.

The boat docked. Where were the crowds? Where was the band? Miller was sure thousands of workers would meet us at the dock "with a band."

Only about thirty feet away was land... Soviet Land! In another half hour I should be walking on the streets of Soviet Russia, the Workers' Fatherland!

2

Yes, there *was* a crowd at the dock, but no band. And the crowd kept getting larger and larger. But what a crowd! Did my eyes deceive me? Was this some kind of a masquerade, one of those horrible Thanksgiving parades? For, thirty feet away, were people dressed, or undressed, in the most ragged clothes that I had ever seen. They were barefooted, too, men, women and children. No miner emerging from the depths after a day's work looked so dirty.

They cried to us with outstretched arms: *"Daite diengee, pozhaluysta! Daite diengee, pozhaluysta!"*

"What are they yelling?" I asked a fellow-passenger beside me who understood Russian.

"They are asking for money," he replied. I turned to Miller. "Why do they want money?"

"I don't know. We'll find out when we get out of here," said Clarence, a little puzzled.

A representative of MOPR, which is the Russian section of the International Labor Defense, met us in-

side the Custom House. The MOPR comrade had it all
fixed up with the Customs inspector not to make a thorough examination of our luggage. I appreciated this
after witnessing the mauling the other passengers' luggage received. Everything was turned upside down.
One woman carried a few fancy pillows. These were cut
open and a careful search made for something. The
feathers flew all over the place. Every new article the
passengers had was confiscated. I was told that they
could have them back when they left the country.

The five of us walked down the gang-plank onto
Soviet soil. Ragged urchins pulled at our coats. Some
of them danced around us in their bare feet, yelling:
*"Americanetz, Americanetz! Otchen mnogo diengee . . .
da?"*

"What do they want?" we asked our MOPR escort
who understood English.

He laughed, but I thought he looked a little embarrassed when he replied: "They ask for money—American money. They say Americans have very much
money."

"But why do they ask us for money? Don't they
work? Can't they get jobs? And why are they so ragged
and dirty?"

"These people, the old ones," explained our MOPR
comrade, "are of the former privileged classes. They do
not want to work. They beg foreigners for *valuta* (gold
currency) so as to disgrace our Soviet Government.
They were the exploiters once."

From the looks and dress of the people on the streets
there must have been more exploiters than workers in
Leningrad, I thought.

"But the kids? Where do those kids come from?"
Bill McGinnis wanted to know.

"They became orphans as a result of the Revolution. There were millions of them in Soviet Russia, running wild. But the Government is trying to put them in schools and factories," was the explanation.

We were walking to the MOPR headquarters. Leningrad truly looked like a desolate city! Had it been visited by a cyclone or tornado? The débris was piled in the streets and on the sidewalks. Most of the stores were empty and the window-panes were broken. Our escort said these conditions were a heritage from the former régime. (After thirteen years of Soviet rule!) He added that the Soviets were now laying sewer pipes, which accounted for the streets being all torn up.

A man with a huge mop of red hair and a tangled red beard passed us. He wore a long purple faded garment which nearly touched the ground and carried an umbrella under his arm.

"What is that?" exclaimed Joe.

"That," replied our Russian comrade, "is a priest. He has no power now but he still fools many people."

We arrived at last at the House for Political Emigrants—Leningrad Section. So reads the sign over the door. Our good MOPR comrade informed us that the house belonged to a Baron before the Revolution. We were met at the door by the "commandant," a middle-aged woman with a red kerchief wrapped round her head. A "commandant" in Soviet Russia is what a hotel manager or house superintendent is in America. The "commandant" took us up a flight of marble stairs and across inlaid floors to a large room containing ten cots, ten chairs, ten dressers and a center table with a lamp.

The head of the MOPR in Leningrad arrived and called us downstairs for a conference. She had a program mapped out for us. It went something like this:

we had two weeks' stay in Leningrad. Then we should go to Moscow. While in Leningrad we were to speak at factories and clubs about the conditions of the workers in America . . . how they suffered under capitalism. She explained that there would be no grand reception for us because the Soviet Government could not afford to antagonize the American Government on account of negotiations for recognition. The American Government must not know of our being in the Soviet Union. The United States might demand our extradition and this would put the Soviet Government in an embarrassing position. Besides, she said, our case was in the hands of the Comintern. We should know in a few days the decision on whether or not we were to remain in the Soviet Union indefinitely. That the Comintern was deciding our fate without our presence was a surprise to us. Hendricks and I were especially concerned. But we still did not believe the Comintern would act without listening to what all of us had to say in the matter. The head of the MOPR gave each of us twenty-seven rubles apiece from the unemployment fund, which is what bona fide unemployed workers receive monthly from the State. With this information came the comment that the Five-Year Plan had not as yet given work to all.

3

MOPR provided us with good meals at a workers' restaurant. We had a special eating room to ourselves in the center of the dining hall. This was known as the visitors' room. To reach it we had to pass hundreds of people already eating, or standing in line for food. We had borsch (cabbage soup), beefsteak, cutlets and compot, the latter a sticky substance made from cranberries.

I got used to the black bread after a while, and preferred it to the white. I thought the Russian workers were certainly lucky to be getting so much food, judging by the amount we received. The beggars and ragged people must indeed be "bums" who would not work for Socialism, just as the MOPR comrade had said, I almost decided. But the waiter who served us killed this thought, he looked so scrawny and wasted. And, after we were through with our meals, he would eat the leavings. A few days later we discovered that the workers in this same restaurant were not getting the kind and amount of food we were receiving. They ate thin cabbage soup, black bread and tea. Three days a week this menu was varied with boiled fish.

At the first opportunity we had, we asked a high Communist Party official, who invited us to his home for dinner, about this condition. He explained that there was a shortage of food because the Party decided to export food and other products to capitalist countries for machinery. "The workers agreed to limit their food supply in order to carry the Five-Year Plan to a successful conclusion," he said. "You Americans have a higher standard of living than we, Russians, ever had. But we'll catch up, we'll catch up with America, through sacrifice and struggle...."

We finished our beefsteak and proceeded to sip hot tea with lemon. Miller offered our host an American-made cigarette, and the comrade went into a spasm of joy while puffing it. "A good cigarette," he said, "a good cigarette. We make good ones for export."

Little did Miller realize at the time that American cigarettes were at a premium in Russia and that any cigarettes were on the luxury list. Practically the only obtainable cigarette in Leningrad was Nasha Marka

(Our Mark) made from floor sweepings. Each worker was entitled to two packages a week; speculators sold them on the street at exorbitant prices. The wild and woolly "Bill" McGinnis rolled his own from a mixture made of the veins of tobacco leaves which the Russians call "Mahorka." It is said to be very strong, but "Bill" seemed satisfied. Like the Russian workers, "Bill" used scraps of the daily newspaper in the absence of regular cigarette paper.

Our host, in answer to questions, told us further that the Soviet Government divided the Russian people into three categories for the purpose of distributing food, clothing and other articles. In the first category were high Communist and G.P.U. officials, technicians and workers whose toil involved danger or unusual physical strain. In the second category came the great army of clerks, professional people and ordinary workers. In the third were included priests, speculators and other disfranchised elements. The first category could buy eggs, butter, sugar, shoes and clothing at a government store, within a set limit, cheaper than on the open market. The second took what was left or else paid the excessive open market price. The third, of course, could only buy in the open market, or bazaar, operated by the peasants under strict supervision of the government.

Our host described to us in detail how the Proletarian Dictatorship worked, how it fought the former ruling class which was hampering in every conceivable manner the Bolshevik program of building Socialism. The Communist Party, he said, was the advance guard of the working class. It won its right to rule in Russia because of years of struggle in the interest of the working class. No other party was permitted to exist because the Communists did not believe in free speech, which was fit only for democratic countries. In order to suppress the former ruling class, the Communist Party created the State Political Police (G.P.U.). On its shoulders rested the Dictatorship of the Proletariat. "The struggle for Socialism has just begun," he said. "It will be years before Socialism is a fact and *our* generation will never see the Communist State."

4

There and then I had to readjust my Utopian ideas about the Soviet Union. I had gathered from reading the *Daily Worker* and other Communist publications in America that Socialism was already an accomplished fact in Soviet Russia. Socialism, I believed, was in force when workers owned and collectively operated all the factories and when the farmers owned all the land. But I had not taken into account the opposition of the former ruling class nor that within the working class itself. I had clearly been doing a lot of day-dreaming in America, and my host was now doing his best to bring me back to realities. "Red" Hendricks felt the way I did. But Clarence Miller had a firmer grip on the situation. Perhaps this was due to his close association with the theoreticians who shuttled between New York and Moscow.

The road in front of the Political Emigrants' House was dug up for blocks. Next to the old cobblestones lay new sewer pipes. The Soviet method of laying pipes was to dig up the neighborhood first and then lay all the pipes at one time. This was done, I was told, to prevent sabotage. From the porch of the Emigrants' House I watched a young barefooted girl carry cobblestones from one pile to another. She was the only one working.

Further down the street, where the sun was strongest, the sewage workers, for the most part men, were taking sunbaths on the huge piles of dirt. The lone girl worker carrying the cobblestones interested me because she did the work over and over again. She would carry one stone at a time to a spot fifteen feet away. I figured out that she carried about three hundred stones in this way, and when she finished with the pile, she returned the stones to the original place!

My curiosity got the best of me. Accompanied by the MOPR interpreter, I went to the girl and asked her why she carried the stones from one place to another and back again. She didn't know why: she was told to do it. But I wished to probe further into the matter. We went looking for the boss of the project. Unable to find any one in charge, we poked a sunbather in the ribs. My interpreter explained to him what I wanted to know. He said the girl was one of the many peasants who came to the city for a job, but knew nothing about factory work. I told him she would be more useful at present on the farm since the food situation in Leningrad was so desperate. He replied with a shrug: "Nitchevo" (it's nothing). Then he stretched out for another sunbath.

My interpreter explained that the government encouraged peasants to leave their farms and to go into industry. Communist agents were even sent to the villages for this purpose. In many respects this was analogous to the industrialization of the South in America. The southern farmers and hardy mountaineers had little or no knowledge of machinery when they started their trek to the cotton mills. Mill agents enticed them to the city and the machine with the same promises that

Fred E. Beal on lecture tour throughout Usbekistan, U.S.S.R., 1930.

Fred E. Beal in conference with farmers on Collective Farm,
Fargana District, Usbekistan, U.S.S.R., 1930.

the Russians made to the *moujik,* the betterment of their social economic conditions.

Nearly a week after our arrival we received notice from Moscow that the Comintern had come to a decision in our case. We were to jump bail and remain in Soviet Russia!

"What right," argued Hendricks and I, "had the Comintern to make any kind of decision without all of us taking part in the deliberations?"

Clarence Miller and Joe Harrison were jubilant. Clarence read and re-read the letter from Moscow. "That's the time I put one over on that bastardly Central Committee," he said, in reference to the Central Committee of the American Communist Party. "How sore they'll be when they get this news," he chuckled.

"And the liberals and others who'll lose the bail money," I added.

"To hell with the liberals!"

"And the workers, who had confidence in us."

"To hell with them, too. . . . They'll forget us, the damn hill-billies! They'd let us rot in jail."

The other boys had always disliked Clarence. I thought it was due to his superior book learning—a sort of jealousy on the part of the backward Southern boys. But now I knew it was instinctive.

"Don't be a sentimentalist, Fred," he continued. "A revolutionist must be hard-boiled. The Russian revolutionists always made an escape whenever they had a chance. There will be hundreds of Americans that will follow us over here as the crisis over there gets sharper and sharper. . . . I am going to be a General in the Red Army."

Hendricks and I asked MOPR to provide us with immediate passage to Moscow. We would insist on a hearing before the Comintern, and seek a reversal of the decision. We would give plenty of reasons why we should return to America. It was a rather ludicrous position to take: we found ourselves fighting for the right to return to prison.

XVII. THE RED MECCA

1

Moscow! It was a magic name to me. The word was
indelibly carved in my mind. The Boston *American*
once ran a headline: BEAL ACCEPTS MOSCOW GOLD. And
the Southern mill owners thought Moscow had a hand
in every strike that took place in their plants. These
flashes came to me on the train from Leningrad. I still
had to make my first contact of any kind with Moscow.
We were in a "hard" car—equipped with bare wooden
benches as distinct from the "soft" upholstered cars.
Three of us shared a compartment with a young
Russian anxious to further his meager knowledge of
English. The other two, Clarence Miller and Joe Har-
rison, were in a separate compartment with a Russian-
American who had been deported from the United
States for his radicalism. The deportee could not share
Miller's optimism about life in Soviet Russia.

Whenever the train came to a stop, we heard the
voices of children beneath our carriage. They were
bezprizorny on a free ride to Moscow. The pickings
were better there than in Leningrad, according to the
deportee. We were warned to keep a strict watch on
our baggage because these waifs were considered the
slickest crooks in the world. "They pick gold from your
teeth while you sleep," said the young Russian comrade
in his best school English. This comrade, whose first
name was Ivan, was a very enthusiastic young person.
His father had taken a leading part in the Revolution

and died from wounds received while fighting the Whites. Now Ivan was on his way to Moscow to attend a technical school. His joy and happiness radiated over the train. Even the sad, glum and bewildered old people had to smile.

"Say, comrade," I asked Ivan, "why do they wear such heavy clothing and so much of it, when it's so hot?"

"They crazy," he laughed. "They wear everything because they are afraid bandits will steal them. Idiots! See, I am free, like—what you say those things that fly in the air? Oh, yes, birds. I am free like the birds in the air. Me, I have no—what do you call that? . . . Yes, I have no suitcase for bandit to, what you Americans say, pinch!"

We pulled into Moscow.

Faded and weather-torn Red flags hung listlessly from every building. Old straw-roofed houses rubbed elbows with modern apartments and factories. The apartment houses were rough and plain looking, a disappointment after the beautiful workers' apartments I saw in Berlin, but still very heartening. I thought: how wonderful it is for common workers to be living in such apartments. Certainly a great improvement over the Tsar's régime.

At the Moscow station we were again met by representatives of MOPR. One of them carried a large red flag with the letters MOPR written on it. Without ceremony we were hustled through the station, over hundreds of people sleeping or sitting on the floor, to a waiting car and on to MOPR headquarters. En route, one of the Russian comrades proudly pointed to the new buildings, especially the new post office, which he said was the largest in the world. We were ushered into the presence of Comrade Elena Stassova, International

Secretary of MOPR. Comrade Stassova, who comes from a family of nobles, was a close associate of Lenin during the first years of the Soviet Revolution.

She looked like the exact replica of an old-fashioned New England school teacher of mine, Miss Pingree. The only things missing in the likeness were the starched shirt and the little watch with a fleur-de-lis pin on Miss Pingree's bosom. Stassova is blessed with a long nose and a pair of pince-nez. Her gray hair is combed straight back, emphasizing a receding forehead. Her office fitted in with the simplicity of her dress. A plain desk, a few chairs and reclining couch. Pictures of Lenin and Stalin on the whitewashed walls. A large built-in safe with a huge lock. And padded doors to make the room soundproof.

We had a conference. Again we heard the Comintern's decision that we jump bail and remain in the Soviet Union. Comrade Stassova added that, in order to absolve the Comintern and Soviet Government from any blame for the action, we should have to sign a paper, already drawn up, to the effect that all five of us begged to be admitted into the Soviet Union! She cautioned us not to talk to American press reporters and not to frequent places were American tourists were likely to be. I was quite puzzled by the solicitude of the Comintern. From experience I knew that the Communist Party was never concerned over the personal welfare of individuals, except for propaganda purposes. One reason for the decision, I found out, was the use the Russian Communist Party expected to make of us by displaying us to the Russian masses as a horrible example of American class justice. The Russian worker was just then having a hard time trying to keep alive. Applying the old axiom "misery likes company," it was up to us to shake their belief in the American workers' superior standard of living.

2

After the meeting with Comrade Stassova we were taken "home"—to the House for Political Emigrants. It is located in Moscow in another one of those palaces confiscated by the Bolsheviks from former aristocrats. Count Vorontsov once walked through its dark and gloomy rooms. The street upon which the house stands is still named after him, *Vorontsovo Pole*. The House was overcrowded with emigrants from Poland, Hungary, China, and Germany. We were the only Americans. There were no refugees from England or France.

A Polish fellow, insane from six years solitary confinement in a Polish prison, shared our room. He slept most of the day and paced the floor nights. He was found one night, standing over "Bill" McGinnis' bed sharpening a knife. He looked mad and probably took "Bill" for a Polish guard. As luck would have it, another Polish comrade intervened in time. He led the madman to a mirror where he sat for hours grinning at himself.

The plight of these emigrants was pitiful. They had fought against injustice and misery in their own countries where they were the backbone, the élite, of the Communist and radical movements. They sacrificed everything for the Cause. In the Soviet Union they were nothing. They were not treated with the same high respect given to bourgeois writers and preachers and business men whom the Communists in America so roundly condemn. The Soviet functionaries did not grovel at the feet of these revolutionary heroes as they

did before visiting capitalist politicians. The problem
of adjusting themselves to this Soviet code was agonizing to these Communist martyrs. Leaders of the Bela
Kun type did not live in the House for Political Emigrants but in the finest apartments as befits Communist
politicians of the first magnitude. Every day there were
protests against bad living conditions, especially lack of
food. Very little was done about it. Clarence Miller,
who stayed no longer than a week in the House, drew
up a petition demanding the removal of the "commandant" and more food. He was soon put right by
MOPR: one never makes *demands* in the Soviet Union.

Some emigrants, disillusioned by Soviet reality, asked
to be allowed to return to their respective countries. One
German comrade battled for weeks with MOPR for
the privilege of returning to Germany where he had to
serve a prison sentence of five years. The heads of
MOPR and the Communist Party disliked such comrades. They were suspected, and perhaps sincerely too,
of being counter-revolutionists sent in by foreign governments to spy on the Soviet system or to assassinate
certain emigrants. For this reason the House for Emigrants was well guarded. It was surrounded by a high
iron fence and had special police. No one could enter the
House without a special pass. Because of these precau-
tions it was difficult to understand how thieves could
enter in the middle of the night and make off with five
suits of clothes belonging to five recently-admitted
American fugitives. But it happened in our case. On
the second morning following our arrival we woke up
to find our clothes missing, together with money, passports and other articles kept in the pockets. Clarence
Miller lost a valuable watch and a fountain-pen, "Red"
Hendricks over 100 rubles. The suit stolen from me had

been presented to me by New Bedford workers. I had worn it only a few times.

The robbery created a stir in the House and the G.P.U. was hastily summoned. The investigation revealed the following:

About one o'clock in the morning the watchman at the gate was called on the telephone: "Hello, is this the Comintern?"

"No, this is not the Comintern. Wrong number."

Two minutes later the 'phone rang again: "Hello— this *must* be the Comintern. I want to speak to Comrade Stalin."

"This is *not* the Comintern. Comrade Stalin doesn't live here."

"Well, this is 5-04-60, right?"

"Right. But this is not the Comintern."

"Does Comrade Stalin's secretary live there?"

"No, he does not."

"Now, listen, comrade. You must get Comrade Stalin on the 'phone or his secretary. It's important."

"But comrade, you must have the wrong number. This is not the Comintern and neither Comrade Stalin nor his secretary lives here."

The conversation lasted over ten minutes, just long enough for the thieves to jump the fence, enter the house through the open window, and get away with the stolen clothes. The poor watchman lost his job and we our clothes. The passports were found in the gutter. The G.P.U. agents said the thieves would not dare keep the passports, because it was a political offense, making the culprit liable to execution.

These little inconveniences did not shake my belief in the Cause. All the bad food and even the lack of it; the swarms of homeless ragged children; the bewildered and suffering old people; the reports of daily shootings of the "class" enemy; these and other phenomena were justified by the Communist leaders. It was their historic mission, they claimed, as the vanguard of the proletariat to defend the Soviet state with might and force. I succumbed to this line of reasoning, too, as it was cogently presented to me by the Soviet heads who maintained that there was no other course open to them.

3

"Red" Hendricks and I were at this time more concerned about getting back to America than about the troubles of the Russian workers. We decided upon a course of militant action. We got together with "Bill" McGinnis in one of the Russian tea-shops and drew up a letter to the Comintern demanding that we be given a hearing.

"The Secretariat of the American Communist Party unanimously decided that for political reasons the entire seven of us should serve the Party and movement by returning to prison," the letter began. "If the decision has been reversed, it is because five of us and the Comintern compelled the change of 'policy.' We were not given permission by the American Party to come to the Soviet Union. We came on our own initiative, with money raised by friends. The desire to see the Soviet Union but to return to America before the State Supreme Court handed down its decision was uppermost in our minds." We then outlined the reasons why we should return to America and to prison. We stressed largely the promise given to the Southern workers that we should not leave the South until our union was firmly planted and growing. Little did I realize at the time how bourgeois this sounded to the Comintern. Perhaps not since the days when they had to contend with that great American fighter, Bill Haywood, did they have to deal with such questions as honor and truth inside the Communist movement. But there was no getting around it for us. In closing our appeal, we demanded that our case be reopened and that we be given an opportunity to appear before the Comintern to tell our story. George Carter and Louis McLaughlin were still in America.

After some delay we were called to the Comintern to present our case. Comrade Kuusinen, Secretary of the Comintern, a short and pleasant-looking man, the leader of the Finnish Communists, acted as chairman. Others present included representatives of the Russian, German, and American Communist Parties and E. Stassova, director of the MOPR. Clarence Miller presented in five minutes the opposite view, why we should jump bail and remain in the Soviet Union. His arguments in effect were: the American masses wanted us to run away; the revolutionary movement in America would gain nothing from our serving twenty years in prison; the Russian Bolsheviks before the Revolution always escaped whenever they could; and that we could be more useful in helping to build socialism in Soviet Russia.

I spoke about fifteen minutes. I reminded the judges that Communists took a great responsibility in leading the masses, that every true revolutionist should expect prison as his lot. America, I said, cannot be compared, either economically or politically, with Russia of the Tsar's time. And as for Russia needing our help in building Socialism, well, none of us could build a peanut stand, much less a factory. We knew only how to destroy and pull down capitalism. We were trained destructionists; we knew very little about the art of construction. Of course, I finished, we could be given a portfolio job and look wise, or go to school for three years and become Red Professors if it would help the Cause along.

Before the session adjourned, Kuusinen described how he had escaped from Finland over the border, dressed in a woman's clothes, by engaging the services of a prostitute. She kept a border guard busy while he crossed the line into Russia. Comrade Stassova also described her exploits in escaping from Siberia. These stories were clearly intended to influence us in agreeing to our escape from American prisons.

How futile I felt there, before Kuusinen. State of North Carolina vs. Fred Beal. Comintern vs. Fred Beal.... Before the Southern bar—pleading to stay out of prison. Before the Moscow bar—pleading to go to prison. For what? For a Cause. And the Cause I had in mind just then was the working class of the South— the textile union. How was Judge Kuusinen to understand my feelings any more than Judge Barnhill? I didn't want to leave America like a common criminal. I loved America, its hills, its rivers, its people, as much as I hated its miserable system of exploiting human beings for profit. No, I could not bring myself to run away.

4

The Red International of Labor Unions (Profintern) held a world conference in the summer of 1930. The sessions took place in the Dom Soyuzov, the Moscow Palace of Labor. It was before Hitler's rise to power. The German Communist Party, next to the Russian the most powerful section of the Comintern, was strongly represented at the conference. The German delegates displayed their sense of importance. They came with bands of music, red banners flying, marching with raised fists. They even wore uniforms which aroused the admiration of the Russians. According to the German Stalinists, the revolution was just around the corner in their homeland. The English Communist delegation was the most conservative. This appeared at an English caucus that preceded the conference. The Comintern representative demanded that the English trade unions denounce King George for accepting one million pounds a year from the exchequer.

"You're balmy," said a delegate. "The blighty masses wouldn't stand for insulting the King!"

"Hear, hear!"

"Besides, King George is only an ornament on a shelf."

"A pretty expensive ornament," said the Comintern spokesman with a slight frown. "The million pounds could be used better for England's unemployed."

It was finally decided, for the sake of peace and harmony, to "lay off" King George.

The American delegation was ninety per cent proletarian, due to previous commands from Moscow that the would-be Lenins stay home. But it took a genius to report the multifarious political and economic developments occurring in America after one year of the great depression. This is where "Bill" Dunne came in, except that he delayed the American section's report for three days, while he was recovering from a too studious examination of the medicinal qualities of vodka.

The American delegation had a considerable sprinkling of Negroes, in accordance with the instructions given by the Comintern to its American section that

one-third of the American delegates to the conference of
the Red International of Labor Unions must be black
proletarians. This followed the policy laid down by
Moscow a year before that the American Communist
Party should concentrate on organizing Negroes. The
concentration showed little results in numbers. But the
American Party had to send Negro delegates even if
they were picked off the streets. After all, the offer of a
free ride across the seas had its temptations. One of
those who fell for the lure was Jenny, a beautiful
Negress, who came as a delegate from the proletariat
of Philadelphia. She attracted much and rather intimate
attention in Moscow among Russians.

I was scheduled to speak at two Sacco and Vanzetti
memorial meetings with Jenny. One meeting was held
in a hospital in the suburb and had to be reached by
street car. On the way I suggested to Jenny that she
connect the Negro question with Sacco and Vanzetti.

"Mistuh, *who* am this Sacco and Vanzetti?"

At first I thought it was downright sacrilege—for
one to be in the labor movement and not know of Sacco
and Vanzetti. But Jenny looked at me so innocently,
with her large, roaming, coal-black eyes, that I forgave
her ignorance.

"No, Mistuh, Ah don't know dese gennemen. Where
do dey live?"

"Where do *you* come from?"

"Philadelphia."

"Do you belong to a union?"

"No, *suh,* Ah don't belong to no union. Deys have no
union in mah business. Ah onced worked in a shirt factory
and de people dere, dey made me join de union, but
Ah's quit. Why, man, Ah wouldn't work in no factory.
Ah gets more money from my gennemen friends."

"But how did you get over here?"

"One of my gennemen friends asked me. He says: 'Jenny, all you got to do is to speak about the colored people. Tell the Russians how badly Negroes live in America and how you belong to a union.' Ah's pretty run down in health and Ah thought: Well now, the ocean would do me good—and here Ah is."

"Well, Jenny," I said, "you say whatever you want about America and the colored people at the meeting. Our comrade here will interpret what you have to say." And to the comrade interpreter who accompanied us I said, "You'll have to interpret her speech according to Karl Marx."

The meeting was held outdoors and our audience made up of doctors, nurses and patients. I felt sure some of the doctors understood English, so I was quite worried about what Jenny would say. After the Russian comrade translated my speech, it was Jenny's turn. All eyes centered on the beautiful Jenny. She was received with tremendous applause.

"Ladies and Gennemen," she began. "Ah's come here to-day to speak to you about Mr. Sacco and Vanzetti. Ah don't know who dey were except dey is some gennemen from up Boston way who belonged to labor unions and helped de workingman." From here on, for ten minutes, she spoke about America. She was quite patriotic. She said to me afterwards: "Why should Ah come across the ocean to tell dese Russians about bad t'ings in America?"

She was wildly applauded at the close of her speech. The interpreter gave his version of her address in twenty minutes—according to Marx.

The other memorial meeting was held at a textile factory. Jenny made the same speech and the interpreter his. There were many questions here, mostly about the silk clothes and the good shoes Jenny was wearing. These just didn't jibe with what the Communist Party was telling Russian workers about the Negroes. The Russian textile workers were wearing cotton dresses and cotton stockings, when they wore any at all, and many were barefooted.

"If Ah had a'knowed it, Ah'd a' brought cotton dresses and stockings 'stead of silk and then they wouldn't be pawin' me all over," ruminated Jenny, after the meeting, "but that's all Ah had."

XVIII. HELL AND BOHEMIA

1

WHILE the conference of the Red International of Labor Unions was still in session in Moscow and the Comintern was still considering our appeal, a message was flashed from the United States which seemed to seal the fate of the Gastonia fugitives. The Supreme Court of North Carolina denied our appeal for a new trial. The decision was handed down immediately after it had leaked out that five of us were in Soviet Russia. I was prepared for the blow. It was clear now that had we remained in the United States, our case might have been dragged out for years. The Comintern was as prompt as the North Carolina Supreme Court. Moscow decided that we were to remain in the Soviet Union.

To appease "Red" Hendricks and me, the Comintern proposed that the five of us go on a world tour of propaganda in defense of all political prisoners in America, especially in favor of Tom Mooney. In the meantime, we were to journey within the country for one month. There was nothing to do but to consent to the proposition. I had written to my friends in America for money to pay our passage back home, but received no replies to this request. Letters from America came to me opened and I concluded that my correspondence to America was likewise censored. But I found ways and means of sending out a letter to Roger Baldwin, head of the American Civil Liberties Union, who had frequently come to my rescue in the past. This letter not only reached its destination, but eventually made a little history.

I was informed by MOPR that my assignment would take me to Uzbekistan, in Central Asia, about six days' travel by rail from Moscow. It looked as if the Comintern wished to send me as far away from the Soviet capital as possible. Accompanied by an interpreter, I left for a tour of Bokhara, Samarkand, Tashkent and a score of other cities and villages in Uzbekistan. In each place, at specially arranged meetings, I was assigned to tell how and why the workers starved in America.

It was the hardest thing I have ever done in my life. The people wore such a hungry, hopeless look that I just could not paint the American workers for them the way Moscow wanted me to. Even the most exploited and the most unfortunate in America did not have that cowed and pleading look in their eyes. I complained to those about me, to my interpreter and to Communist officials, that I couldn't lie so deliberately.

When I visited the silk mills in Tashkent, I was surprised and disturbed to find many children working. They would plunge their tender hands into near-boiling water to retrieve cocoons, just as children do in the factories in China, owned by Western capitalists. How often had I protested violently in America against the needless cruelty of child labor? I recalled how I drew murmurs of horror from my audiences when I described the tender little hands of children in the Orient turning into crippled masses of boiled flesh! We had pointed with pride to Soviet Russia where child labor was abolished. And now I found Soviet children being forced by the workers' government to do the very thing we had all denounced. I began to criticize the action of those in key positions. In some factories I would be asked to give my criticism and, as a former textile worker, to give my advice. The Communist heads of the silk factory in Tashkent gasped with amazement when I abruptly advised them to close the mills down and turn the children out to play. They thought I was joking or crazy or perhaps just a plain counter-revolutionist. Why shouldn't the children work in the mills when their fathers were doing more important work? They were working for Socialism! They might well have been working for some ruthless capitalist. At least, they would have received enough wages to buy back a little of the goods they produced, while here, from the "proletarian state," they never got an inch of the thousands of yards made by their toil. All of it went for export.

If the workers tried to steal a little of that which they created, they were nearly always arrested and sentenced to even harder labor. The heads of these factories filled with native laborers were Russian Communists sent down from Moscow to speed production and build up profits. The cotton was ready for picking, but the majority of the peasants refused to help gather it on the ground that the greater part of the crop would be requisitioned from them and hauled to the government storehouses. The farmers would get nothing for their labor, certainly less than the wretched sharecroppers in the South of capitalistic America. The Soviet Government then mobilized the city population, men, women, and, in this case, children to work in the fields. To entice the children, the Communist Party leaders did the Pied Piper act: they got out a brass band to lead them to the plantations.

I was the guest of Achun Babaief, President of the Uzbekistan Soviet Republic, and lived at his Tashkent home. I asked the President to be allowed to accompany the children to the cotton fields. He agreed and I started out at five o'clock in the morning with several thousand sleepy-eyed kids. Brass band in the lead, red flags flying, we marched down the principal street, Karl Marx Avenue. The slant-eyed natives lined the road and watched us silently as we tramped toward our objective. Moving picture operators, perched with their cameras upon a shack, called to us to sing and cheer. The children acted well before the camera, but, as the day wore on, there was little energy left to cheer. We tramped in step with the weary band players. We walked all that day in the blistering desert sun, with short pauses from time to time for a rest and a lunch of flat bread and honey-dew melon. We arrived at our cotton collective at nine o'clock in the evening, completely exhausted, and slept under the open sky. At five the next morning, we were aroused by a bugle. After breakfast of bread and melon, we started on a hike to the fields we were to work in. This took another hour. The party leader organized "socialist competition" among the children. At first it was like a game and the children picked cotton in the spirit of play. But soon the children became completely worn out. By three o'clock, most of them were hiding under cotton plants for rest. The leaders rounded them up, but the children revolted against further work that day. The organizers demanded a continuation of work until the sun went down. Some of the children cried and asked to be permitted to return home. The Communist leaders climbed on a little mound and exhorted them, pleaded with them, threatened them. They told them of the need for carrying out the Five-Year Plan and that unless they finished their work that day, they couldn't expect to participate in the good things which were coming along.

With their last reserves of energy the youngsters toiled until sunset. Then they tottered, rather than walked back to their camp.

2

In Tashkent the Communist Party leaders held a banquet in my honor. While the workers were starving to "build Socialism," the Communist bureaucrats partook of the most sumptuous feast I ever attended, either in Russia or in capitalist America. Twenty-five guests were present, all Soviet officials and trade union leaders. Even before the meal began, hundreds of people had gathered at the windows to stare at us. At first I thought they had come to see me, as foreigners were seldom seen in these parts. But it soon became clear that the people were hungry, fiercely hungry. They grumbled at the sight of the rich food the like of which they had probably never tasted. They became menacing in their attitude and the leading Communists gave orders to have them sent away. Soon the police were driving the hungry crowd in all directions. An official drew the curtains together so that no one could look in on that lavish meal. He smiled at me and apologized for the interruption. I kept thinking: How much this scene is like a *Daily Worker* cartoon of capitalists stuffing themselves while the starving workers are looking on!

In Fergana, Uzbekistan, I ran into H. N. Swayse, an American. He was supervising the building of a gin mill for the Uzbekian Soviet. He had two co-workers in this enterprise, an Englishman and a German. All of them were kept in this district against their will. How? The Russians "couldn't find" their passports. Sometimes the passports were supposed to be at the Tashkent office and sometimes in Moscow. The American, upon hearing I was in the district, walked miles to see me and pleaded with me to help him get an exit visa from the Soviet Union for himself and the two others. He had had his fill of "building Socialism." I took up the matter with high officials in Tashkent and they admitted it was true. They said it was necessary to get the mill finished and they would keep the three foreigners, by force, if necessary. They promised to give them extra food allowances.

Back in Moscow I wrote a severe criticism of the many unjust things I had seen on my tour. I sent this to the Moscow *News* and to the Communist International Offices. My interpreter laughed at me for my naïveté. "They'll never print anything like that," she said. "Do you think you are in America?"

I was called before Kuusinen, the head of the Communist International, in the presence of William Weinstone, Moscow representative of the American Communist Party. I was warned not to interfere in Russian affairs and not to send letters to America of a disparaging nature. Then they showed me copies of letters that I had mailed to friends in the United States. In one letter, written to Roger Baldwin, director of the American Civil Liberties Union, I stated my preference for Southern prison hospitality to living in Soviet Uzbekistan. This sentence was underlined in red by the G.P.U. censors. Weinstone fired question after question at me as in a third degree: "Are you in touch with the Trotskyites? Do you communicate with the Lovestonites? Are you taking part in any counter-revolutionary movement either here or abroad?" Heatedly, he warned me to adapt myself to the conditions which prevailed in the Soviet Union.

Kuusinen, who is a rubber-stamp in Stalin's hands, was then nominally the chief figure in the Communist International. Kuusinen's word was law to all the Communist sections abroad. He leaned over to me and said coolly: "Comrade Beal, you must remember you are under a workers' government now!"

"I'm glad you have told me, Comrade Kuusinen," I said, "I shouldn't have known it."

These things shook me to the core. I was sick at heart. What would my comrades and working-class friends in America say if they knew something of the real truth! I had traveled through large parts of the immense Soviet Union as a Communist dignitary, yet I could not fail to observe the incredible conditions. Was it Socialism to drive people to work? Was it Communism to force children to labor for the State in the cotton fields? I had sacrificed my life and freedom to a different faith. I had believed Socialism to mean that the workers were to receive the full value of their labor.

The Soviet Government was building tanks and guns and airplanes and chemical plants to defend the Soviet Union. This was the common explanation for the general privation. But what did the workers of Soviet Russia have to defend? They were hungry. They needed clothes and shoes and living quarters. All my life I had preached that the workers had nothing to lose but their chains. Certainly the Russian workers had nothing more to lose.

I was deeply disturbed, and occasionally gave vent to my feelings and thoughts. Under ordinary circumstances the Soviet authorities would have done something drastic in my case if I had not had a record as a working-class leader in America facing a long prison term for my efforts in the Communist Party. Had I

been a simple worker they would have denounced me as
a bourgeois and either expelled me from Russia or
placed me in jail. But some of my letters had already
got through to the United States. Had I been imprisoned or otherwise abused, it would have proved that the
Soviet dictatorship would not allow the mildest criticism
of its methods and its works. Rightly or wrongly, the
Communists in America and Russia believed that the
workers of the United States were interested in my fate.
The Comintern, therefore, suddenly changed its attitude
and began to treat me with touching solicitude. I was
made at ease in Moscow—good quarters, good food, and
a good income for lecturing and writing for the newspapers.

At that time writing for the Russian press was a special "racket" of foreigners in Moscow. The more horrible the tales they could tell of their native lands, the
better the editors liked it and the more money they paid.
"Red" Hendricks, too, decided to become a literary
man. He would choose the horror tales from the issues
of the *Daily Worker* concerning the lynching of Negroes
and beating up of workers and convert them into ex-
posés of American life. The first time he offered a story,
the editor rejected it as being too tame. After that
Hendricks always had enough blood and thunder to
thrill the most rabid editor. One day we learned that a
textile strike was threatened in Lawrence, Mass. Knowing the situation there, I could predict the number of
workers that would go out on strike—or, at least, how
many the Tass agency or the *Daily Worker* would report as striking. I estimated the number at ten thousand
and "Red" rushed to the editor with a story, headlined:
10,000 LAWRENCE WORKERS STRIKE AGAINST TERRIBLE
LIVING CONDITIONS. A few days later the Tass news

carried exactly that statement. When the editors asked
Hendricks how he had been able to score a beat on the
agency, "Red" reported that his friends in America
wired him all the spot news in code. Needless to say,
"Red" was made then and there.

But these successes and the pleasant life in Moscow
could not shut out one fact which we considered above
all others—we were prisoners in Russia.

3

The American Communist Colony in Moscow was a
little Bohemia worshiping vodka and Stalin. Upon my
return from the Uzbekistan hell, I plunged for a short
time into the life led in the shadow of the Kremlin by
the future commissars of the foreordained Soviet
America. I found it a round of drinking bouts done by
cliques.

There was the clique of Mike Gold. Gold is a senti-
mental revolutionist who has been very successful in
exploiting his sentiments. He is undoubtedly sincere in
his feeling for the working classes and will do anything
to help them—from a safe distance. But he bravely attacks all liberals, whom he detests even more than
capitalists. Any opinions other than that of the ruling Communist group Mike considers anathema even
though they were once his own. Like all emotional people, he prefers to consider himself a thinker and wears
a frowning expression, like one accursed. But he is really
a very jolly and likeable fellow, anxious to impress people with his "proletarian" childhood among bedbugs,
rats and roaches. Gold was followed by the intellectuals
among the American Communists, each of whom expected to write a "best seller" or a popular play about

the coming revolution and settle down on a farm in Pennsylvania.

"Bill" Dunne, who could guzzle down more liquor than any of the others with the possible exception of "Tom" Bell, had a smaller clique because he was rather particular about his company. He preferred bolting the door of his room and spending the whole night drinking with a few of his cronies. These were chiefly men who had participated in the radical trade union movement, tough, rough men who had taken hard knocks and given them. They scorned the Mike Gold clique and they would not even associate with the third group, the Soviet sympathizers who did not belong to the Communist Party in America.

Noticing my despondency, "Bill" asked me to join him one evening. "Take a drink of vodka, Fred. Best thing in the world to cure the blues. I know how you feel. Come and drink some vodka and forget it."

In the United States I seldom touched liquor. Whether it was my Puritan upbringing or the knowledge that my type of work and liquor did not mix well, I do not know. Anyway, I never felt it right to drink and never really wanted to. Now, here in front of me, were quarts of the hardest sort of liquor. "Tom" Bell was also there, already drunk. It was Bell who, in 1925, had promised to cut my throat, ear to ear, if I told the Party officials secrets he had disclosed to me while drunk. The American Communist Party had sent him to Moscow to sober up. He had been there five years without any signs of soberness. Bell, like "Bill" Dunne, liked to shock people by pretending to be frank and outspoken. He hated me as all drunkards hate people who are teetotalers.

"That sanctimonious labor preacher wouldn't take a drink!"

So I did.

John Little, representative of the Young Communist League in America, came in. He evidently had contributed his share of the liquor because he protested that two bottles were missing from the lot.

"This hop-head has drunk over a bottle already," said "Bill" Dunne, rolling his eyes in the direction of "Tom" Bell.

"We've got Beal off the water wagon," said Bell.

"The thing for you to do, Fred, is settle down," advised Dunne. "Take unto yourself a wife."

"That's what he needs," said Little. "A sleeping dictionary. That's the only way to learn Russian."

"Say, Beal," said Bell, changing the subject, "why do you insist upon living when there's no reason for it? You Gastonia phoneys are all washed up. You can't get back to America. The Party won't let you. You're on the spot here, Beal, and you'll do as you're told. Too good for us, ain't you? Even Stalin isn't good enough for you."

He had in mind my refusal to call on Stalin. Clarence Miller, who worshiped Stalin, begged MOPR to arrange an audience with Stalin for the Gastonia boys. It was arranged, on condition that all of us should come, so as to prevent other individual appointments later. Miller came to the Political Emigrants' House with the exciting news. "Bill" McGinnis and I, not having any great desire to see Stalin, but mainly to spite Miller, said: "To hell with Stalin. If he wants to see us, let him come here." This angered Miller. We never got to see Stalin.

The night passed quickly. And others like it. For a few weeks I went on drinking sprees with other Party members. In the company of Gold, Hendricks, Philip Mason, and Eric Burroughs, I joined parties held here and there by various Americans. Eric Burroughs was a cultured, good-looking Negro whose mother had charge of the Negro Section of the Comintern. Mason was a young enthusiast from America who had come to Russia to study Soviet moving pictures. These and others were pleasant people. At their homes, at the Opera, on picnics along the Moscow river, one could forget for a while. But even vodka was not potent enough to drown the realities.

XIX. AMERICA CALLS

1

In North Carolina, the state prison was eager to receive into its cells the seven Gastonia fugitives. In Moscow, several of these victims of capitalist justice were spending nights conspiring how to flee from the promised land back to the America of the textile barons. "Red" Hendricks, "Bill" McGinnis and I, all determined to return to the United States in defiance of the decision of the Comintern, discussed in whispers various means of leaving the happy Communist fatherland. One would urge an attempt to smuggle ourselves across the border—a most perilous adventure in Soviet Russia. Another would suggest going to the ports of Leningrad and Odessa to watch for some American freighter, in the hope that the captain might consent to let us sail back to America as members of his crew.

True, we were "guests" of the Communist International. Was it not preferable by all odds to the status of being "guests" of the North Carolina prison? But like young colts we balked in the harness of our host—the Stalin dictatorship. Its arm reached farther and its grip was more implacable than that of the Gastonia mill owners. For two of our comrades, Louis McLaughlin and George Carter, were still fugitives in America. Neither of them wished to jump bail. The Communist International thought otherwise and forced them to sail quietly for the Soviet Union. I had been unable to get in touch with them, to warn them, because all my mail was under

rigid censorship. But the one letter I had managed to
transmit to Roger Baldwin in New York did cause quite
an explosion, and its reverberations were all in our favor.
It is strange how the defiant Soviet Government cowers
before the blow of publicity in the capitalist press.

On September 20, 1930, the front page of the New
York *Times* carried a long and complete account, on the
authority of Roger Baldwin, of the fate of the Gastonia
fugitives in Soviet Russia. It reported that "Red" Hendricks and I were set upon coming back to the United
States even in violation of orders of the Comintern. The
news created a sensation. It struck the American Communist Party like a cannon-ball. Indeed, what would
the American workers say at the spectacle of the Gastonia martyrs returning from the Soviet Utopia to serve
long, very long, sentences in Southern jails? But the
effects of the bombshell in the press did not react upon
us for several weeks. In the meantime I was enrolled in
the Lenin School, one of the higher Communist acade-
mies for the training of revolutionary Marxist leaders.
McGinnis and Hendricks were attending a political
school of a lower category. "Bill" had escaped the edu-
cational system in America. Unable to read or write, he
had remained an unaffected simple soul. Imagine "Bill"
coming along one of Moscow's streets with a volume of
"Capital" by Karl Marx under his arm!

At this time the great public trial of the so-called
Industrial Party took place in Moscow. It attracted
world-wide attention and was dramatically staged by the
Communist Party with that purpose in view. For, about
two months earlier, the Moscow newspapers had published a matter-of-fact announcement of the execution
of forty-eight men and women, chiefly scientists and
technicians, who had held important posts in the eco-

nomic departments. This summary execution of people condemned by a secret tribunal, which was subsequently described in detail by the Tchernavins, had created an international furore. Protests signed by Albert Einstein and other world figures were circulated abroad and the act was compared with the bloody incidents of the Tsarist régime. The Soviet Government decided, therefore, to hold a public exhibition of the manner in which it administered justice and it chose the Ramzin case for its exhibit. It charged that the Industrial Party had plotted with the connivance of foreign powers to overthrow the Soviet Government and it specifically accused a noted Soviet engineer, named Ramzin, and nine other defendants of the alleged conspiracy.

All the students in the Lenin school of which I was a member were compelled to parade past the Dom Soyuzov (Palace of Labor) the night of the trial and to shout: "Death to the wreckers! Death to the enemies of Soviet Russia! Death! Death! Death!" It seemed as if the Communists enrolled in the Lenin school had but one aim—revenge. We tramped the snow-covered streets. The Kremlin, the crevices in its walls lined with snow, made a beautiful sight. The masses were tramping, tramping, to shout, "death!" The factory workers were there, because they had to be, for fear of losing their bread cards or suffering worse penalties. And the American comrades were there too, shaking their fists at the building where the trial was being held, and shouting murderous slogans. The representatives of the foreign press were watching the march and making notes on this "spontaneous" outburst of mass indignation.

How I burned with shame at the sight of this organized mob inspired with lust for blood. I, too, had faced death at the hands of biased justice, a system of justice which

I had fought to the limit. Was this to be the system of the new society, this drilled and cowed crowd led by packs of bloodhounds, and all in the name of Socialism? My thoughts went back to another night, an August night in Boston three years earlier. Sacco and Vanzetti were to be executed in the Charlestown prison there. With a group of comrades I had fought my way through a cordon of police and troops to protest against the taking of two innocent lives by capitalist class justice. The square around the prison was filled with a mob, mostly come out of morbid curiosity. Some cried: "Let the Dagos burn!" That night made a Communist out of me.

I was now on the sacred soil of Communism. I was participating in the staging of a blood bath. No random mobs here. Like myself, the thousands on the streets had been driven by some strange power to fill the air with cries of "death." And all my life I had believed that Socialism meant Life, a new life, a free life, the really true song of life.

Inside the building where the trial was proceeding, the leader of the "plot," Ramzin, declared: "I am aware of the crime committed by me. We aimed at the overthrow of the Soviet power with the help of foreign intervention. We committed treason, not only against the Soviet Government, but against our country. I am the leader and I am to blame."

The Ramzin "confession" provoked wide discussion and speculation within and without Russia. In the Lenin school, it gave rise to several arguments. "How is it that they always get 'confessions' out of them?" I asked. I really knew the answer. There had been hundreds, thousands of executions in the Soviet Union that year. There had been numerous "confessions." We had discussed the matter before and it was understood that the G.P.U.

knew how to make its victims confess. Sometimes torture was used, at other times threats of harming members of the prisoners' families were applied. As a rule, the G.P.U. was successful.

"We were always sore when the American cops did this to us back home," I remarked to one of the stalwart comrades. "We Communists always raised hell when the third degree was employed in the United States!"

"That's class justice," came in reply. I was silent. I had known capitalist injustice. I now knew Communist injustice. But justice, I wondered, where is it to be found?

2

In capitalist countries, the issue of wages is ever a subject of agitation and free controversy. In Communist Russia, I had occasion to discover, it was a most delicate point, one which people had learned to avoid in conversation. At this time the wages of workers in Soviet Russia were fairly well equalized. The differences in pay which had formerly embraced as many as twenty-one categories were now reduced to but four divisions. Thus, the technician and the highly skilled worker received only about three or four times as much as the common laborer. Because the man who received high wages had to pay more for food, clothing and shelter, the difference in buying power was not so great. In other words, the system had some semblance of wage equality.

One night, at the Foreign Workers' Club, the discussion turned to the wage question and the condition of Soviet industry. The latter was suffering from an acute shortage of skilled and efficient workers. The wage scale suited many of the unskilled workers who had no ambition to rise above the grade of a floor-sweeper or machine-tender. One of the habitués of the Club, a former I.W.W. in the United States, whom I have already designated as Dan, joined the discussion. He cited chapter and verse from the chaos existing in Soviet industry. Casually I expressed the thought that perhaps the remedy for the crisis lay in a change of policy by Stalin. I said something about a wage scale which would encourage the unskilled to advance themselves by raising the pay and the standard of living of the skilled workers.

A chorus of sh-s-s-s greeted my suggested reform.

"See that slogan up there?" said Dan, pointing to a long red cloth banner stretched from one wall to the other. It bore a Russian inscription in white letters. Dan translated it: ADVOCATES OF INEQUALIZATION OF WAGES ARE COUNTER-REVOLUTIONISTS!

I made haste to inform the group that I didn't advocate wage inequality. I had just been thinking aloud.

"There's plenty of Russians pushing up daisies for thinking that out loud, too," Dan said.

All my life I had fought for higher wages. In fact, was I not a fugitive in Russia because of that? And now I was in danger of being regarded as a counter-revolutionist for merely expressing an idea designed to promote a discussion as how best to advance Soviet industry. There was plenty of food for thought in Dan's warning.

Two years later Stalin proclaimed the new policy of "inequalization"! It became a counter-revolutionary act to suggest equality in pay or to criticize the differences in the wage categories. The devout comrades who had silenced me when I gave vent to the heretical suggestion now defended the policy based upon it in good orthodox Marxist fashion.

3

I was determined to get out of Soviet Russia. The office of the Moscow Soviet furnishes exit visas. It occurred to me to try my luck there without the knowledge of the Comintern. With my passport in the name of Jacob Katz I applied for such a visa. But the passport was not enough to establish my identity with the Soviet official. He asked me to produce other documents proving that I was Katz. And all my other papers were in the name of Fred E. Beal. In this predicament, I hit upon the scheme of going to the headquarters of the MOPR. There I applied for an identity paper in the name of Jacob Katz. I explained that I did not want the American reporters in Moscow to bother me and preferred to stay in the Soviet Union under my assumed name. The MOPR officials swallowed the explanation. Without telephoning the Comintern, they immediately issued a pass to me in the name of Katz. I made a dash for the Moscow Soviet. Here I produced my new credentials from the MOPR. It worked like a charm. My passport was stamped with an exit visa, entitling me to leave the country within a week or so. I felt jubilant.

But my stratagems and exertions were unnecessary. The Gastonia men were suddenly called before the mighty Kuusinen. We were told that we were free to choose our course, whether to return to the United States or remain in the Soviet Union where we would be assured of good jobs and accommodations.

What had happened? It was the effect of the New York *Times* story of September 20. The Comintern also learned that the American Civil Liberties Union had placed two hundred dollars at my disposal with the White Star Line in Poland to pay my fare to America.

As a result the Communist Party and the MOPR began to display a keen interest in my welfare. They decided to pay for my trip out of their funds rather than let me go at the expense of Baldwin's organization. And they opened a fierce barrage of attacks against Roger Baldwin. He was denounced in the Communist Press as a man "with a shopkeeper's soul" who was more interested in saving the bail put up by the Civil Liberties Union than the lives of workers! The International Labor Defense in New York echoed these sentiments. It issued a statement which was headlined in the *Daily Worker:* LOVESTONE AND BALDWIN WANT LIVING DEATH FOR GASTONIA STRIKERS.

The Comintern wanted us to sign a statement exposing the New York *Times* story as "a pack of lies," and denouncing Roger Baldwin for his part in helping us escape from Russia as an *agent-provocateur* and an enemy of the workers. At the height of the argument in our midst as to whether we ought to sponsor such a document, "Bill" McGinnis decided to sign it as John McGinnis, for the New York *Times* had reported his name that way. "Bill" was determined to return to the United States and hoped that his assuming the name of John would save him from arrest.

A few days before my departure, "Bill" was all ready to leave for America. His things had been packed. His visa had been granted. But he was detained at the Communist school he was attending! The guards refused to let him out when he was ready to go to the railroad station. He ran back to his dormitory and smashed loose the leg of his iron bunk. With this piece of iron he attacked eight men. He was on the point of getting out when the police appeared. They leveled their guns at "Bill." He stood there panting, intent upon breaking out, even to the point of daring the officers to shoot. The comrades at school prevailed upon him to accompany the police to jail. "Bill" was locked up in a Soviet bull-pen. He demanded to see Weinstone. It was reported later that Weinstone was in the middle of a meal when the telephone call came through. He bolted from the table and made a dash for the prison to free "Bill." After all, there was danger of the incident reaching the capitalist press. But "Bill" lost his train that night. He left Soviet Russia soon afterwards and made his way to the United States. I was told recently that he died in his native South a couple of years later, forgotten and unmourned by the Communist Party.

In the first week of January, 1931, I left Soviet Russia for the United States. "Red" Hendricks was to follow me. At the time he was lying sick in a Moscow hospital. It was our intention to return to prison. I would continue my fight for the textile workers from a Raleigh cell, just as Tom Mooney was keeping the struggle alive from a cell in St. Quentin. I found myself penniless in Berlin and the police were on my trail. The wife of a famous American novelist came to my help at the crucial hour by giving me twenty-five dollars. I proceeded to the United States where I arrived in March.

Roger Baldwin who had fought to get me back while the Communist Party endeavored to persuade me to stay in the Soviet Union, welcomed me. I saw a great deal of him, and told him of the horrible conditions in Soviet Russia. Baldwin did not seem surprised. One of his protégés, a youth by the name of Truman Peebles, was full of romantic ideas about Stalin's country. Peebles had studied forestry and wanted to give Soviet Russia the benefit of his services. Roger Baldwin asked me to discourage Truman from going to Russia. But I advised the young man to go and learn the truth for himself.

When I imparted to Baldwin some of the epithets which the Communists in Moscow applied to him, such as stool-pigeon, *agent-provocateur,* and Department of Justice man, he brushed it aside with the comment: "Politics, Fred, politics."

Roger Nash Baldwin is a politician of the modern age. He flirts with the anarchists, he hobnobs with the communists, he fraternizes with the socialists, he chums with millionaire radicals. He is a Red among conservatives and a conservative among Reds. He is a divine among liberal ministers and an atheist among freethinkers. He is a friend of democracy and a friend of dictatorship. He is a champion of civil liberties and an apologist of Stalin's system of terror.

Roger Baldwin is a New Englander of noted ancestry, a Harvard graduate and member of the university's fashionable clubs, who has directed the Puritan attitude of mind into social channels. For ten years he was at the head of a St. Louis settlement house where he learned the true condition of the laboring classes in the United States. When the war broke out, he publicly proclaimed his position as a "conscientious objector" and was sent to prison. In his speech before Judge Mayer, just before his sentence, he declared: "Some six years ago I was so discouraged with social work and reforms, so challenged by the sacrifices and idealism of some of my I.W.W. friends, that I was on the point of getting out altogether, throwing respectability overboard and joining the I.W.W. as a manual worker."

Socially Roger is a very pleasant, likeable person but he has a good deal of Puritan fanaticism in his make-up so that to many he appears obstinate and dictatorial. In my own case that was well illustrated when Travers Hoke, a writer who was living in Baldwin's house, argued against my going to prison. Roger would get furious at these arguments and became more convinced than ever that I ought to serve my sentence. Nevertheless, he always said: "Fred, in the end, you are the judge. If you don't want to go, it will be all right with me. But for the good of the labor movement, I think you should go."

The leaders of the Communist Party, William Z. Foster, Clarence Hathaway, Josephson and several others held secret conferences with me. They all urged me to return to the Soviet Union.

"It will do tremendous harm to the prestige of Soviet Russia if you return to prison," said Foster.

"It will give the Soviets a black eye," said Hathaway.

"The Soviet Government should never have let him out," said Leon Josephson, the Party's G.P.U. representative in America.

"If you go alone," continued Foster, "back to prison, without the other boys, it will look as if you want to play the part of martyr. Go back and give the Soviets another chance. It will not always be so bad over there."

After all, it was certainly not an easy decision to make. Now that I was no longer in Russia, the twenty-year prison sentence in North Carolina did not seem so tempting. The Communist Comrades played on that cord. They also played the old line: "Things have changed for the better in the Soviet Union." They decided to remove me from Baldwin's influence. They chose Clarina Michelson for this task and they could not have picked a more effective person. Mrs. Michelson is one of the most sincere and devoted workers in the

Communist movement. From the time of the Sacco-Vanzetti case, when she abandoned the Socialists and joined the Communist Party, she has given her time and money to the "cause." Like Baldwin and myself, she is a New Englander, descended on one side from the Beacon Hill Brahmins of Boston and on the other from Nancy Hanks, Lincoln's mother. As a débutante, she was presented at the Court of St. James but she has retained none of the aristocratic airs and manners of her youth. In fact, like so many other people of a fine upbringing, Clarina believes that in order to belong to the working-class one ought to be "tough": eat in the worst places, wear ill-fitting clothes, and generally ignore all the finer aspects of life. No one could question her idealism. She had made sacrifices for the movement and she had faced its dangers as few of the Party leaders ever did. When she urged me to reconsider my stand, I began to waver in my decision. At her suggestion I moved to her Connecticut farm where I could wait for "Red" Hendricks, who was to surrender with me to the prison authorities.

But months passed and I heard no word from Hendricks. I suspected that our letters were being censored and destroyed. Subsequently that suspicion was confirmed. Meanwhile all I knew was that all of the Gastonia boys were in Russia and apparently determined to stay there. There seemed little purpose in my going to prison all alone.

In the United States, the Five-Year Plan propaganda was at its zenith. Magazines and newspapers, capitalist publications all, were overflowing with exuberant reports, fantastic statistics, prophetic interpretations of Soviet progress. Travelers returned from Russia with ecstatic accounts. I was bewildered. I could no longer get my bearings in this topsy-turvy scene. Why, even Roger Baldwin privately knew one truth about Russia and publicly professed another. I, too, was persuaded to withhold my criticism of Soviet Russia. "Do not give comfort to the enemy by telling the truth about Russia," was the maxim often employed by my comrades. With it went this set of arguments: "Just give them a chance! They are going to do marvelous things for the workers. One cannot make a revolution with silk gloves. One cannot build Socialism without sacrifices. What are the difficulties of today as compared with the glorious future of Communism?"

I finally yielded under the pressure of my comrades. Perhaps they were right, a voice within me said. I had gotten off on the wrong foot while in Soviet Russia. I would start all over again. I would go back and co-operate with the powers that be and do my bit in the construction of the new order. After an "underground" sojourn of six months in the United States, I slipped out of the country just as secretly as I had entered it, and in September, 1931, returned to the Soviet Union resolved "to be good" and make my peace with the Stalin régime.

XX. ON THE INSIDE

1

THE officials of the Communist International received me with open arms upon my arrival in Moscow. All the Gastonia fugitives were now in the Soviet Union, with the exception of "Bill" McGinnis. One of the boys, Clarence Miller, was making a career for himself in the Soviet bureaucracy. Others, like Joe Harrison, were having a hard time of it. "Red" Hendricks, still sick, was not daunted by my return. He was determined to leave for the United States as soon as his health improved. "I'd rather die fighting in the American labor movement than die here in a Soviet hospital," he said to me. I promised "Red" that I would do everything in my power to help him in the event of his arrest in America.

The food situation in Russia had taken a decided turn for the worse during my nine months' absence. But I still had some American dollars and I patronized the Torgsin stores. What an extraordinary institution was the Torgsin! It developed out of the shipment of food packages from abroad to relatives and foreigners in Russia. The appeals of the latter to individuals in America and elsewhere started a stream of food parcels to the Soviet Union. The Soviet Government quickly saw in this trade an opportunity to obtain the much needed foreign currency, and monopolized the commerce. It gradually developed into a nation-wide chain where the recipients of orders from abroad as well as Russians owning gold or foreign currency obtained food supplies. The vast majority of the population could only pass the Torgsin stores and look hungrily into their windows. For the Soviet currency was not valid in these shops. Fortunate were those who had generous kinsfolk in America, the land which according to the reports in the Soviet press at the time was in the throes of hunger and on the verge of collapse.

There was one American in Moscow who did not take stock in these Communist reports, an aged Negro woman, known to everybody as Aunt Emma. She had come to Russia with a troupe of colored actors before the Revolution, and played for the Tsar and imperial family. She had lost her passport and was stranded in Russia during the Revolution. Emma learned Russian. For a while she worked in a Soviet textile factory. Later she became a cook for Americans. And still later she held the job of clerk in a Torgsin store. The Americans loved her. She always wanted to get back to the United States. Many had tried to arrange for her return before American recognition of the Soviet Government, but without success. Emma liked to be called "Mammy," much to the discomfiture of the American Communists in Moscow. But her apple pies atoned for her "bourgeois" manners. She gave a party in my honor and made a few dozen pies for the guests. The flour and the apples came from the Torgsin. Many an American firebrand extinguished his revolutionary ardor in feasting on Emma's apple pie. In 1934, Emma was enabled by the American Embassy in Moscow to go back to the United States.

2

Aside from American Communists and sympathizers, all kinds of driftwood from the United States floated

into the Soviet Union. Why not? People in this country
were reading the most flamboyant articles about the
Communist Utopia. Communist orators declared that it
was "the workers' paradise." And those who believed
what they read and heard contrasted it with the capitalist depression and decided to seek the new and better
life across the seas. They came with every intention of
settling into the pattern of communist existence; they
found that it was an existence without pattern and yet
without freedom, either. One of the victims of this confusion was William Gedritis, a lad of sixteen, who had
been sent by his communist parents from Chicago "to
help build Socialism." Bill knew nothing about Socialism but, like any American boy, was enthusiastic about
the trip. Moscow was not so enthusiastic about Bill's arrival. The American leaders there were in a quandary
as to what to do with him. They dared not send him back
because he had received a handsome farewell reception
in Chicago at which much reckless propaganda had been
issued about the opportunities of Soviet Russia; and
they feared to keep him because Bill had already begun
to organize the American youth on hand into a group
which was extremely embarrassing to the Communists.
In fact, they called Bill, "king of the bandits," a description which owed more to the boy's origin in Chicago than to the activities of the "bandit gang." They
were just a group of healthy American kids, full of
mischief, but to Russian Communists American horse-
play is "hooliganism," a word which has terrible impli-
cations there.

The editor of the Moscow *News* was very anxious to
rid the city of its All-American problem, Bill Gedritis,
and I was asked to take him with me to Kharkov where
I had just been assigned to take charge of the political

propaganda among the foreign workers in the newly opened Tractor Plant. I took him along and the lad remained with me for two years and finally helped me to get out of Russia. But for his assistance I should never have reached Paris.

A curious misfit who finally did establish himself was Tony Sponza. He arrived in Moscow shortly before my departure for Kharkov as a deportee from the United States. Sponza was a prize-fighter who had been arrested in America for rioting with Italian Fascists when the latter were on parade. He was not a Communist and knew nothing about the aims of the Party. His fight with the Fascists was strictly personal. The immigration authorities decided to deport him to Italy. The Communist International Labor Defense took up his case and fought it in the courts to change the deportation order so as to give him the privilege of going to Soviet Russia. Now Tony, though completely ignorant of Soviet Russia, thought it would be better than Italy. The American Communist Party gained prestige by defending his case. So that every one was happy when it was finally decided to deport Sponza to the workers' republic.

I met Tony when he arrived in Moscow. He had already spent two weeks in Leningrad. This was enough for him. The adventure was over. Now he wanted to go back to America. Day after day he made trips to the MOPR begging to be sent back to the country that had thrown him out. He hadn't the slightest idea what was meant by the class struggle. The MOPR tried to put him to work, but he refused. Being a boxer he tried to induce the Russians to let him put on an exhibition bout in Moscow. But they threw up their hands in horror at this bourgeois suggestion. Besides, there probably was

William Gedritis and Fred E. Beal, Kharkov, Ukraine, U.S.S.R.,
1932.

American Section, Red Front (Osoaviachim), Fred E. Beal,
leader, 1932.

not a pair of boxing gloves in all Russia. Failing to get up a fight, Tony lived off American tourists and hung around the hotels and restaurants to beg from foreigners. The MOPR gave him more rubles and warned him to keep away from the tourists. He was, indeed, in a pitiable condition. He pleaded with me to write to some sympathetic persons in America to secure for him permission to return to the United States. I gave him a ray of hope when I wrote to find a way for Tony's return on the ground that he had a wife who was about to have a child. He sat beside me, biting his finger-nails, while I typed the letter to Roger Baldwin. Tony's wife in America was a young Jewish girl. She had left him when he was arrested.

"Is she really going to have a kid?" I asked, feeling that Tony would hatch any kind of a plot to get back.

"I don't know, but I'll write her to get one. She hasn't written me a letter for months." He then insisted how much he loved her and yearned to be in her arms again. "These Moscow broads are a dirty bunch, they never take a bath," he complained.

I mailed the letter to Roger Baldwin. Tony was to write his wife pleading to be forgiven and to ask her if she was going to have a child. If not, to get one some way—through an orphanage, if need be.

In due time I received a letter from Baldwin that nothing could be done. Tony despaired. He was afraid that if he refused again to go to work, he would certainly be sent to prison. The MOPR did give him notice—to get out of the Political Emigrants' House as his bed was wanted for another political refugee. Then Tony thought of the idea of getting a job on one of the Russian boats, with the intention of deserting in some foreign country. "I'll go back to Italy," he exclaimed, "and take a chance on getting caught by Mussolini!"

But to his dismay he was told that only those who had worked five years on inland boats could travel to foreign lands, and then only those who belonged to the Communist Party. So Tony started on a five-year plan of his own. He would work five years inland, then make his escape!

Nearly two years later, on our way out of Soviet Russia, Bill Gedritis and I met Tony again in Odessa. He was surprised to see us. He had a good job. He boasted of it. It was cleaning up the prostitutes in Odessa. As long as he could hold this job, he was satisfied with Soviet life. He was a Communist now. And Communists had an easier life, he confided.

"How do you do it, Tony?" I asked.

"I bring her to my room and put her through a test. After it's over, I put her under arrest. I've rounded up plenty, and the best of it is, I get twenty rubles a head."

3

Kharkov was then the capital of the Ukrainian Soviet Republic. There was a colony of several hundred foreign workers and specialists, mostly Americans, Germans, and Czechoslovaks at the tractor plant. I was to be in charge of propaganda and cultural relations, and serve as the contact man between the Soviet authorities and the foreigners. My chief in this work was Isadore Erenburg, a Los Angeles Communist, a native of the Ukraine. The instructions that I carried specified my duties as follows: to supervise the food supply and the housing conditions of the foreigners and take measures to satisfy their complaints; to organize political classes,

excursions and cultural entertainments. Before leaving
Moscow, my instructions were amplified at the Communist International by Clarence Hathaway, at the
time Moscow representative of the American Communist Party and later editor of the *Daily Worker* in
New York. Comrade Hathaway explained my duties to
me in the following fashion: "Do *not* yield to the ma-
terialistic desires of the foreigners, but cajole them and
try to make them happy with as little as possible in the
way of food and other requirements." He made it clear
that the idea was to get the most out of the foreigners
in the way of showing the Russians how to produce
tractors without giving way to their individualistic tendencies and loose political notions.

Upon my arrival in Kharkov, I realized how important my position was. I was thrown into contact with the
highest Soviet officials, such as Petrovsky, the President
of the Ukrainian Soviet Republic; with Skrypnik, Vice-
president of the Council of People's Commissars and
member of the Central Committee of the Communist
Party of the Soviet Union; with the all-powerful Posti-
chev, who had been sent down by Stalin from Moscow
to weed out the rebels in the Ukrainian Communist
Party; and with the leading officials of the G.P.U.

My first thought upon assuming office, based upon
many years' experience as a union leader, was to
organize the foreigners at the Kharkov Tractor Plant
into one group in order to increase their efficiency. All
the foreigners received much higher wages than the Russians. Many were paid in *valuta*—in foreign currency.
I wanted the Soviet Government to get its money's
worth out of the foreigners. My first act was to call a
meeting of the most active foreigners, who were either
Communists or Communist sympathizers. The meeting

was a huge success, if judged by the number of complaints received about living conditions and the food service. The Soviet officials were angered by my calling the meeting. I had done it in my naïveté without their knowledge and they had no representative present. I discovered shortly afterwards that only an American with such a record as mine could have gotten away with such an unheard-of step—daring to hold a meeting at which no agent of the Stalin dictatorship was present.

The chief of the G.P.U. in Kharkov, Comrade Potapenko, invited me to call on him. He told me not to organize the foreigners, because those inclined toward Fascism might take up political matters. I replied that having been entrusted with a job by the Soviet Government, I could be trusted to do that job in the best way to meet the needs of the situation. Potapenko made it unmistakably clear to me that the only meetings I was to call were those in connection with factory work, and added: "And then *only* when told to do so by the Communist Party leaders. A party representative must *always* be present at such meetings."

"Why couldn't the foreign workers organize into groups and make known their feelings in matters concerning their own welfare, even on political issues?" I blew up in reply to Potapenko. "The majority of the foreigners consists of Communists or Communist sympathizers."

"Ah," the chief of the G.P.U. spoke up significantly, "now you'd better forget your American bourgeois-democratic ideas! You are now under the dictatorship of the proletariat!"

The irony of the situation was beyond words. I could almost see cartoons in the capitalist press in America depicting that interview, in which a soviet bureaucrat was upbraiding Fred E. Beal, Red Gastonia fugitive, for his bourgeois ideas.

"Of course," I mumbled in answer, "I know that this is the dictatorship of the proletariat. But I had supposed that workers enjoyed democratic rights within the framework of the Bolshevik system."

I learned my lesson. It was obviously my mistake. The workers' democracy which I had believed to exist in Russia was to be found only on the forgotten paper known as the Soviet Constitution and in the bristling columns of the Communist newspapers abroad. In reality, the Soviet régime was a dictatorship *over* the proletariat!

4

The several hundred foreign workers at the Kharkov Tractor Plant formed a privileged upper class, divided by a chasm from the ten thousand Russian workers employed there. The standard of living of these foreigners was the envy of the great mass of Russians. What was this standard of living?

After the G.P.U. had told me not to organize the foreign colony, my job settled down into a continuous effort to keep the foreigners from rebelling against their living conditions. It was not an altogether successful job, as the reader will see. I visited each family individually, according to the class to which the foreigners belonged, whether specialists or common workers. They overwhelmed me with complaints. I took notes and handed in a lengthy report to the factory administration. Here are some random items from the copy of that report in my possession.

House V-2, Room 46. This comrade gets no wood. He and his family have to run around stealing it wher-

ever they can find it. There is insufficient food at the
foreign store. No eggs, flour, onions or other vegetables.
He finds the working hours too long. They are supposed to be eight, but actually he is asked and forced to
work from twelve to fourteen hours each day. He does
not get his pay regularly and keeps borrowing from his
friends. Because of the late working hours, he and his
friends are unable to get together and organize any
kind of social life. He finds life after work very monotonous and his friends complain about this also. He would
like to have a change of bread now and then. (Some
white bread.) This comrade had been a party member
in the United States for years.

House V-2, Room 10, third floor, 1st entrance (eight
Americans). These eight Americans find it hard to get
their wages. They find their wages of one hundred rubles
a month totally insufficient. Some of them are unable to
go to work because of being hungry. They complain of
not getting enough wood and coal. They have to steal
wood to cook their meals with. The laundry is too expensive, costing one and a half rubles for the washing
of a union-suit and seventy-five kopeks for shirts and
they have to furnish the soap. Their room is unheated.

House V-2, Room 34. Cannot get things they want
at the store. The father of the family would like to be
paid for straight time instead of on a piece-work basis.
On piece-work, he has to sacrifice quality if he wants
to make enough money for a bare living. Has the same
complaints as above.

House G-1, Room 33. This comrade has been in the
Soviet Union for six months. The house is poorly managed and the manager supplies wood and coal only to
those who can afford to give him cigarettes. He has to
forage around for wood. The lights in the hall are off at

night and on in the daytime. He cannot get eggs and vegetables.

House G-31, Room 31. This comrade says the meetings are too long. The razors in the barber shop are dull, the bread at the store is stale.

House V-2, Room 91. (German, wife and two children.) This comrade has only one room for his family. He wants two. He wants coal. He is freezing. He cannot buy clothes and shoes at the store for his children. They want springs on their beds instead of the boards they now sleep on. They would like a wardrobe to put their clothes in.

There were numerous other complaints of this nature. Then came the revolt. One day the women of the foreign colony, mostly Germans, went on a Hunger March to the office of the Kharkov Tractor Plant. That is just what it was called by themselves and by the whole foreign colony. What a surprise to the meek starving Russians! The women demanded from the dictators something to eat. They were starving. Their men brought nothing to eat when they came home from work. They were always cold from lack of wood and coal. They marched right down to the factory and demanded to see the officials. The officials called out Erenburg and me to try to calm them. We spoke to them. We spoke about starvation in Germany and America, about the complete breakdown of capitalism and about unemployment. This had some effect. Then Ronin, our local Communist leader, attacked them full blast, scolding them for daring to march on the factory.

In the meantime, Erenburg and I drew up a resolution for them to endorse. The resolution, typical of what we had to put out in such cases, proclaimed to the world the wonders of Socialist construction, the solving of unemployment and the fight against the kulaks and the wreckers, agents of imperialist powers trying to sabotage the Workers' Revolution! We threw in a few cheers for our leader Stalin and condemned the complainants as Fascists. What excellent and manifold uses the word Fascist has been put to!

The foreign correspondents in Moscow never got hold of this sort of news. If they did, they could not send it out to their papers. Moscow would expel them. If a piece of news like this hunger march had got out to the capitalist press, Moscow would have sent down a few of the special G.P.U. men and it would have been all over with such small fry as Ronin. All the difficulties would have been attributed to his mismanagement or, worse still, to sabotage.

The hunger marchers went back to their homes, feeling for the moment they had grossly overestimated their longing for food. But their stomachs could not forget! The women became more angry and threatening. It was not easy for the families to break their contracts and go home immediately, although some did this. But they did write stormy letters to relatives in Germany telling how rotten Stalin-land was. Coming from Communist women, the letters were read in German radical clubs and printed in German newspapers. This called forth another round of resolutions from Kharkov stating the letters were forgeries or sent by some isolated Fascist!

Incidentally, this is one of the answers to the question as to why Hitler rose to power. The German workers, who were closer to Soviet Russia than the people of other countries, saw through the chicanery of Stalinism and lost faith in the Soviet system.

XXI. LABOR UNDER THE HAMMER AND SICKLE

1

THE large colony of privileged foreign workers at the Kharkov Tractor Plant subsisted on a starvation diet. How then shall I adequately describe the condition of the Russian workers? Did the Russian workers have the barest necessities of life? Did they have warm clothes? Were the barracks in which they were quartered warm? Was the factory heated? Were they happy and free, as the Stalinist propagandists abroad tell us? Could the Russian workers leave their jobs and go to look for a better place? Could they go on strike to improve their conditions? Could they protest in any way against injustices?

To begin with, there was a restaurant at the factory for the great mass of unskilled labor, the so-called "black workers." This is what they were served for the noonday meal: a bowl of cabbage soup with a herring bone or two swimming in it, one slice of bread, and a few ounces of barley gruel. That was all. The common workers received no meat, except on special occasions, such as Soviet celebrations or the arrival of foreign tourists. The workers ate in shifts. Many times, those in the last shift got nothing at all. The food ration allowed for the rest of the day consisted of a ticket entitling one to a pound-and-a-half of black bread priced at twenty-five kopecks. When the bread supply ran out, as it did every day or so, the worker was compelled to buy in the open market at the price of three rubles or more for the same quantity. Butter, cheese, eggs, milk were almost never obtained. These were even difficult for the specialists to secure.

In the filthy barracks, in which the common workers lived, heat was sometimes obtainable. In our factory—never! During the long, cold winters, the interior of the plant was an iceberg, little warmer than outside. Every one wore a coat if he had one and jumped up and down and clapped his hands together to keep the blood circulating. Thus were the workers supposed to engage successfully in the complicated work of producing good workable tractors. The sanitary conditions are impossible of description. Toilets were horrible. Water pipes froze often in the winter and the men would be without running water for days at a time. An allowance of one cake of soap a month was made to a worker. It would disappear in one washing. It was that kind of soap. There was a terrible lack of clothes of any sort. If one was an *udarnik*—shock troop worker—he might with great effort secure a pair of shoes or a coat. The common worker got nothing. Every man and woman in the plant was surrounded by stool-pigeons, members of the G.P.U. and other secret agents. They would turn the worker in for the slightest grumbling against his lot, not to speak of an attempt to organize any resistance to it. Sometimes members of the Communist Party and even the privileged *udarnik* would act as spies upon the common worker, inform upon him and turn in even supposedly good friends either by reason of fear or in the hope of advancement and getting favors from the authorities. The only weapon the common Soviet worker has in his agonizing efforts to throw off the shackles of his masters is the weapon of *silent sabotage*.

The fear of getting shot or of starvation in exile threatens any one who resorts to this means of protest. So inexorable is the terror that a strike among the Russian workers or a hunger march is almost inconceivable. Yet so extreme was the despair that all over Russia the workers were engaged in a great spontaneous campaign of silent sabotage.

The shock troopers at the Kharkov Tractor Plant were inspired or coerced by the Communist Party leaders to slave day and night, often in freezing weather, for the "workers' government." When these *udarniks* did an enormous amount of work and exceeded the piece-work quota, which was already high enough, then they received as a reward somewhat better living conditions and a little more food. Poems and songs have been written about these shock brigadiers. Undoubtedly some of them were moved to make sacrifices by their ideals and hopes for the future. Most of the shock workers were simply stool-pigeons, however, who delivered their less fortunate and more exhausted fellow-workers to the terrorist authorities. In the factory restaurant, they were the first to be waited upon and, once in a while, they were allowed to buy a few small cookies and cakes. They were sometimes given free tickets to the "entertainments" where more propaganda was offered up to them. Some were given a chance to live in the apartments where foreigners and party officials lived, but these chances came few and far between even for the *udarnik*. There is a class division between the shock troopers and the so-called "black workers." The latter who formed the preponderant majority stayed away from the *udarniks* and preferred to pour out their bitter hearts to the foreigners without fear of being betrayed to the Communist functionaries.

2

I visited other cities and factories in the Soviet Union. With the exception of the cities of Moscow and Leningrad, where conditions were somewhat better, I never saw any Russian workers whose average life was easier than that of the mass at the Kharkov Tractor Plant. I did see worse conditions. Beneath the privileged classes of the soldiers of the Red Army, of the officers of the G.P.U., of the specialists in charge of technical departments, of the higher Communist bureaucrats, and of the select *udarniks,* the vast class of the Russian workers was in a state of serfdom which defies exact definition.

The Kharkov Tractor Plant was one of the most important Soviet undertakings and conditions there were supposed to be among the best in Russia. Yet factory life in this exemplary establishment was far and away worse than anything I had ever seen in America. Piecework was universal in production. Quotas were high and workers had to put in inordinately long hours to make even their minimum. If they failed to make this a few times, they were fired as quickly as in any capitalist plant. They had no recourse to law in such cases. I remember one fellow in the foundry who, weak and emaciated, asked his foreman for a leave of absence for the purpose of resting and trying to get a little food in the open market to rebuild his energies. The leave was refused. The next day this man walked out of the foundry door to get a breath of fresh air and dropped on the ground from weakness. They took him away and, later, I asked one of the foremen what had become of him. He shrugged his shoulders and would not answer. I knew that the hospital services were reserved for specialists, Communist Party members and sometimes *udarniks,* if the latter had enough "pull." The foundry worker had probably been taken to his bunk in the barracks where he had died, which was a usual occurrence.

Workers tried heroically to keep up the fight. One mistake, one let-up and their places would be taken by others; they would be "removed" or sent out into the open without a food ticket, without shelter or without a job. If by chance a worker lost his passport, he would absolutely be without a place in the economic structure of the country. Poor as his job might be, it was the only path to stave off complete starvation.

At the Kharkov Tractor Plant, the foreigners were in despair at having to work alongside starving, stupefied and dazed Russian workers. Not only was it extremely depressing to the spirits to see the emaciated condition of the men, but they could get little coöperation from them in that state. One American, working in the machine shop on production, delivered a speech at the noon hour: "This food is not fit for pigs," he said. "I learned in the labor movement in America that those who do not work shall not eat, and it seems to me about time that those who do work shall eat!" This man was out of the Soviet Union in two weeks, branded by the American Communist Party as a "Social-Fascist."

The American specialist, Tom Stewart, demanded from the plant director, Swistoon, that foundry workers be given at least a pint of milk in the foundry every day. He threatened to quit the job and go home if the order was not carried out. The order was carried out. How the factory workers loved Tom Stewart!

The factory minimum wage was sixty rubles a month. The unskilled workers received this much. Others received up to one hundred and fifty rubles, and, in the case of Russian specialists, two hundred and fifty to three hundred, according to the quota set for them. Some food was obtainable on the food ticket, but suppose a factory worker wanted to go to Kharkov and get a square meal? I have before me a typical menu of one such meal I had at the time with a companion: two soups, two beef-steaks (stringy meat), two pieces of bread . . . fifty-nine rubles. This, to a wandering tourist, would mean twenty-eight dollars, according to the legal exchange, and a month's wages to a common Russian worker. And that was by no means a high-priced meal in comparison with others I had.

Communists in America fought against piece-work. It was our stock demand: *Abolition of piece-work!* In many of the capitalist factories production men have found they could get a better grade of work and more of it if they left it to the man to work on his own initiative. In Russia, however, piece-work is one of Stalin's main levers of production. Every department of the Kharkov Tractor Plant was on piece-work. They do not trust the workers on straight time. And the speed-up! Another one of our stock demands in America was: *Abolition of the speed-up!* But in our plant efficiency men from the Soviet Tractor Trust worked day and night figuring out how to speed up the workers, how to make the belt move faster.

Communists in Detroit rave against the monotonous life-sucking belt system operating at the Ford plant. Had I not done so myself in Pontiac, Michigan? But I never heard a word uttered against its use in Soviet Russia. The belt system is in the assembling department. It is here that the tractor or automobile comes to life, beginning with the placing of the chassis on the moving platform. The assembly line (belt) moves on, workmen on each side slip in the various parts needed in

building the machine. Finally—the line moving all the
time—all the parts are fitted and the finished car moves
off the conveyor. The trouble with the Kharkov Tractor
Plant was that the belt or conveyor never moved fast
enough for the Communist bosses.

The Stalinists justify piece-work and the speed-up by
saying it is for the greater cause of Socialism. Every
hardship, every iniquity and every injustice was being
perpetrated in the holy name of the Revolution and the
Classless Society! At the same time the Stalin policy
created more classes among the Russian workers than
under capitalism and suppressed with a mailed fist every
true radical and revolutionary manifestation on the part
of the masses.

3

There is no unemployment in Soviet Russia—is the
familiar line of the Communists in America and other
foreign lands. What are the facts? At the Kharkov
Tractor Plant there was not a day that I did not see
large groups of people waiting outside of the gates
looking for work. When a man was taken on, he had to
go through a great deal of investigation. The applicant
had to answer where he worked before and why he left
his job. Were his parents workers or dirt farmers? Had
they come from "kulak" stock? Had the applicant left
a collective farm of his own free will? Many
hungry wanderers looked for work at the plant. Most
of them were turned away, particularly those who came
from collectives. I remember one old man, ragged and
freezing, begging for a job. Being hungry he was ready
to do anything. He pestered the young official who did
the hiring. "Go away, old man," said our young Communist bureaucrat, "go to the field and die!"

As the old man silently and quiveringly turned away and walked down the ice-covered road, the young man's eyes followed him with contempt. "It's time we put these old people out of the way," he remarked.

The Tractor Plant, one of the glories of the "workers' fatherland," is surrounded by a high brick wall. Every entrance is guarded by a soldier with loaded rifle and fixed bayonet. In addition there are watchmen at the entrances to the factory grounds. To get in one must show a pass. Every person entering the plant, including all the workers, must have a pass with the bearer's photograph on it, stamped and signed by the chiefs of the factory G.P.U. Only guided tourists are excepted from this rule. A worker has a hard time getting to his job if, by accident, he leaves his pass at home, or, what is much worse, if he loses it. In the latter case, he has to be hired all over again. I have seen men, old plant workers, pleading with the guard for a chance to get to their jobs, panicky lest they lose their food allowance for that day. Every few months, the administration changes the type of pass and every worker and employee must get a new identification card. This unusual passport system was devised to enchain the workers and restrict them to certain zones. On the whole, it has accomplished the purpose of forcing the men to stay on their jobs regardless of working conditions. Thus, a worker in Kharkov having a passport good only for that zone, could not get a job if he moved, for instance, to Rostov or Stalingrad.

We had a school attached to the plant in which "engineers" were turned out by the dozen. These engineers, supposedly picked for unusual ability or political loyalty, would be rushed through the courses and let loose upon the factory as highly qualified men. They would attempt at once to correct the work of the foreign spe-

cialists, bringing untold confusion and wrecking the
activities of the really able technicians. Fine and expensive machinery was ruined because of the total incom-
petence of these novices who had been put in positions
of authority. Production was hampered time and again.
Parts made of inferior metal would quickly wear out.
Makeshift belts would quickly go to pieces. Measure-
ments would be wrong. The average tractor sent out
from the plant had a very short life. There were spasms
when production slowed down to practically nothing.
The same system prevailed in other great plants all over
the country. But on paper the results somehow looked
impressive. The industrialization of the Soviet Union
appeared to be going ahead by leaps and bounds, and
helped to disguise the appalling starvation and enslave-
ment of the great masses.

4

Wherever I went in the Ukraine, I saw thousands of
homeless outcasts about the streets with great watery
blisters on their feet and ankles resulting from diseases
of malnutrition. I would see them sit down on the
ground and prick these blisters to let out water and then
get up and drag themselves about their begging. Of
course, they stole anything they could lay their hands
on and the factories, whose workers had planted vege-
table gardens and cabbage patches to supplement their
own slim rations, would be compelled to post guards
with orders to shoot to kill these pitiable foragers. In
some instances they waylaid, robbed and killed some
better-faring compatriot in the dark, but they were usually deterred from this sort of thing by the thought of
some awful retaliation of the G.P.U. I saw this state of

things in Kharkov. I saw it in Odessa, Kiev and other
cities. The condition existed all over the southern part
of the U.S.S.R. All these people were called "kulaks,"
and the government slogan was: "Liquidate the kulak!"
They were not allowed to have passports. They were not
allowed to ride trains. They were not allowed to have
jobs in the factories because the factory authorities could
not feed them, although the official reason was that "they
might wreck the machinery." The Soviet Government
had further given orders that no one might feed these
runaway peasants. Such is the spell of fanatical propaganda coupled with unparalleled terror that the workers
in the cities, themselves living on the lowest of rations
and under nigh unbearable living conditions, would
often denounce these peasants to the G.P.U. But they
continued to run away from the collectives by the millions. They robbed freight trains. They plundered co-
operative stores for food. The Central Committee of the
Communist Party issued orders and decrees, threatening these "anti-social" elements with "the highest meas-
ure of social defense"—capital punishment.

The starving peasants and workers stormed the foreign colony at the Kharkov Tractor Plant every day.
With piteous cries for food, they went from house to
house and from door to door whenever they could get
past the guards stationed there. It was the only hope
of getting bread. There was none on the land. The
Stalin clique was determined, however, to teach the
famine-stricken people "a lesson in Communist dictatorship." These crowds of roving peasants were augmented
by discharged workers from factories, workers who
couldn't keep up with the Stalin pace or who had grumbled, protested, or fallen into disfavor with their overseers. For a worker to get fired in Soviet Russia means
death by starvation, unless he can learn the art of beg-

ging or is fortunate enough to have some kind relative in the capitalist countries. For when a worker is fired, he loses his work-card. And when he loses his work-card, he loses his bread-card and the right to live in the government-owned houses or barracks. The discharged worker cannot depend on help from friends who have barely enough food for their own existence. Besides, the G.P.U. "discourages" any aid to such victims. And when the G.P.U. "discourages," it means a threat to life or freedom. So the Tractor Plant and our foreign colony there was besieged by droves of begging and pleading people, seeking a few crumbs of bread, some potato peelings, or some fish bones. Not a day passed without groups of these disinherited peasants and workers, young and old, men and women, knocking at our doors. They would dig into the garbage boxes and fight like packs of wild dogs for food remains.

The Stalin clique positively hated these intruders, especially the peasants. The hungry folks stood in the way of the bureaucrats anxious to make a good showing before the visiting delegations and tourists. Indeed, of what use was the propaganda put out in America, claiming that the Soviet worker was prosperous and always employed, if these hungry, shelterless, jobless "beggars" were permitted to expose the truth? The Soviet authorities, with the aid of the Communist Party members of the factory, who were eager to win favors from the high officials, would round up the starving people in the streets, collect them in great herds, and turn them over to the G.P.U. I saw it happen many times. It was a weekly occurrence. Sometimes a raid would be improvised a few hours before the arrival of a foreign delegation. I confess that I even took part to some extent in these inhuman dragnets.

XXII. FAMINE

1

THE Stalin dictatorship frowned on any attempts on the part of even foreign Communists to see what was going on in the country. When I organized an expedition at Kharkov for some members of the foreign colony to go out into the villages, the G.P.U. immediately quashed the idea. One fall day, in 1932, a Russian factory worker and I started on a long hike out into the countryside. We started early in the morning of our rest day and arrived back home very late at night. I will call my friend Maxim. I don't want to get him into trouble with his masters. The things we saw are not what the visitor to Russia sees. The tourists would see only the special farms. One of these is the G.P.U. Commune located in the Kharkov district. It is called the "Red Star." The peasants working on this farm are hand-picked members of the Communist Party and the Young Communist League. They are well-fed and housed. The cows are contented and the tractors, under the management of strapping young shock troopers, actually plow the fields. But 95 per cent of the collectives and state farms are radically different from this.

Maxim and I hiked south from our place, crossing the ravine in back of the tractor plant town where the beggars stewed up the fish bones and we passed the new laundry beyond, the new laundry which never seemed to be in running order!

After some miles of walking, we came upon two men

and a woman working in a field. We knew they were DOPR (prisoners' corps) workers, but we wanted them to tell us. At first the woman, whose uncovered legs were all broken out with boils and scabby places, started to run. One of the men called her back, saying that it was an "Inostranetz" (foreigner).

"Why did you run?" Maxim asked.

"I was afraid the police had come to shoot me," she answered.

"Why should they shoot you?"

"Because they took my husband and my son. They killed them, I'm sure, and now they want to kill me," the woman cried and became hysterical. With this she fell heaving to the ground, pounding and flaying it with her fists.

The man who had called her back explained her case to us. The father and son had been shipped to some unknown place for failure to make the quota. The quota is the tax in kind set by the Soviet Commissars. It had to be met—or else! This woman did not want to run away from this vicinity, because she hoped she might hear from her husband and son some day. The man told us the story of his own past. He was a cabinet maker. During the war, he was captured by the Germans and put to work at his trade. Considering conditions in Germany at the time, he was making a comfortable living. Then the Bolshevik Revolution broke out in Russia. As he was a Socialist he went back to his native land to help build Socialism. He fought in the Red Army against the White Armies and, after they were defeated, he became a member of the Communist Party. He followed the leadership of Lenin because Lenin had promised land to the peasants. He received a small bit of land and had worked hard and was beginning to prosper.

He owned a cow, a horse and a plow and always met his taxes until the Government began to make them impossible to meet. A year and a half before he was short four bushels of wheat and three of potatoes. They sentenced him to forced labor, one year for each bushel short of the required tax! Now he was a convict.

"There seems to be no one watching you, why don't you run away?" I asked.

"What for ... where will I go? Here I get some bread every day and all the tomatoes I can steal. If I run away, I'll starve."

I thought of the Sokolnike Prison and that other show-place, Bolshevo, near Moscow, where the prisoners never ran away. And how the Bolsheviks boasted of it! How the tourists had marveled at the supposed model Soviet penal system!

"What else do you get to eat?" asked Maxim of the prisoner.

"Nothing ... nothing else at all, other than a pound and a quarter of bread a day. If we walked eight miles we could get borsch (soup) with sun-flower seed oil on top. But we would rather steal tomatoes. Want one?" He took from his faded blouse three or four small tomatoes and offered them on the palm of his hand. We hesitated. "Please take one, it is all I can offer you."

We did and our cabinet maker and his two prison comrades looked happy. In return we gave them a box of matches. Even a measly box of matches made them happy! Now, they could boil the tomatoes and make a soup!

We went on and saw many others like these working the field in a dazed and feeble way. This was a State farm (Sovhoz) and the majority of the peasants were prisoners. All were in a bad condition, weak and undernourished. Miles further, we came to a collective farm. Here we met a woman with two buckets of water swinging on a stick over her shoulder. Nearby was a village of thatched houses. We asked the woman for some milk, offering to pay for it.

"We have no milk," she replied. "We haven't had any for six months."

"Isn't this a collective?" asked Maxim.

"Yes, this is a collective." And we couldn't get another word out of her.

We went on to the houses through a wide field of weeds and tomatoes. The weeds were higher than the tomatoes and absorbing all the nourishment from the ground. The tomatoes were sickly and small. A woman sat close by under the shade of a tree.

"Comrade, why don't some of you get out and pull the weeds? They are choking the tomatoes," I said.

"What for?" she answered us. "We had some nice tomatoes last year and the government came and took them all away from us. The same with the potatoes and everything else we raised. We had nothing to live on through the winter. Citizen, do you think *I* can pull all those weeds? There were two thousand of us here once. Now there are only about one hundred left, and God knows what will happen to the rest of us this winter!"

"And where are the rest?"

"They died or ran away. Now, there are only a few children and one sick cow."

2

My friend Maxim and I continued our journey through the Ukrainian countryside and wandered around a village on the way to the Stalin Commune

which was our destination. In the backyard garden of
one of the thatched houses we found two boys of about
fourteen. Here the vegetables looked healthy, compared
with the sickly products of the fields. One of the boys
was hale and strong, as if the earth had given him the
best it had. The other looked starved and listless. We
asked the healthy one:

"Is this your garden?"

"Yes, and my father's."

"Where is your father and the other people of this
collective?"

"They are out stealing tomatoes!"

The straightforwardness of this answer amazed me.
Maxim said it was because I was a foreigner. The lad
had no fear of foreigners.

"Aren't your father and the other people afraid of
being arrested for stealing tomatoes, and can't you get
them from the collective?"

"We'll die if we don't get the tomatoes, and we can't
get them from the collective. We have no flour or anything except what comes from these gardens. The government took all our food."

The listless boy said he came with his mother from a
long way off, he didn't know where. His mother had died
in a field near this collective and the father of the healthy
one took him into his home. The starveling had some
vague recollections of his father fighting soldiers. These
children were raised since the Revolution. They know
nothing about the old ways except what they have heard
from the older folks.

"I like my own garden best," the healthy one ventured,
pointing to it proudly.

We gave the lads a few lumps of sugar, a luxury in
these parts, and went on in the direction of the Stalin

Commune, advertised as one of the highest Communist achievements. Mile after mile we walked through uncultivated ground. Maxim said it hadn't been cultivated for over two years. As far as the eye could see, the land was barren save for weeds. At other times, I saw similar vast stretches of idle ground. Yet at this very time the Moscow *News* was telling Americans that Ukraine was one hundred per cent cultivated! Near a brook, we came upon the decomposed body of a man. Flies, ants and worms were feeding on his remains. We had seen numerous fresh graves marked with crude Greek crosses pushed into the earth, and skeletons of horses and cows. But this was the first dead human being in the open we saw that day. Another hour's walk and we came to a wheat field, or I should say a weed and wheat field. Maxim pulled at the wheat and showed me a few undeveloped kernels. "The wheat is sick, the weeds are thriving." At last, we came upon two men plowing a field with a tractor. A real tractor it was and running, too. A young man, the driver, was cursing the older man for not being able to hold down the plow.

"You're not digging deep enough," said Maxim.

"It's the fault of this old bag of bones!" complained the young man.

The older one, who was doing his best to bear down on the plow, got somewhat excited. He must have thought we were government officials. "Citizens, I'm doing my best, but I don't know this thing!" he cried and pointed to the tractor. "If they would give me a 'sokha' (wooden plow), I'd show them."

We went on to a small group of houses, passing in the field an abandoned John Deere Combine of late model. It was rusted and out of order. A few more rains and it would probably be beyond repair. I wondered how many thousands of bushels of grain were taken from the peasants to pay for it in American dollars. The group of houses was the Stalin Commune. Inside the largest of these was a row of cots. Each cot, made up, was covered with a single gray blanket. The place was empty except for the cook and a helper in the kitchen making supper. The workers of the Commune would be back from the fields in half an hour, said the cook. We could meet them. We rested ourselves.

Now, at the "Red Star" Commune, of the G.P.U., the workers had come rushing in from work, happy, full of life and energy. But not these men and women. They dragged themselves in sad, hungry, and completely exhausted. They sat at the table like so many mechanical men, not talking to each other, just waiting, each with a tin spoon in his hand, for the cabbage soup to come. A dirty-aproned kitchen girl brought in a trayful of bowls of soup. Hundreds of flies followed her as she deposited each bowl, with a slice of bread, in front of each worker. The soup course was followed by hot tea, without sugar.

They were mostly young people, thin and gaunt. They stared at Maxim and me in silent resentment, I thought, at our presence. The manager came in and sent them back to the fields again. He asked us what we wanted and who gave us permission to come there. I showed him my special documents and told him I was a political refugee. He became almost obsequious. I asked why conditions were so bad on the Commune. He did not agree that they were bad. "We are much better off here than on the collectives," he said. He had been manager of the Commune only a short time. The previous manager had been "removed" for inefficiency. Many of the workers had run away, too.

"Why did they run away?" I asked.

"Because they would rather work in the factories."

"But we don't give them work at the factories! We have enough workers in our factory!" I protested.

"Comrades, that is my answer!"

We left him and talked with a barefoot girl, who straggled behind those walking through the field. "Why do they run away from here?" I repeated the question to her.

"Because there is nothing to eat and too much driving," she offered unhesitatingly. When she found out that I was from America, she wanted to know if America had Communes and if the people there were dying from hunger as the manager had told them. "He said the workers in America live worse than we do. Is this true?"

I couldn't think of any worse food I had consumed in America, save perhaps in one or two of the jails I had been in.

3

In the spring of 1933, when the last of the winter snows had melted away, I made a random visit to a Ukrainian collective near the village of Chekhuyev. In company with a Russian-American comrade from the factory, I took the train from our little station of Lossevo and rode for two hours to Chekhuyev. From this place, we walked east for several miles. We met not a living soul. We came upon a dead horse and a dead man upon the side of a road. The horse still lay harnessed to the wagon. The man was still holding the reins in his lifeless stiff hands. Both had died from starvation, it seemed. The atmosphere itself seemed filled with death and desolation.

The village we reached was the worst of all possible sights. The only human there was an old woman who passed us on the village street. She hobbled along with the aid of a stick. Her clothes were just a bunch of rags tied together. When she came close to us she lifted the stick as if to strike us but the movement petered out in weakness. She spat at us and mumbled something incoherent, something my friend could not make out, though he knew the language well. Her feet were dreadfully swollen. She sat down and pricked her swollen feet with a sharp stick, to let the water out of the huge blisters. There was a large hole in the top of her foot from continuous piercing of the skin. She was stark mad. She laughed when she sat down and screamed with pain when she squeezed her foot. She spat again at us. We moved on.

There was no other life. The village was dead. Going up to one of the shacks, we looked into a window. We saw a dead man propped up on a built-in Russian stove. His back was against the wall, he was rigid and staring straight at us with his faraway dead eyes. I shall always remember that ghastly sight. I have seen dead people who had died naturally, before. But this was from a cause and a definite one. A cause which I was somehow associated with, which I had been supporting. How that deathly gaze pierced me! How it caused me to writhe in mental agony! As I look back, I think that unforgettable scene had more effect than any other in deciding me to do what I could do to rectify my horrible mistake in supporting the Stalinists of Russia and the Third International.

We found more dead people in what had been their homes. Some bodies were decomposed. Others were fresher. When we opened the doors, huge rats would scamper to their holes and then come out and stare at us.

At one house, there was a sign somehow printed on the door in crude Russian letters. My friend read it: "God bless those who enter here, may they never suffer as we have." Inside two men and a child lay dead with an icon alongside of them.

There was a sign on the door of another house. It read: "My son. We couldn't wait. God be with you." Two old people were dead in there. We took it to mean they couldn't wait for a food package to arrive, possibly from Moscow or even from America. Maybe their son had been in the Red Army; perhaps he was a factory worker. If it was food they had been waiting for, either the boy had not sent it or it had been stolen by some hungry mail-censor.

Many of the houses were empty. But, in the rear, the graves told a story of desolation and ghastly death. More signs were stuck up on these graves by those who buried them:

I LOVE STALIN. BURY HIM HERE AS SOON AS POSSIBLE!

THE COLLECTIVE DIED ON US!

WE TRIED A COLLECTIVE. THIS IS THE RESULT!

I had seen enough of villages and collectives and communes. On our way back, near the station, people told us that *that* village was to be burned. Three or four others in the vicinity had already been burned. Not a trace of the houses or of the dead bodies in them was left. A terrible weight of sadness and hopelessness settled upon me. These horrors could not make me hate the responsible ones any more than I did, but I felt completely helpless about getting out of Russia. And where to go? It would be hard to take up life again in the world outside without helpful friends, and most of my friends were Communists or Communist sympathizers. They, perhaps, would hate me for upsetting their beliefs and illusions as to Stalin's glorious way out for mankind.

4

I was editor of the American Communist factory paper, *Tempo,* in the Kharkov Tractor Plant. My work often took me into the city of Kharkov ten miles distant. I constantly saw the most unbelievable tragedies. It was common to see people drop dead from starvation. On no occasion that I can remember did I fail to see a death from starvation during my travels to the city.

The Stalin dictatorship has one thing which works in its favor: the horrors of Soviet life are such that few people in the Western World could be brought to believe them. As I am writing this, it all seems like a ghoulish dream. I've never been in an insane asylum, but I should compare my Russian memories to those of a man cured of insanity and trying to recollect the visions of a ghastly past. At the city bazaar I saw a woman lie down and die. Her begging days were over. Wrapped tight around her and hugging her breast was an infant sucking at her nipples. The people about paid little attention.

Death meant freedom! The few who hovered around shook their heads in utmost sorrow. A militiaman blew his whistle and when another came, they both took her body and the suckling to the police station. This police station was crowded all the time with homeless workers and peasants who had been picked up during the day. These were destined to receive a bullet of mercy or to be shipped in cattle cars to some prison camp. On a visit to Odessa, I saw many such freight cars loaded with these unfortunate people. As they passed our train, I could smell the stench of these cooped-up beings. It was particularly terrible to see young people in these groups. But they were there, along with the old ones.

Once, I saw a lad of about nineteen walking in the gutter. He was smiling and brave-looking, as if he were proud of whatever he had done. Behind him was an officer with a drawn pistol. When an officer parades an individual down a Russian street with a drawn gun, it means *that* person is to be shot. Since capital punishment is reserved for political prisoners, other crimes receiving a maximum of ten years, it meant that the young fellow had committed some political act contrary to the wishes of the rulers. I wanted to cry out to the world: *"Save him! Save him!"* as I had done so many times for Sacco and Vanzetti! I wondered what Vanzetti, a simple noble being, would have said if he had lived to see the Russia of to-day?

Another young man, walking under police escort, but without guns, seized a loaf of bread from a fat woman standing at the curb. The woman, with three round loaves, seemed to be inviting some wretched one to make a pass for that bread. She screamed!

Before the policeman could take the bread from the youth, he had gulped down a few mouthfuls. The cop gave him a terrific shove, but the lad just laughed and laughed, as if to say: "It's in my stomach now, try and get it!"

I yelled: "Good for you, good for you!" The officer looked at me in puzzlement. Fortunately for me, he couldn't understand English.

There is a shallow river running through Kharkov.

So many people jumped into it in attempts to commit suicide that special guards were placed on the river banks to arrest the would-be suicides. On the part of some, it was a trick to get arrested and taken to jail, so that they might get a little to eat, if only a little.

5

In 1933, I had occasion to call on Petrovsky, the President of the Ukrainian Soviet Republic, in his office in Kharkov. I was accompanied by Erenburg, my superior in the cultural-propaganda work at the Tractor Plant. "Comrade Petrovsky," I said, "the men at our factory are saying millions of peasants are dying all over Russia. They see poverty and death all about them. They say that five million people have died this year, and they hold it up to us as a challenge and a mockery. What are we going to tell them?"

"Tell them nothing!" answered President Petrovsky. "What they say is true. We know that millions are dying. That is unfortunate, but the glorious future of the Soviet Union will justify that. Tell them nothing!"

Now the Ukraine is known as the bread-basket of Europe. Its soil is as rich as that of Nebraska, Iowa, and Kansas. That black earth will grow anything, given only the seed and care. What then was the cause of this general starvation? One of the answers is Stalin's forced collectivization. The peasants stubbornly fought the campaign ordered from the Kremlin. Their seeds were confiscated and distributed only to collective and state farms. Their horses and cows were expropriated. The right of disposing of their crops was denied the individual peasants. Farm implements were made unavailable to them. Heavy taxes were placed upon peasant holdings and collected at the point of a gun. Scores of thousands were killed outright because they refused to go into the collectives. Red Army detachments were sent into the villages for that purpose. The inhabitants of hundreds of villages literally died in their tracks and, in thousands of other villages, the peasants abandoned their homes after the forcible seizure of from 60 to 90 per cent of their grain. Great numbers took to the roads, flocked to the cities, and wandered as far as their legs could carry them. The tragedy of these living corpses, who were often without even the customary rags in the coldest weather, was more grewsome than the tragedy of the dead.

Heart-rending was the condition of the great swarms of homeless children let loose by the Stalin policy. It should be remembered that this new crop of waifs was not inherited from the Tsarist régime, from the early period of the Revolution. The Stalinists have a way of blaming the Tsar and the World War of nearly two decades ago for the latest wave of homeless children. These youngsters hated the Soviet factories, the G.P.U. and all government institutions and restrictions. They preferred to ride freight trains, to beg, to steal. Their parents had been starved to death, shot, sent to concentration camps far away, or were still roaming over the land lost to their children forever. All the stations and railroads of the country were infested with these waifs. They had a way of getting through the cordons of guards despite the vigilance of the G.P.U. officials.

On a trip that I made to Moscow from Kharkov and back, I encountered many little derelicts pleading for food. I was on board the International train and ate in the restaurant car. Across from me sat a characteristic Soviet bureaucrat with shaven head. He carried a brief case. Into this he put the remains of his meal, such as pieces of bread. Outside the window a dirty-faced kid, wearing a cap much too big for him, appealed to the bureaucrat: *"Dyadya, dai kusok khlieba!"* (Uncle, give me a piece of bread.)

"Go to work. You ought to be arrested for begging!" the bureaucrat said.

I gave the youngster my bread. The bureaucrat, who could speak English, told me that I should not spoil the waifs by giving them food.

"He is too young to work," I answered, estimating the boy's age to be about twelve.

"He could go to a Soviet institution," was the retort.

"But perhaps he does not want to go to an institution," I replied, thinking of the disgraceful Gorky Commune near Kharkov where the children received very little food and plenty of discipline.

"Well, he ought to be made to go! He and the rest are a nuisance to the government!"

Indeed, the more I saw of Russia the more convinced I became that not only the homeless children but all the common people of the country were a nuisance to the Soviet Government.

XXIII. "THIS IS NOT UNION SQUARE!"

1

A MIXED delegation of Americans, Englishmen, and Germans came to Kharkov. The local Intourist office notified us a few hours ahead that the visitors were scheduled to visit our plant and that we should have to serve them a meal at the foreigners' restaurant. Our director, Ravinsky, called for my chief Erenburg. "You and Beal," said Ravinsky to him, "get busy and clean up the place before the delegation arrives."

We had to get in touch with the Communist Party officials to remove the beggars and prepare a grand meal for the visitors. And how our officials like the latter duty! At a given signal, the agents of the G.P.U. and the Communist members, scattered throughout the grounds, pounced upon the weary, almost lifeless people who were either stewing some fish bones or pawing in the garbage for scraps of food. Some of the "beggars" were swaying with the wind beneath apartment windows, crying for bread. The raiders swooped down upon them and forced them in the direction of the corner house, known as A-1, because it was near the road, convenient for transportation.

I watched on the side lines, ashamed of being a party to the system that was murdering these innocent people. Often I thought: "It won't be long, I cannot stand it!" It was horrible to see the starved people dragged along the road, their bare swollen feet scraping against sharp rocks. Their looks and dress could not be described. For months they had been slowly starving to death. Hardly any of these people could ever again eat a square meal —their stomachs would not bear it. Scurvy and boils covered their bodies. Their legs were bloated. Some were insane and spat at the guards and the Young Communists who teased them. Huddled together by the well-fed G.P.U. men, the hundreds caught in the round-up and roughly thrown together in one batch made a sight which mocked at humanity.

The children of well-fed Communist officials, Young Pioneers, stood by and parroted phrases of hate learned in school. When some of the younger "beggars" tried to escape, the Pioneers warned the G.P.U. men and helped to recapture the fugitives. This cut me to the bone. How terrible it was to put such hatred into the hearts of little children. Then two trucks made their appearance on the road beside apartment house A-1. A cry went up from the corraled women in the crowd: "Citizens, citizens! Don't send us away!"

They knew that they were about to be carried off a long distance, where they would be dumped into the wilderness, miles away from cities, so that they would perish without embarrassing the Soviet Government before foreign delegates and tourists.

I had never dreamed that Communists could stoop so low as to round up hungry people, load them upon trucks or trains, and ship them to some wasteland in order that they might die there. Yet it was a regular practice. I was witnessing myself how human beings were being tossed into the high trucks like sacks of wheat. Right there and then I was determined to make a complete break with the Stalin gang and return to the capitalist world, no matter what the consequences

would be to me. As the two trucks were being loaded
with the human cargo consigned to perdition, some of
the victims fought back, but due to their weakened condition their blows had little effect. The children among
the prisoners climbed in of their own free will. They
apparently looked upon it as a joy-ride. Many of the
young ones did manage to escape en route and reach the
cities again. There were cries of pain rending the air as
the swollen and blistered captives were tossed into the
trucks. When the two vehicles were jammed full, they
started with their human freight and disappeared from
view. An hour later the foreign delegation arrived to
inspect the boasted Soviet industrial giant and to enjoy
a hearty meal. More than one speaker exhorted the
foreigners to bear witness to the world that there is no
starvation in Russia.

There were many such raids. The Stalinists, after
dumping their victims in the barren fields, trusted that
none would ever come back alive. But some did, and they
would tell us foreigners what happened to them in the
wilderness. Such was the case of the lad who gathered
my wood in return for a few slices of bread and whatever
scraps of food I could give him. He had been captured
three times, but always made his way back. He reported
to me that the older and the weakened folks perished
in the fields or by the roadside. The poor youngster had
seen so many deaths and so much suffering that he
seemed to think it all part of life. There was no other
life to him. The children always accepted the horrors
of their environment as a matter of course. Only the
older people could dream of a past that treated them
more kindly. One day my youngster came in with a
basket of wood and announced that he had solved the
problem of escaping the dragnets. He would simply al-

ways carry a basket under his arm, as the people do
who can afford to buy anything at the stores. The trick
worked. The G.P.U. was fooled, by the "respectability"
of the lad with the basket.

2

Soviet Russia has in recent years become a Red
Mecca. Every summer large streams of tourists go there
from the capitalist countries lured by colorful advertis-
ing or propaganda. These "observers" are a new phe-
nomenon of our times. In the pre-war days tourists to
Tsarist Russia or to the Kaiser's Germany were just
sight-seers and did not undertake to report upon political and social conditions in the countries visited. To-day
tourists are pilgrims; they go in quest of a faith; they
come back as missionaries; and they are listened to, regardless of their qualifications, as if they were trained
students of history, economics, and sociology.

One of the reasons why there is so much confusion in
ascertaining the truth about Russia is this annual tide
of superficial tourists. Now it was part of my job with
the Soviet Government to steer foreign visitors and even
newspaper correspondents around the Kharkov Tractor
Plant. And how gullible the average tourist turned out
to be! I was particularly struck by the gushing enthusiasm of these well-fed pilgrims over the happy and contented Russian workers who had at last "come into their
own." These tourists could stand by watching Russian
workers sweat beads while carrying heavy loads on their
backs or almost faint from hunger and heat in the foundry and get lyrical about it!

Women paving streets and laying railroad ties in the
hot sun or in sub-zero weather were, to these tourists,

emancipated. The poor western women were still slaves because they were not permitted to perform such manly labor. Children could be cajoled and egged on to work any number of hours, and it seemed a glorious achievement to these "students" of the Soviet system. After all, the children of Soviet Russia should be taught the art of manual labor. Nearly all the tourists flitted lightly from one city to another and swallowed all that was handed to them by the officials. Some spent only a month or so romancing around tourist hotels and felt informed enough to write a book, to give interviews, to deliver lectures on the Communist progress when they returned to America.

The tourists to Russia can be divided into two classes. There is the large group of those who come over already convinced by Communist propaganda and by their own illusions that Bolshevism is the way out of the capitalist crisis. These pilgrims, who are in the majority, are so cleverly guided about on their short visits that they leave the Soviet Union strengthened in their faith. It is enough for a Communist official to tell such "observers" that "the Five-Year Plan is a hundred per cent fulfilled," or to proclaim that "the tremendous enthusiasm of the Bolshevists can conquer every obstacle," and they take these statements as incontrovertible facts. The will to believe makes these people blind to the most patent realities. Then there is a minority of tourists who are penetrating discerners of the real situation. But some of these, members of radical organizations in America, are fearful of returning home and telling the truth. They would lose their friends and might even be denounced as "Fascists." One such radical comrade from New York, a member of the John Reed Club, told me in Kharkov that he would not dare tell his friends back home some of the things he had seen in Russia. "They wouldn't believe me," he said to me in my room, "and I'd be an outcast."

I have already described how thorough was the preparation around the Kharkov Tractor Plant on the eve of the arrival of foreign visitors and how cruel was the cleaning-up process in which hundreds of starving Russians were seized and carried off into the wasteland. From the moment of their arrival in the Kharkov station, the tourists would be taken in tow by the Intourist officials, escorted to waiting cars, driven to the Red Hotel and given the best rooms in the city. The tourists had to eat their meals at the hotel—elsewhere the cost would be ten or more American dollars per person for a luncheon or dinner. One full day, seldom over two, was the schedule for the city of Kharkov, and few tourists wandered from this course. We always got the press photographer out when tourists arrived and rushed them through the Kharkov Tractor Plant as quickly as possible.

The American labor delegations, well-dressed and healthy-looking, were a source of embarrassment to the Soviet officials guiding them. Their appearance did not quite fit in with what the Russian workers are being told about the starving proletarians in America. One such American labor leader, after seeing the slave system in our foundry, remarked to me: "Is this what the Revolution gave us! Me for slavery in the States!" But he quickly added: "Don't tell the others what I said. They might think I am a counter-revolutionist."

There were many Americans whom I had known back home, and who would take me into a corner alone, asking questions such as these: "Tell me, Comrade Beal, do you think this is really a success?" . . . "It will be better in the future, won't it?" . . . "America is fully industrialized; we won't have to go through this suffering, will we?" But most of the time the tourists raved to me about the wonders of Soviet construction.

Sometimes, I would ask them: "Would you like to live and work here? I can get you a job, right here in the factory."

Then there would be a sudden change of front. I could read the thoughts in their minds: "What! I live in all this filth and starvation! No, sir, not I.... The States for me and *three* square meals a day!"

3

In the spring of 1933 the Stalin government feared that a general peasant revolt might break out at any time. The collective farming system was a shambles and the ruling dictatorship was afraid that the factory workers would be left completely without food. Orders were issued to every industrial plant in the Soviet Union for all workers to put in so much of their time in planting their own gardens and raising their own products. It was decided at the Kharkov Tractor Plant that the five hundred foreigners employed there should organize their own gardening collective.

Now the overwhelming majority of our foreign colony was composed of Communists. The experiment in actual Communism, by Communists, under a Communist government provided a memorable lesson. We started off with a general meeting and elected committees to take charge of the organization of the gardening collective. In the beginning all the foreigners, such ardent internationalists in their respective homelands, were in on the venture, the Americans, the Germans, and the Czechoslovaks. But it soon appeared that these three nationalities could not work together. The Germans wanted to boss everything. The Czechoslovaks wanted to be by themselves. So we separated into three committees.

About one hundred and twenty-five acres were placed at our disposal in the rear of our apartment houses by the plant administration. Timekeepers were assigned to check the working hours of each man so that each would get paid in produce according to the working hours put in. We managed to get a tractor from our own plant. This tractor circled the field a few times, coughed . . . and died! It was never resurrected and eventually carted away. We then took to the shovel and the lowly hoe, and did our own digging. Sometimes we would rest on our shovels and look at the great buildings of the Kharkov Tractor Plant which turned out tractors, it was said, at the rate of fifty, seventy-five, and one hundred a day for "socialist" farms. Occasionally we would think of the striking photographs of the plant printed all over the world as irrefutable testimony of the success of the Five-Year Plan. And then we'd laugh—a bit wildly!

Soon the foreign collectivism began to weaken and grow discouraged. The Russians could not give us many seeds. Some of the group were lying down on the job. Others did not want to work on a collective basis, pointing to comrades who were putting in the hours but not the labor. There was a clamor for *individual* gardens. We obtained the consent of the administration to divide up the collective into separate patches, so much land per family. The gardens began to take on life with the arrival of a large box of seeds from the United States for one of the Americans. All through the season most of the foreign Communists kept a sustained interest in their *private* gardens! Various crops came up and flourished.

In the midst of the terror and starvation surrounding us, the gardening venture was the one bright spot in our lives. Although the foreigners had privileged food cards in restaurants, the provisions were expensive, inadequate, and often unfit. The coffee was made from acorns. During my entire stay in Russia I never had a half dozen cups of real coffee. The "omelets" for which we paid one ruble often had no eggs. If they did, the eggs were rotten. The beef stew was just a name for potato soup with a bit of gristle in it. In the foreigners' restaurants the cooks, waiters and managers were under constant surveillance because of food thefts. They watched each other. They checked and double-checked. The cook would let the waiter have food for service only on an O.K.'d slip from the manager. This happened in the case of each item and each order. From time to time the managers were "removed." One day I would go into the restaurant and find a new manager who would have to be coaxed or browbeaten for some food. "What happened to the last manager?" was a frequent question. "I don't know, comrade, I don't know," was the usual answer. But we all knew. He had dipped his fingers into the eggs and was in a box-car on his way to Siberia.

The foreigners were always in a state of wrath. They would have to spend hours buying a little food at the *Insnab*—foreigners' supply stores. The service was almost unbearable. One would have to stand in line to have the supply book registered for the quantity wanted, then stand in line at the sugar counter for half an hour, until the supply ran out, then stand in line for another half-hour at the milk counter, unless the word passed around that the milk had gone sour. The same procedure applied at the bread and meat counters. When there was meat, it was covered with dirt and sawdust, and it would be thrown on the scales and given to the customer without wrapping. The only things that one could buy without waiting in line were perfume, lipstick and wine. The store clerks would steal food. Despite armed guards, hungry people would break into the shops at night. After such a robbery, the foreigners' store would be out of things for a day or longer.

Now since I was in charge of the welfare of the Americans, I made every effort, sometimes storming and sometimes pleading, to improve conditions. Most of the chiefs would merely shrug their shoulders. I discovered that to report an individual case of mismanagement to the factory G.P.U. was useless and only served to put the man or woman "on the spot," subjecting the offender to capital punishment or to exile. The real offenders were the confusion, the red tape, the inefficiency of the bureaucracy fostered by the Stalin dictatorship.

4

The downtrodden and hungry Russian workers in Kharkov dared not rebel, but the five hundred foreign "enthusiasts" at our plant, enjoying preferred treatment, were finally up in arms against the conditions. Especially militant were the Germans who had a way of organizing themselves and demanding better conditions. We had a difficult time restraining the foreign colony from headstrong action. The American preferred individual methods of protest. When an American reached the limit of his endurance, he just packed up his things and demanded his exit visa to go home. Word of the turmoil among the foreigners reached Moscow. Comrade Smith, political Tsar of the foreign section of the All-Soviet Tractor Trust, hotfooted it to Kharkov.

Smith is a Finn. His face is disfigured by a deep scar. He has been in New York, acting as Moscow's representative to the American Communist Party.

At this critical moment, when the foreign workers, especially the Germans, were on the warpath against the unbearable conditions, a meeting was called to celebrate the anniversary of the Red Army. At that time the Americans, who had heard that the Ford plant was about to reopen, talked about going home. An attempt had to be made by Moscow to renew their dwindling faith and keep them on the job. They had to be given more inspiration to keep them from starting their own little revolution. At the meeting, Smith spent two hours talking about the Red Army. The foreigners moved nervously about in their seats. When the time came for questions, an American spoke up abruptly: "Do you know people are dropping dead from starvation here on the streets?"

Instantly, Smith was on the alert. "Where did you read that—in the Chicago *Tribune?*" he asked brazenly.

The foreigners laughed, a kind of laugh which said: We don't have to read American papers for this kind of news; we see these things all about us.

Smith shouted to his audience: "What do you mean— coming to the Soviet Union to criticize and make demands? Where do you think you are—in Union Square? Here the dictatorship rules with an iron hand! It is unmerciful to its enemies! We will not let bourgeois sentimentalities stand in our way. . . . Bread!" sneered Smith. "You comrades ask for bread! What about the Russians who are not getting a third of the bread you get— are they complaining? *No!* It's some Fascist dog, creeping in our midst from some capitalist country, who is trying to bring dissension and disruption to the forward swing of Socialist construction and, in the end, keep us from having a Communist Revolution in America and from freeing the Scottsboro boys!" Smith said all that in one breath. Before the meeting closed a prewritten resolution glorifying the Red Army was endorsed.

After the meeting Comrade Smith and I motored to the city of Kharkov in the plant's car and partook of a fine dinner at the Red Hotel. Smith paid one hundred rubles for the meal. He criticized me for being so soft with the foreigners. "See how I handled them," he boasted. "They were like putty in my hands. The bourgeois bastards, we'll show them! You know," he suddenly looked at me slant-eyed, suspiciously, "there is funny business going on around here. The foreigners at the plant are restless; there must be a German Nazi spy among them. All these complaints are not coming out of thin air. There is something behind it all. Have you any suspicion?" His eyes narrowed to mere slits. He trusted no one. He was nervous and obviously anxious to find some goat upon whom he could place the blame for planting the seed of rebellion among the foreigners.

Dropping all pretense, I leaned back in my chair, looked him straight in the eye, and said: "Comrade Smith, your speech to-day was just a lot of meaningless phrases. Why didn't you tell them the truth about the state of things and have it over with? I thought we were trying to do away with treating adult workers like eight-year-old children. The foreigners, sooner or later, are going to discover the mess here with the collectives and industries, and, if the situation is not explained to them, there will be hell to pay. The peasants are running away from the collectives by the millions. They come to our colony to beg for food, right at our doors. The American Party members are asking why so many peasants are

Political class in the Red Corner, Kharkov, Ukraine, U.S.S.R.

Fred E. Beal on tractor, Kharkov, Ukraine, U.S.S.R., 1933.

being arrested and why so many of them are being shot and exiled. You can't continue calling them ALL 'kulaks.' The truth is the foreigners are to undergo a terrible shortage of food this coming summer, and next winter it will be worse. It will be hard to fool them much longer. You know, you 'phrase slingers' and 'slogan repeaters' are going to be blown off your lid when the pressure from below works up to a ferment!"

Comrade Smith was amazed at this. He wanted to know how the Party saw fit to put me in charge of the foreigners when I didn't seem to understand the ABC of Communism. "Tell them the TRUTH!" he snapped at me. "Why should we tell them *anything!* Most of them are bourgeois-minded, even if they are Communist Party members, having come from lands under the influence of the bourgeois ideology. All we want of them is their brains and skill to get the plant running and to teach the Russians how to run the plant. After that, we can dispense with their services and they can go back to their capitalist fatherland."

5

But why did most of the American correspondents in Moscow fail to reveal the truth of the insufferable conditions described by me? One reason is that most of the foreign correspondents were not allowed to go into the famine-stricken areas during the critical years. Another reason is that the few correspondents who know their Russia are careful not to send out reports distasteful to the Stalin dictatorship and censorship, so as not to be expelled from the country and thus lose their jobs. Independent and fearless correspondents, such as William Henry Chamberlin, of the *Christian Science Monitor,*

Isaac Don Levine of the Chicago *Daily News* and the New York *American,* and Eugene Lyons, of the *United Press,* were obliged to leave Russia in order to tell the full truth. The fundamental reason why this truth from Russia does not reach the world is to be found in the corrupting influence of the autocratic state. All governments have their satellites in the form of semi-official press correspondents who disseminate "inspired" news. In the case of an absolute dictatorship, such as prevails in Russia, the foreign correspondents are even more restricted as fact-finders. They become "rewrite" men. They cannot collect and report news from their own sources of information. They are confined to translating and transmitting items which appear in the rigidly censored Soviet newspapers. Now the Soviet press is a government press. Its servility to Stalin is beyond comprehension abroad. It practices an almost inconceivable deception upon the Russian people and indirectly upon the outside world. Its weapons are denunciation and prevarication. It exists for propaganda and not for information. Its aim is to proselyte and not to seek the truth.

In the United States, I used to denounce the capitalist press as a "kept" press. More than once I attacked newspapers controlled by textile interests and other privileged groups as prostitutes of opinion. My experience in Russia taught me that only under a dictatorship is the complete prostitution of the press possible. In a capitalist country, some predatory interests will hire a pack of writers and make them serve the ends of privilege and injustice. But no one is powerful enough to corner all the papers, to acquire all the printing presses, to own all the publications, to employ all the writers, and to outlaw all opposition. Only an absolute dictatorship can do this. And the Stalin dictatorship has just that kind of a press. It is polluted with untruth. The foreign correspondents in Russia, the visiting delegates, students, and tourists, have all been drawing upon that source of pollution to give the outside world a picture of the people's life under the Soviet system.

XXIV. THE CHALLENGE

1

FOR us seven Gastonia fugitives the Soviet Union was a shortcut to freedom, just as it has been and still is a spiritual shortcut to the millennium for thousands and tens of thousands of believers in the Stalin utopia. But the shortcut led us into a blind alley. There was but one retreat—back to prison in North Carolina. Try as I would, I could not stand the suffering of the Soviet workers and farmers. And I could not protest against the system, criticize the acts of the dictatorship, contribute as a Communist to the policies laid down by the Communist Party. During the last months of my stay at the Tractor Plant, I was not even permitted to serve as chairman at any of the meetings of the American workers and engineers. I had many private discussions with them in their homes, and nearly all of them were in opposition to the Stalin régime. It was at this time that I learned that the leadership of the Communist Party had been considering ways and means of disposing of me. I planned my own retreat from the "socialism" of Stalin as carefully as I had planned my escape from the perils of capitalism.

I had a great battle with my conscience about remaining in the Soviet Union. If I kept my mouth shut there, I should be free from prison. This much was clear. It was also clear that in America I faced a twenty-year sentence if caught. And if not, I should become a part of the army of fifteen million unemployed. Yet I felt that I had to go. The things that were going on around me were just unbearable. I decided to go—*anywhere*. But the fate of "Red" Hendricks changed this vague decision into a determination to return to America.

2

To this day, "Red's" case remains shocking evidence of the Comintern's attitude toward such political prisoners and victims of capitalistic injustice as dare to disobey the orders of Moscow. Hendricks started for America on what he described as a "Five-year plan" of his own. He risked seizure and serving his sentence of five to seven years in the Raleigh prison.

One day in July of 1932 Bill Gedritis was reading one of a batch of American papers which had just come. "My God, Fred, they've got Red," he suddenly exclaimed. "Look here, it's in the *Daily Worker*."

I grabbed the paper and read the following small, obscure item which betrayed in every phrase the attitude of indifference that Communist officialdom intended to adopt in the case of this victim of the class-struggle. Most significant of all was the fact that this boasted defender of revolutionary workers carefully avoided mentioning that Hendricks had just returned from Soviet Russia:

MAN HELD COPS SAY IS HENDRYX
If Gastonia Victim
ILD Will Fight

New York.—According to capitalist press reports, police claim to have arrested man described by them as K. Y. Hendryx, who in 1929 faced a prison term of seven years following his conviction with six other workers in the Gastonia, N. C., strike.

Detectives made the arrest, according to the report, at a rooming house at 361 E. 10th St., last night.

As the *Daily Worker* was going to press, lawyers for the International Labor Defense, which defended the workers framed up in the Gastonia trial, were unable to check up on the identity of the jailed worker.

The I.L.D. announced, however, that if it is Hendryx the police have arrested, that they will wage a bitter fight to prevent his extradition to North Carolina.

Subsequent issues showed that the *Daily Worker* and the I.L.D. had decided to ignore the entire affair. And I realized very soon that in this, as in all other things, they were following the lead of Moscow.

This was the first word we had in Kharkov of "Red's" capture. The Comintern, the MOPR, the American Communist leaders in Russia, all of whom are on the alert for a good reason to make propaganda against capitalist justice, were strangely silent about Red. Was it possible that they preferred to ignore one of the Gastonia martyrs because he had left Stalin's refuge? I immediately sent off a batch of letters to various persons and offices in Moscow and in the United States. I wrote to the Comintern demanding that a campaign be started at once in behalf of Hendricks. The first reply from Weinstone, who was at the time representing the American Communist Party at the Comintern headquarters in Moscow under the name of Randolph, was to "mind your own business." Another American Communist in Moscow, Mary Reed, who was "Red's" best friend and who had collaborated with him in preparing articles and pamphlets published by the Soviet government, wrote to me.

> Dear Fred:
> I have sent your letter on to Comrade Minor in N.Y. and also asked Comrade Randolph, the Party rep. here, to take the matter up at once, which is being done.
> Of course there is no excuse for neglecting "Red" now or at any time, and I hope that already everything is being done that can. The letter from "Red," written on his way to prison, which I turned over to the Party rep. here, seems to be lost. He has promised to look for it.

Some weeks later I received a letter from "Red," written on July 4th, while on his way to prison. "Red" often addressed me as "Sam." I am reproducing the letter here as originally written, spelling, punctuation, and all, for Hendricks believed in writing words as they sounded:

> Hello Sam how is the boy fine I hope well Sam I am feeling fine and looking forward to my great future. well Sam I hav flatly refused to make any Statemints to any press on the case but will later and I wood love for you to giv me some advice as to what kind of a Statemint to make in regards to the other 6 boys. well Sam theas jails in the East is quite differn to those in the South whin I wint out for a hearin I was closed in a ware cage like a wild man and no wone has bin aloud to speak to me sinc I was caut.
> you must rite to me very oftin and tell me all the news and sind me the moscou news and any other paper that you can. and another

thing some money will come in good for smokes
and ice cream for it will bee hot on the Rock
pile this sumer. well you ansor soon I hav lost
your adress but I am shure that my Brother
has mail for me from you. You rite to this
addres. M C Hendrix. Martinsville, Va.

I flooded Moscow with letters about Hendricks. The
summer passed without any favorable action in response
to my pleas. It was October, 1932. The misery of the
Russian workers reached a new climax of terror. I
sought to escape this oppressive environment and at the
same time I aimed at an organized fight for "Red"
Hendricks. On October 3rd I wrote to Comrade Randolph, at the Comintern, as follows:

Two matters I want to take up with you in
this letter. One, about the renewing of my
passport and the other about K. Y. Hendricks,
now, I understand, in the Raleigh prison serving his sentence. My passport ran out last
May. I went to Moscow to see about the renewing of it, but the rep. was out of the city
with a group of American delegates. It is now
five months over. Don't you think it time that
I had it renewed? I hope this time, Comrade
Randolph, that I will not be compelled to raise
the small sum of twenty-five dollars, needed for
the trip to a foreign country for the renewal,
from friends in the States. . . . Now about Comrade Hendricks. I have written indirectly to
you regarding him (thru Mary Reed) but have
received no reply. All I want to know is why
the Party or ILD apparently is doing nothing
for him. Nothing is said in our press about
him. As one of the Gastonia prisoners I am
entitled to know the facts of the case and I
don't want to make a trip to Moscow to find

out. I was told by Comrade Reed that he wrote me a letter on the way to Raleigh and that now you have it. Will you please forward me a copy? Red told me in Moscow before he started that his intentions were to again take part in the movement in America. He was so sick with tuberculosis that he thought he might die any time here in the Soviet Union. He decided, like the best fighters that we have, that it would be better to die fighting in the movement in America. However it seems that he got caught before he had the chance. The MOPR paid his way over, so they have the right to defend him, as they should all political prisoners. Please give me an immediate reply to the above.

The foregoing letter elicited an answer from the Comintern. Weinstone finally stated in a communication to me the position of the Communist Party with respect to the defense of Hendricks. The document is worth preserving for the benefit of those innocents who believe that Communism and idealism are synonymous terms.

Comrade Beal:
The case of K. Y. Hendricks has been considered by the Comintern. We can not do anything for him in the line of a campaign in the open to free him, as you request. Hendricks left the Soviet Union at his own volition without consent from the Party, even though his fare was paid to America. To make an open campaign for Hendricks would put the Soviet Union in an embarrassing position. The workers in America would be asking: Why did he return to America? Is American jail better than living in the Soviet Union?
You are not to give the Hendricks case further consideration.

About renewing your passport. When the
time comes for us to send you out of the Soviet
Union for Party work, you will be given a
passport. We have ways and means of furnishing you a passport. There is no need of
your renewing your present one.

William Weinstone.

But the last thing in the world that I intended to do
was "not to give the Hendricks case further consideration." I had received a letter from the United States
which showed me that nothing could be expected from
the American Communist Party. It was written by
Harry Eisenman, a member of the Young Communist
League and "Red's" friend. It informed me how Hendricks had been captured. "Red was staying at my
apartment from the time he arrived in New York until
the time of his arrest," wrote Eisenman. "Red had met
an Irish kid and also brought him up to the house to
sleep. The kid was very active in trade union work so
I let him stay. They both became rather good friends.
The result was that the kid turned out to be a Department of Justice agent. The apartment was raided and
every one placed under arrest on some phoney charge of
assault on some scab. When they got Red down in the
Radical Squad headquarters and started grilling him
about beating this scab (You understand that all this
questioning was only to cover up Red's arrest) then
they suddenly began asking Red whether he was wanted
for murder. In spite of his dyed black hair and his assumed name of John Grey and though he kept denying
this charge, he was finally forced to admit it and signed
a statement to that effect. Red was extradited to the
South to serve his sentence. The International Labor
Defense and the Communist Party have not breathed

one single word about his arrest, in fact they denied that it was Red Hendricks. I think that all this keeping quiet is a disgrace and something should be done about it. I can't understand why not a word has been said in our papers, the capitalist papers were full of it. The stool-pigeon's name is Raymond Healy. He was a member of the Party."

3

The conduct of the Comintern in the case of "Red" Hendricks boded ill for those of us fugitives who contemplated a return to the United States. "Red" did not go back on the Communist Party. His sole crime was that he did not like Soviet Russia and chose the precarious life of an underground revolutionist in America against the wishes of Moscow.

Here was a challenge which I could not ignore. I made frequent trips from Kharkov to Moscow in connection with the Hendricks case. But all my efforts were futile. On one of my trips to Moscow, I ran into Mary Hillyer of the League for Industrial Democracy. She was touring the Soviet Union. I interested her in the fate of Hendricks and she promised to do all she could upon her return to New York. She would place the case before Norman Thomas and through him bring it to the attention of the wide public. In order to aid this campaign with the masses I went over the heads of the Communist leadership and wrote an appeal to the workers of America not to desert Hendricks and to fight for his release. This letter I gave to Mary Hillyer. Later I received a report from her that Norman Thomas had taken the matter up with Roger Baldwin and the Civil

Liberties Union. But the expected action in behalf of Hendricks did not materialize.

I was puzzled and embittered by the strange silence with which the Socialist and Communist leaders in America received all the appeals in favor of Hendricks. I could not understand the indifference of the International Labor Defense and of the Civil Liberties Union. Did the status of "Red" Hendricks under capitalism undergo a change as soon as he left Soviet Russia? Was he innocent in 1929, in Gastonia, when the Communist Party and the I.L.D. collected thousands of dollars in our defense campaign, and was he guilty in 1933? Or was it, as Comrade Weinstone of the Comintern had written me, that the people in America would be asking if the Hendricks case were reopened: "Is American jail better than living in the Soviet Union?"

I could not bring myself to face the full truth at the time. But one fact was clear. The Communist and Socialist leaders who had so often exploited the most trifling labor difficulties in order to agitate against the iniquities of capitalism, turned deaf ears to all my appeals to do something for Hendricks. The extent of their indifference was revealed to me in the pathetic letter which is reproduced below. I received it at a time when the Comintern was answering all questions concerning Hendricks with the information that he had died in prison. As the letter shows, he was indeed dead for them.

Raleigh NoC
April 23, 1933

Dear Fred:
  Your letter was received Some Time ago and was very glad indeed to hear from you. Am Getting Along As Well as Could Be expected under the circumstances Which are

very Poor. Am looking forward to the Time When I Will Be free, Which is a Mightly long Time I Suppose.

At the Present Time Things look Mighty dark for Me, Fred! I Hate to State This, But it is the True Condition as have Been With Me Since I Came here last July. The party has only given Me Ten dollars Nine dollars Was Given until January 1st This Year and Since Then until This date I have received only one dollar for over Three Months. Now it is very Necessary for There is Things I Must have, Because This Place Gives one Nothing But rotten food and Clothing. They do Not even Give You Soap to Wash With; Nothing to Smoke, No Tooth Paste, No brush, No Shaving Articles Not even a face Towel. One Cannot live in here Without These Necessities. There is only one favorable Point and That is, They Will Allow You to Buy These Things. It is Very Necessary I Should have at the least five dollars each Month, for the above Things, and for Such as the expense of Mailing letters Which Cost me 25c each, as They do Not Allow any letters Written and This is done Thru Secret Channels. This is the reason I have Not Written You More often and I am Surprized That You Have Not Written Me oftener Than You have.

I Have Never Heard from the Other Boys Since I came here.

I don't Know But in My opinion There is Nothing being done for me Whatever. The last I Heard Was Something about a parole Which I am Bitterly against and Will Not accept. I am Sure if Proper Procedure Was Taken in my Case, They Could Get me a Time Cut to Where I Would Not have to Make over Two Years at the Most.

In other Words I am Buried Alive in a Morgue and forgotten by the Outside World, especially Those Who Are Supposed to look after me. I often Wonder if the other political Prisoners in Jail Are Neglected as I am.

If there is anything you can do about this Matter in Seeing that I Get Necessary Aid while I am here I will Greatly appreciate it. Also I trust You Can do Something along the line as Suggesting to the Party that they Work toward a Time cut for me instead of a parole. Of Course I realize there is very little You can do about it But I am Sure You Will do what You Can. I do not Know the outside Condition or What is Happening, Because I do Not Get Any News from the Outside. Very Seldom I ever See a News Paper.

I guess You Will Get Tired of reading this hard luck Story. I am not Criticizing the Party for I do Not Know their financial Condition. Regardless of What happens to me, I am a Social Revolutionist and Will Continue on With the Struggle. There is No More News to Send You. Am wishing You the Greatest of Luck. Hope to hear from You Soon.

Comradely Yours

R.

If I was to help Hendricks, there was only one course open to me and that was to get out of Soviet Russia. I felt sure that an open letter from me to the workers of America would at least get for him some funds to lighten his lot in prison and I was just as sure that such a letter would never get by the Soviet censorship. I resolved to try a trick whereby I could slip out of the "Workers' Fatherland"—this time forever!

The American technicians at the Kharkov Tractor Plant periodically went to Poland, where American consulates functioned, to renew their passports. Early in August, 1933, I applied to the Communist Party committee at the plant for permission to go out to renew my passport and declared in the application that I was doing so upon orders from Moscow. This was believed by the Kharkov authorities and they issued to me the following certificate for the purpose of securing a Soviet exit visa. Although the Comintern knew nothing of this testimonial, it opened the border gates for me. The text follows:

THE COMMUNIST (BOLSHEVIK) PARTY OF THE UKRAINE

PARTY COMMITTEE OF THE KHARKOV TRACTOR PLANT

August 7, 1933.

To the Central Committee of the International Labor Defense of the U.S.R.R.

The political refugee Comrade Fred Beal, employed at the Kharkov Tractor Plant, has been doing great political-educational work among the American workers and specialists.

At present Comrade Fred Beal is leaving for Poland to extend his foreign passport. The Party Committee of the Plant requests that assistance be given Comrade Beal in the matter of adjusting his passport problem, so that he can return in the nearest future to the Kharkov Tractor Plant.

Secretary of the Party Committee of the Kharkov Tractor Plant

(*signed*) *Potapenko*

Chief of the Propaganda at the Kharkov Tractor Plant

(*signed*) *Ronin*

(Seal of the Communist Party Committee of the Kharkov Tractor Plant)

4

This out-going visa gave me the right to go to any foreign country in order to renew my American passport. It was taken for granted by the authorities that I should make my way into Poland or Germany and return within a few days. But I had other ideas. One of them was to see Leon Trotsky who was in guarded exile in Turkey for having dared to challenge the rule of the Stalin gang. Although I had never been a Trotsky follower, I had an enormous admiration for the man, for his intellectual powers, for his great work as revolutionary and as war commissar during Russia's most critical period, and, finally, for his friendship and support of Lenin. I also felt that Trotsky might help me resolve my personal problem—my belief in Socialism and my hatred for the Socialist State which existed in Russia. Some months previously, when I first thought of the possibility of seeing Trotsky, I wrote Albert Weisbord and Vera Bush who were New York Trotsky-ites. Vera Bush had been one of the defendants at the first Gastonia trial and Weisbord, her husband, was the leader of the 1926 Passaic textile strike. I received a reply in code that they had arranged with Trotsky to see me about the same time as I got my visa. I was greatly excited and decided to risk everything on the attempt to get to Turkey.

Accompanied by young Bill Gedritis I went to Odessa to take a boat to the land of the Turk. But my joy was short-lived. The Turkish Consul in Odessa refused to give us a visa to his country unless we could show two hundred dollars apiece. Bill's folks had written him that there would be a hundred dollars awaiting him at the American consulate in Constantinople and

we had about fifty more between us, but that was still
a far cry from the sum we were expected to produce.
For several weeks we hung around Odessa trying to get
through but finally had to give it up. On September 17,
1933, we left Soviet Russia for Riga and reached Berlin shortly afterwards. The ever-present question of
finances became very serious in Nazi-land for I was
there with a Jewish name on my passport and had no
other connections than the Communists who were being
hounded for their lives by Hitler. The great Reichstag
fire trial was on at the time and Arthur Garfield Hays
was present, representing an international committee
of famous lawyers. I had met Hays, of course, when he
came down to Gastonia as one of the attorneys at our
first trial. He walked into the prison one day with a
number of other lawyers and I was surprised to learn
who he was. Now I decided to appeal to him for help.
He was very cordial. After a long talk about conditions
in Russia, he invited me to come back for dinner that
evening.

Hays had a suite of rooms at the Hotel Adlon and
dinner was served there for us, his daughter, Laura, and
some other friends of theirs. At the table Hays asked
me to repeat the things I had told him earlier in the
day for the benefit of his friends. In fact, he was so
interested in this information that he urged me to write
a book on the subject. He proved equally generous in
money as in ideas and when we met again in Paris, just
before he sailed for America, he gave me enough cash
to carry me along for a while and arranged for his
daughter to give me one hundred francs a week until
further notice. Hays promised to take up my problem
with Roger Baldwin as soon as he returned to the
States and it was his opinion that Baldwin would ar-

range for me to come back to the United States and take up the fight against the Gastonia sentence. But evidently Baldwin thought otherwise and managed to convince Arthur Hays for the latter wired his daughter not to give me any more money and Baldwin cabled me, "Go back East," meaning to Russia. That left me on my own again, except that Laura Hays continued my little income out of her own allowance.

Hays sailed on the *Berengaria*. On the same boat, in the "royal suite," Maxim Litvinov, the Foreign Commissar, was traveling to the United States to arrange for American recognition of the Soviet Union. Also on that boat, in steerage, Bill Gedritis, the lad who had gone "to help build Socialism," was returning to his native land, his fare being paid by the American Club in Paris. Bill's experience inspired me to appeal to the American Consul for help, not as Beal, of course, but as Jacob Katz. The Consul sent me to the American Aid Society of Paris and the secretary there agreed to get me passage home and a railroad ticket to Cherbourg if I could raise twenty dollars toward these expenses. I went to my lovely treasurer and informed her that she could stop my weekly drain on her allowance by finding that much money. It was just before Christmas and Laura was "broke" but she begged, borrowed and extorted enough small sums from her friends to make up the amount and the Aid Society furnished me with a ticket on the *Albert Ballin*.

5

A new year had dawned when I arrived in New York. To America, gradually pulling out of the depression, it was a year of hope. For Russia, too, which had just been recognized by the United States, it was a time of good omen. The changed attitude of many capitalists, who were looking forward to large commercial deals and huge profits in the Soviet Union, was evident in the press. Led by Walter Duranty of the *Times,* a chorus of praise for the Communist régime resounded throughout our country. Thus I found myself, in spirit and in attitude, entirely out of step with my country-men. I had resolved on ship-board that, whatever the consequnces to myself, I should devote myself to two chief tasks: to get help for Red Hendricks and to disclose the truth about Russia. I set out to do so among my old comrades and the response brought stark dismay to my heart. Communists, Soviet sympathizers, and even liberals of the old school obviously did not want to hear the facts about the "Workers' Fatherland." They preferred the picture which had been drawn for them by the propagandists; it fitted in so much better with their ideals and their illusions. And whenever I brought up the case of Hendricks in circles which always seethed with indignation at capitalist injustice, the air would suddenly grow chilly. The defenders of labor, the upholders of civil liberty disowned the man who had dared to imply that life in America was preferable to existence in Stalin's utopia.

There were exceptions, of course. From Sidney Howard and from Isaac Don Levine I received encouragement in the suggestion made by Arthur Hays that I pen my observations and experiences in Russia. Howard told me to write the story of my life. "Put in everything," he advised, "all the names, all the incidents, all the truth." I have followed this advice. I am aware that it does not make pleasant reading. The story of "man's inhumanity to man" never does. And one who is ever conscious of the threat of a life-long prison sentence, who is aware that he has been abandoned by those to whom he could look for help and support, cannot call up the cheerful moments of his past to relieve the gloomy facts and their depressing effect. The optimism with which I looked upon the world from early childhood, the hope I cherished of a happier life for the workers of America, the faith I had in the Socialist experiment in Russia—all these have suffered disillusionment. I have not abandoned either of the first entirely; but of the last I despair.

POSTSCRIPT.

"Turn a liberal inside out and you will find a reactionary."

Was Lenin right when he uttered this maxim? Did he foresee the march of the Stalin soldiers, recruited from among the liberal ranks, to the Soviet banner? Did he not fear the rise of the reactionary force of Stalinism, with its natural attraction for every other reactionary force in society?

I have been ground under the pressure of these two forces ever since my return to the United States as a fugitive. Was it blindness, cowardice, or intellectual serfdom which made the American liberals join in a virtual alliance with Stalinism? Or was it their consciousness of belonging to a parasitic class which drew them to the parasitic power of the Stalinist rule?

We who consider ourselves class-conscious workers, look forward to and advocate a system of society without classes, a society in which those who produce shall be the sole rulers.

My proletarian journey through life, my struggles through strikes, prisons, escapes, and the written word, would be robbed of all meaning if I were to lose my ideal of a classless society. Yet the professed aim of all the liberal and radical groups which worship Stalinism is the same as mine.

But how is one to arrive at this classless goal? At present Stalin has a corner on the class-conscious market. The Stalinists vociferously claim to be the sole custodians of true Communism, the only rightful leaders of the working class. Stalin alone holds the key to the Communist heaven. To enter its Pearly Gates, all must pass through his purgatory.

As I write these lines, that purgatory is still reeking with the odor of the burned flesh and bones of the organizers of the great Russian Revolution, the comrades-in-arms of Lenin, the erstwhile apostles of Bolshevism: Kamenev, Piatakoff, Serebryakoff, Zinoviev, and many other Communist grenadiers. Unable to confer the blessings of his purgatory upon Trotsky, the one surviving founder of the Soviet Government, Stalin found it possible to make all the capitalist nations of the world serve the ends of his purgatory. What a triumph for Soviet Communism it is that no country in Europe dares to offer an asylum, even in jail, to the greatest living Communist!

As for myself, I am beyond the grasp of the direct arm of the Stalin purgatory, but not beyond the reach of its American watchdogs. If you do not shout pæans of praise for the Stalinist empire, you are branded with all the foul names which our rich English language offers to the Communist propaganda machine. If you dare expose the truth about the Soviet Union, you may be delivered by the Stalinist *agents-provocateurs* of the American Communist Party to the American agents of capitalist justice, if you happen to be, as I am, a fugitive from such justice.

The degeneration and degradation of Soviet Communism under Stalin during the last seven years are reflected in the conduct of its American adherents and mouthpieces. Consider the road traversed by the official Communist spokesmen from 1929 to 1937, as measured by their attitude towards me. It is significant not because of my personal fate, but as an illustration of the prevailing "revolutionary" morale.

In 1929, in a little book entitled "Gastonia, Citadel of the South," one of the high priests of the American Communist Party, "Bill" Dunne, wrote:

"In February, 1929, Fred Beal was sent to Gastonia by the National Textile Workers' Union to begin organization work. Well known for years to the textile workers of Lawrence and New Bedford, Mass., as one of the most courageous and experienced leaders of their struggles, fresh from the battlefield of New Bedford, where 25,000 workers had rallied around him and the N.T.W.U. against attempted wage cuts in 1928 and where the strike was won in the face of mass arrests of pickets (800 being held for trial), Fred Beal came to Gastonia and went to work to build the N.T.W.U. in the Loray mill."

On January 12, 1936, another high priest of the American Communist Party, Joseph Freeman, in the course of an attack on me in the columns of the *Daily Worker*, wrote under a Stalinist caption:

BEAL OUT OF JAIL

But Beal is not in jail. At this very moment he is freely circulating somewhere between New York and California.

"But Beal is not in jail" is more than an open expression of regret. It is an invitation to the agents of capitalist justice in North Carolina to do the Stalinist bidding. In this incredible denunciation of one of our leading "artists in uniform" one can discern the disappointment over the inefficiency of the capitalist police as compared with the beloved Ogpu.

What had happened in the intervening years? Did not the Communist Party, with all its liberal and radical subsidiaries and appendages, wage a national campaign in 1929 to keep Fred Beal out of jail? Did not the same *Daily Worker,* on August 27, 1930, when the matter of our escape to Soviet Russia became a national scandal, justify even our bail jumping which I had opposed? Under the caption, "The Gastonia Defendants," the Communist organ then wrote:

"They are quite justified in escaping from the vicious sentence imposed upon them, by placing themselves beyond reach of the Southern capitalist class justice.... The working class as a whole should glory in the fact that they got away. The workers should support their escape despite the howls of the bourgeoisie.... Let the bosses take the bail; it is better that they have $27,000 than the seven Gastonia fighters serve 117 years in their prison."

Now consider the strange destinies of the seven Gastonia fighters who fell into the Soviet realm.

William McGinnis fought his way out of the Stalin haven, secretly returned to the United States at the risk of being imprisoned, and is reported to have died amidst the silence of his former comrades of the *Daily Worker*.

K. Y. Hendricks also battled his way back to "freedom," to a long prison sentence in America, where he was seized amidst the studied silence of the Stalinist organization, ignored and forgotten in his cell by the brave Communist leaders.

Louis McLaughlin felt the pangs of hunger in Stalin's land of plenty. He was arrested in Moscow for stealing bread. To avoid a scandal abroad, he was shipped off to Odessa.

George Carter was a physical and mental wreck when

I last saw him. He was glad to get potato peelings for food when he visited me in Kharkov.

Joseph Harrison was forced to live in an unspeakable workers' barracks, infested with rats and vermin, in a Moscow suburb.

Only Clarence Miller, who was never a worker and whose connection with the Gastonia strike was accidental, blossomed out in Soviet Russia as a "Red professor" and occupied a comfortable apartment in Moscow, enjoying the prosperity of the Soviet bureaucracy.

As for myself, I left Russia with the realization that the radical movement was at the crossroads, and with the determination not to remain silent.

I became convinced that the road taken by Stalin to the goal of a classless society is not the right road. It is advertised as a short cut. It has taken a terrible toll of life. But it has done something even more frightful to the living. And the end is not in sight.

At close range I watched the results of the Stalin drive. I saw the dead and the living. I saw a man-made famine in which millions perished. I stood aghast at murder becoming a normal function of the state—the state of my dreams.

With a twenty-year prison sentence hanging over my head, I made my way back to the United States to speak out somehow, to tell the truth, to call my comrades to take another road for the happiness of the workers.

But my former comrades, my former defenders, indeed, the entire radical-liberal world which took such a seemingly deep interest in the Gastonia case in the name of justice and truth, would not even listen to the truth from Soviet Russia.

The press which was most keenly concerned with the

problems of labor was the press which barred from its columns the greatest labor story of our times, the tragedy of the working masses under the whips of the Stalinist taskmasters.

There was one labor paper in the country which did print throughout the years the facts about Soviet Russia, the Socialist Jewish *Daily Forward* of New York. The account of my Soviet experiences was therefore first published in a language which I do not understand. This did not prevent the Stalinist press in America from opening a barrage of vilification against me.

In the beginning of my narrative I had declared that I was not concerned as to where the truth of my story appeared, so long as it reached the greatest number of workers and served to open their eyes to the horrors of the Stalin dictatorship.

A veritable storm broke loose when, through an agent, my story was placed for publication in the Hearst newspapers. It brought down upon my head the entire arsenal of vituperation and falsification at the disposal of the Stalinist agents and their stooges.

I make no apology for printing the truth in the Hearst press. To me, the Hearst newspapers are essentially like the other capitalist journals and magazines to which the Stalinists contribute their propaganda. If there be a difference, it is that the Hearst papers are read largely by the working masses, and have always had a distinct bias in favor of labor.

The Hearst newspapers, I was only too well aware, had fought for Tom Mooney long before any other capitalist papers took up the cudgels for that great martyr of the American revolutionary labor movement. If it was right for Fremont Older, the outstanding champion of Mooney's innocence, to wage his unremitting battle in the Hearst press, why was it wrong to fight for justice to Russian labor in the same press?

If it was right for Anna Louise Strong, Lincoln Steffens, Jerome Davis, and a host of other Communist and near-Communist writers, to sing in the columns of the Hearst press the praise of would-be Soviet achievements, why was it wrong for a worker like myself to tell in the same press of the conditions of the Russian workers as I found them?

It was the Hearst press which first crusaded for the recognition of the Soviet Government by the United States. That was in the days when there was still reason to hope that the Russian Revolution might bring a new and better social system into the world. Now that Stalin had beheaded nearly all of the original makers of that Revolution, had betrayed the masses of Russia and of the world, had enthroned himself in the Kremlin like an Asiatic demigod, the Hearst press was the first to discover these truths and to expose them to the public.

The publication of my articles on Soviet Russia in the Hearst press completely blotted out my record as a strike leader and as a victim of the Gastonia frame-up in the eyes of the Communists and their liberal lackeys. What did it matter if I was a fugitive from North Carolina justice so long as I committed the cardinal crime of telling the truth about Russia? Although it was obvious that I had nothing to do with the Hearst policies, that I could no more approve of them than of other capitalist newspapers, my act was sufficient to induce the Stalinists to try to deliver me to the North Carolina police.

Yet my status had not changed between 1929 and 1937. My ideals had not changed. I discovered that Soviet Russia is the grandest fraud of history I learned that there is still nothing mightier in the world than truth. I found that the Stalinist road leads to calamity and darkness. But I am as convinced as ever that there is another road to a free and classless humanity, a road which is worth the quest, and which can be found only by minds liberated from the worship of false gods and by spirits strong enough to face the truth in the quest for the truth.